Praise for *Emotional Intimacy*

"Understanding and working with our emotions has never been more important. Personally, relationally, globally—the maturing of emotion is the first step toward peace. In *Emotional Intimacy*, Robert Masters creates a thorough geography of the heart, offering detailed understandings and extensive ways to practice being human. A true resource for individuals and those in the helping professions."
—MARK NEPO, author of *Seven Thousand Ways to Listen* and *The Book of Awakening*

"There is wisdom and power in this remarkable exploration of emotional intimacy. Robert Augustus Masters journeys into unexpected regions of the human heart, and with rare discernment explores the dark and light of that which allows for a new order of coming together."
—JEAN HOUSTON, PHD, author of *The Search for the Beloved*

"*Emotional Intimacy* sets out a perfectly clear and accurate map of the all-too-often confused dimension of our emotional territory. The result is everything you could ever want from a book on this topic: it is concise, useful, beautifully succinct, exquisitely well-executed, and a deeply joyful book to read. I highly recommend this book for professional and laypeople alike—it has something deeply important to offer each."
—KEN WILBER, author of *A Brief History of Everything*

"*Emotional Intimacy* is a godsend. Open it to any page and you will experience the truth within your emotions. I recommend this wonderful book to everyone!"
—CHRISTIANE NORTHRUP, MD, author of the *New York Times* bestsellers *Women's Bodies, Women's Wisdom* and *The Wisdom of Menopause*

"This is one of the best books on human emotion I've read. What I particularly like is its practicality. Few explorers venture into the heart of emotion at the depths Dr. Masters navigates."
—GAY HENDRICKS, PHD, author of *The Big Leap*

"In *Emotional Intimacy* Robert Masters offers a primer on emotions—from the most primary to the more subtle. Whether you are currently in a relationship or wish to be in one, this is a worthwhile book to pick up and select a chapter from which to taste, digest, transform, and heal. As a couple's therapist, it is a book I will recommend to my clients."

—STAN TATKIN, PSYD, author of *Wired for Love*

"This remarkably helpful, lucidly written book provides an exceptional road map for how to work creatively and constructively with all of our emotions. I was particularly impressed by Masters' emphasis on intimacy throughout the book, including the art of developing intimacy with each of our emotions. For those of us who wish to deepen our capacity for emotional intimacy with another human being, Masters' offering is a beautiful place to begin."

—KATHERINE WOODWARD THOMAS,
author of *Calling in "The One"* and creator of the Conscious Uncoupling Process

"For millennia, spiritual inquiry and practice has been dominated by the masculine psyche. The rich world of our emotions has been viewed, in most traditions, as something just to master, overcome, and transcend. This book is a lucid expression of a new balance of masculine and feminine awakening, through which we can surf emotion as a wave to take us deeper home into our true nature. Masters shows us, through highly articulate explanation as well as an abundance of very practical exercises, how every aspect of our emotional life is another doorway into love."

—ARJUNA ARDAGH, author of *The Translucent Revolution* and *Leap Before You Look*

"With a poet's facility with language, a psychospiritual guide's skill in teaching us how to work practically with our most challenging emotions, and a scholar-practitioner's light but firm grounding in the current literature on emotions, Robert Masters brings together in one volume a wonderful combination of wise perspectives, great depth and breadth, exercises, and practices to help us explore our emotional lives. And his book exhibits deep care and compassion for the reader, for all of us."

—DONALD ROTHBERG, PHD, author of *The Engaged Spiritual Life*

Emotional Intimacy

Emotional Intimacy

A Comprehensive Guide
for Connecting with the Power
of Your Emotions

ROBERT AUGUSTUS MASTERS, PhD

sounds true
many voices, one journey

Sounds True, Inc.
Boulder, CO 80306

Published 2013

Cover and book design by Rachael Murray
Cover photo © R.S.Jegg, Shutterstock

Printed in the United States of America

Masters, Robert Augustus.
  Emotional intimacy : a comprehensive guide for connecting with the power of your emotions /
Robert Augustus Masters, PhD.
    pages cm
  ISBN 978-1-60407-939-5
  1. Intimacy (Psychology) 2. Interpersonal relations—Psychological aspects. 3. Emotions. I. Title.
  BF575.I5M28338 2013
  158.2—dc23
                            2013000544

Ebook ISBN 978-1-62203-047-7
10 9 8 7 6 5 4

For Diane, my wife, ever-deeper beloved, and cojourneyer
to the far reaches of relational and emotional intimacy,
meeting me as I've never been met before, holding
my all with a love I'd not imagined possible

To be intimate with all that we are—including our every emotion—
is to fully embody and awaken to who and what we truly are.

CONTENTS

Introduction **Into the Heart of Emotion** 1
What Constitutes Emotional Intimacy?
Navigating This Book

PART ONE Orientation 9

1 **The Anatomy of Emotion** 11
Emotion Is More Than Feeling
Emotion and Reason
Containing and Expressing Emotion
Identifying an Emotion

2 **Cultivating Intimacy with Our Emotions** 21
Four Steps to Developing Emotional Intimacy
Practice Developing Intimacy with Difficult Emotions
Having a Conscious Rant
Being Emotionally Vulnerable
Empathy and Emotional Intimacy

3 **There Are No Negative Emotions** 35
Worry, Hostility, Hate
Practice Making Wise Use of Hate
The Shadow of Trying to Be Emotionally Positive

4 **Emotional Disconnection** 43
The Anatomy of "Cool"
Turning toward Emotional Disconnection

5 **Emotion and Language** *Exploring the Use of Metaphor for Emotional Experience* 49
The "Container" Metaphor for Emotion
Making "Inner" Synonymous with "More Real"
Other Metaphors for Emotion
Conceiving of Emotions as Untrustworthy

6 **Emotional Intimacy in Relationships** 57
Turning toward Our Fear within Relationship
Practice Sharing What We're Afraid to Share
Gender Differences in Beginning Relational Work

7 **Gender and Emotional Intimacy** 65
"The Masculine" and "The Feminine"
Gender Differences in Emotional Intimacy
Deepening Emotional Intimacy Regardless of Gender
Differences

PART TWO **Meeting the Emotions** 75

8 **Fear** *Stepping into the Dragon's Cave* 77
Meeting the Dragon: Getting Acquainted with Your Fear
Fear Is Excitement in Drag
Practice Fear and Excitement
Fear and Its Relationship to Anger
Practice Fear and Anger
Adaptive and Maladaptive Fear
Practice Getting to Know Your Fear
Getting Under the Dragon's Skin: Working with Fear
Practice Working with Your Fear
Embracing the Dragon: Bringing Your Fear
into Your Heart
Fear in Intimate Relationship
Practice Working with Fear in Relationship

9 **Collective Fear**
        Letting Others' Fear Break Open Our Heart 97
        Psychoemotional Numbing
        Our "Solutions" to Collective Fear
        Practice Meeting Collective Fear
        Working with Collective Fear
        Practice Working with Collective Fear

10 **Shame** *From Toxic Collapse to Healing Exposure* 109
        Practice Staying with Our Shame
        The Nature of Shame
        Strategies to Evade Shame
        Shame Deflates Us
        Aggression, Shame, and the Inner Critic
        Healthy and Unhealthy Shame
        Practice Taking Shame to Heart
        Working with Shame
        Practice Working with Shame
        Evicting the Inner Critic
        Practice Evicting Your Inner Critic
        Shame in Intimate Relationship
        Practice Shame in Intimate Relationship

11 **Anger** *Moral Fire* 129
        The Nature of Anger
        Anger and Aggression Are Not Synonymous
        Practice Getting to Know Your Anger
        Four Approaches to Working with Anger
        Practice Four Approaches to Working with Anger
        Clean and Unclean Anger
        Practice Toward Clean Anger
        Practice Conscious Anger Rant
        Gender and Anger
        Expressing Anger, Receiving Anger
        Practice Sharing Anger Nonverbally
        Practice Sharing Anger Verbally
        From Reactive Rage to Wrathful Compassion

12 **Sadness** *Loss Taken to Heart* 155
     Sadness and Gender
     Shame over Sadness
     Sadness and Depression
     Working with Sadness
     Practice Opening to Your Sadness
     Connecting through Our Tears
     The Importance of Crying
     Practice Allowing Old Sadness to Surface

13 **Joy** *The Unbound Feeling of Being* 165
     Types of Joy
     Shadow Forms of Joy
     Working with Joy
     Practice Joy and Deeper Joy
     Practice Gratitude Meditation

14 **Grief** *The Heart Broken Wide Open* 175
     Practice The Experience of Grief
     Grief Undammed
     Practice Allowing Grief to Flow and Expand

15 **Disgust** *Oral/Moral Rejection* 181
     Practice Experiencing and Expressing Disgust
     Healthy and Unhealthy Disgust
     Working with Disgust
     Practice Working with Your Disgust

16 **Guilt** *A Stalemated Parent-Child Bind* 187
     Practice Guilt's Parent-Child Dynamic
     Cutting Through Guilt's Dramatics
     Working with Guilt
     Practice Working with the Shame in Guilt
     Fear Is Part of Guilt
     Practice Working with the Fear in Guilt
     Practice Working with Both Sides of Guilt

17 **Depression**
>> ***A Pain That's a Solution to a Deeper Pain*** 197
>> Working with Depression
>> *Practice* Working with Depression

18 **Contempt** *Disdainful Dehumanizing* 205
>> *Practice* The Experience of Contempt
>> Contempt as Moral Condescension
>> Working with Contempt
>> *Practice* Working with Contempt

19 **Self-Doubt** *Fearfully Myopic Inner Questioning* 211
>> *Practice* Exploring Self-Doubt
>> Working with Self-Doubt
>> *Practice* Working with Self-Doubt
>> Doubting Your Doubt
>> *Practice* Cutting Through Self-Doubt's Content

20 **Paranoia** *Fear-Driven Delusion* 217
>> *Practice* Bringing Compassion to Paranoia
>> Self, Sanity, and Paranoia
>> Cultivating Intimacy with Our Paranoia

21 **Jealousy** *Heart-Stabbing Rejection* 221
>> How Jealousy Can Manifest
>> Jealousy and Envy
>> *Practice* Exploring the Elements of Jealousy
>> Working with Jealousy
>> *Practice* Getting Better Acquainted with Our Jealousy
>> *Practice* Holding Your Jealousy
>> Jealousy and Attachment
>> Jealousy and Love
>> *Practice* Turning toward What We Reject in Ourselves

22 Exultation *Fiery, Elated Affirmation* 233
   Practice The Experience of Exultation

23 Schadenfreude
   Finding Joy in the Misfortune of Others 235
   Practice Experiencing Schadenfreude
   Schadenfreude as a Vicarious Shame-Fest
   Schadenfreude as Armchair Judge
   Schadenfreude's Lack of Compassion
   Practice Working with Schadenfreude

24 Envy *Sideline Craving* 241
   Envy's Relationship to Greed, Resentment,
      Jealousy, Shame
   Envy as Inspiration in Passive Drag
   Practice Working with Envy

25 Surprise 245

26 Awe *The Full-Blooded Intuition of Innate Mystery* 247
   The Shadow of Awe
   Awe as Self-Transcending Intimacy with Mystery

PART THREE Deepening Emotional Intimacy 251

27 Directions Feeling Can Take
   Feeling Into, Feeling For, Feeling With 253
   Feeling Into
   Feeling For
   Feeling With

28 De-Numbing *Thaw Until Raw* 257
   Working with Numbness

29 Collective Overwhelm 261

Working with Collective Overwhelm

30 **Connected Catharsis** 267
Considering the Value of Emotional Discharge
The Nature of Connected Catharsis

31 **Phantom Limbic Pain**
Emotional Healing and Breakthrough 275
Working with Phantom Limbic Pain

Epilogue **The Feeling of Being** 281

Appendix **A Meditative Practice for Establishing
Grounded Spaciousness** 287

Acknowledgments 289

About the Author.. 291

Into the Heart of Emotion

TO BE ALIVE IS TO feel, and to feel is to experience emotion. Whether our emotions are overwhelming or subtle, fiery or chilling, dark or light, they are always present, finding expression in an extraordinary number of ways. Our emotions are ever-moving wonders, bringing together physiology, feeling, cognition, and conditioning, allowing us to connect and communicate in more ways than we can imagine. The more deeply we know our emotions, the deeper and more fulfilling our lives will be.

However anatomically complex our emotions are, they are simple in their felt immediacy, providing us with the opportunity to participate more fully and more consciously in them so that we might make use of them as wisely as possible. For all too many of us, emotions remain a largely untapped source of strength, freedom, and connection. They are so much a part of us that we tend to take them for granted, losing touch with their sheer mystery and with the marvelously varied ways they transmit our inner workings, facially and otherwise.

How well do you know your emotions? To what degree are you at home with them? How do you view them—are they more ally or foe? Do you distance yourself from them, or get lost in them? Do you keep them tightly reined, or do you let yourself get carried away by them? Or do you cultivate *intimacy* with them, however dark or unpleasant or disturbing they may be?

Whatever we are *doing* with our emotions will not be clear until we know them well. We simply won't be close enough to them to see what directions we may be channeling them into. For example, we might not recognize that hostility is not something that simply arises in us, but it

1

is something that we are *doing* with our anger. The more intimate we are with our anger—which is far more about being close to it than about controlling it!—the more easily we can see the choices we are making with it.

The capacity for emotional intimacy—a greatly undervalued capacity—is essential not only to truly fulfilling relationships, but to having an uncommonly vital life in which awareness, passion, love, action, and integrity function as one. What I mean by emotional intimacy is twofold: (1) becoming intimate with our emotions, including their arising, expression, historical roots, and relational functioning; and (2) becoming intimate in our relationships with significant others through how we express and share our emotions.

To be intimate with our emotions is no small undertaking; doing so requires far more than simply being able to openly express and talk about them.

Being intimate with our fear, for example, means getting close enough to it to see it clearly—and in detail—in its mental, psychological, and physical dimensions, but not so close that we fuse with our fear or get lost in it. So we remain *slightly* separated from our fear even as we openly feel and closely connect with it, maintaining just enough distance to keep it in focus.

To take this example further, cultivating intimacy with our fear doesn't necessarily lessen it, but it does put us in a position where we are neither identified with it nor disconnected from it. We see our fear for what it is, we sense its location and coursings in our body, we recognize its impact on our thinking processes, we become more aware of our history with it, we register its degree and quality of contractedness. As such, we become increasingly capable of working with it and skillfully sharing it. As we become more intimate with our fear, we lessen our fear of it and eventually adopt a nonproblematic orientation toward it.

The more intimate we are with our emotions, the more adept we'll be in both containing and expressing them, so that their presence serves rather than hinders us and those with whom we're in contact. In this sense, there are no unwholesome or negative emotions—only unwholesome or negative things we do with them. Emotional intimacy allows us to make the best possible use of all our emotions—and it enhances relationship.

Without emotional intimacy, relationships founder on the reefs of emotional discord or flatness—no matter how heated the sex, no matter how much we hold in common—leaving us marooned from the interpersonal closeness for which we yearn. If we are parents, our children will pay the price of our lack of emotional intimacy, learning to normalize emotional reactivity and disconnection. All too easily, we may simply act out our unresolved wounds and mishandled needs through our emotional expression or lack thereof, while remaining unaware of what we are doing! Such *re-acting* keeps our relationships in the shallows, cut off from the emotional depth and resonance needed for genuine intimacy. When we wake up to this and begin doing what it takes to develop and deepen emotional intimacy, our relationships start to become less of a battlefield or flatland and more of a sanctuary. They become more vital, more nourishing, more authentic.

∾

Emotional illiteracy infects many relationships, regardless of how effectively it might be camouflaged—or compensated for—by "rational" discourse, material success, erotic intensity, or spiritual practice. Despite the obvious presence of emotion in everyone, as well as the plain-to-see emotional difficulties or challenges many of us have, emotional education has yet to take a significant place in the majority of our schools. It simply does not appear to be a priority for those in charge of "educational" policy. This, of course, is not just a failing of our school system, but of our culture. Intellectual intelligence tends to get the lion's share of attention, with moral and emotional intelligence getting far too little focus, and many relationships reflect this.

Modeling a healthy relationship to our emotions is one of the biggest gifts we can give our children. Many of us grew up suffering the consequences of our parents' unresolved emotional wounds, and we developed an understandably problematic orientation toward our emotions. For example, we may have learned to associate the expression of anger with danger or the loss of love, and so have a reaction to anger that works against relational well-being—unless we've worked through this. We have an obligation not to pass on our emotional wounding to our children, or at least to minimize such transmission. This means doing our very best to face and work through that old hurt, as perhaps optimally done through high-quality psychotherapy.

How we treat our children is closely akin to how we treat the child within us. If we're uncomfortable with our emotions, especially those that are particularly vulnerable, we'll very likely be uncomfortable with our children's emotions, especially when they are fully expressed. If we were shamed for crying when we were young, the odds are that we'll find ourselves shaming our children for crying at least some of the time, despite our intentions to do otherwise—unless we've worked through this dynamic in us to the point where we no longer shame ourselves (via the finger-pointing of our inner critic) for our more vulnerable emotions and their open expression.

When emotional intimacy is all but missing from a relationship—with emotional reactivity and dissociation at the helm—and nothing significant is done about this, it might be more accurate to say the partners have an *association* rather than a relationship. There may be similar values, the overall tone might be friendly, and there may be some sex occurring, but at best what is happening is basically akin to a successful business in which both partners are doing their part to keep the ship afloat. There's nothing necessarily wrong with this, but it's a far cry from the kind of relational mutuality they could be sharing and living. It's as if we're thirsty and are relying solely on the bottled water that's on sale nearby, even though a crystal-clear river of clean water is also within reach, asking only that we turn toward it and take the necessary steps.

If we want more depth and connection and joy in our relationships, we're going to have to develop more emotional intimacy with our partners, our friends, our family, our coworkers. It's that simple and that challenging. Connecting only through our upbeat emotions is not enough—we also need to find, and keep finding, relationship-deepening connection through *all* our emotions. And there is no way we can do this if we are not significantly intimate with our emotions. How can we share our anger in a way that brings us closer if we are not close enough to it to know it well?

~

It is quite natural to feel uncomfortable as we embark on the journey toward emotional intimacy—given that along the way we'll very likely have to encounter whatever first drove us into emotional darkness, numbness, or dissociation—but developing this closeness with our emotions is an immensely rewarding and liberating passage, regardless of its challenges. When I began this journey, catalyzed by an extremely painful relationship breakup in my midtwenties, I, being strongly inclined to suppress my vulnerability, was far from willing to approach my emotional hurt. Anger came easily to me, but not tears. I was tightly contained, but my circumstances were sufficiently intense to crack the container beyond repair. And so my walls crumbled and my grief emerged, flooding through my defenses, my numbness, my denial of how much pain I was actually in and had been in for a long, long time. In this process I had to encounter the early-life dynamics that had generated the construction of my emotional walls; this was excruciating at first, but after a while it felt very natural to me. I had broken down and broken open, and through that very breaking gradually emerged into an increasingly life-giving sense of wholeness, at the hub of which was my emotional life.

So many of us feel our emotions (or at least some of our emotions) only partially. We may be used to suppressing them; we may not feel sufficiently safe; we may find it just too vulnerable to feel fully. But when we become intimate with our emotions, we come alive—full-bloodedly alive—feeling with an exquisite sensitivity, depth, and breadth. And then vulnerability takes on a new meaning; we realize that it can be a source of *strength*. Our senses are heightened, our empathy deepens, our intuition sharpens, and we begin to fully know in a deeply embodied sense the uniquely essential presence that is us.

This newfound vitality is coupled with an ability to be more tuned in to the impact we have on others. We are more able to cut through our tendency to let ourselves off the hook when we have hurt others, knowingly or unknowingly. Integrity becomes not a "should," but a given.

Deepening our capacity for emotional intimacy awakens and grounds us, connecting us with palpable immediacy to the pulse of what really matters, rendering us more able to respond optimally to life's inevitable challenges. This is an inherently liberating process, unchaining us as it does from much of our conditioned way of being.

WHAT CONSTITUTES EMOTIONAL INTIMACY?

Emotional intimacy happens as a result of multiple factors in synergistic combination:

1. Being sufficiently well acquainted with our emotions so that when one arises we recognize it, can name it, and acknowledge what we are doing with it.

2. Relating *to* our emotions rather than just *from* our emotions, so that we neither fuse with nor dissociate from them.

3. Listening to others deeply, both to what is being said and to what is not being said.

4. Remaining emotionally transparent and nondefensively expressive of whatever is arising in us, be it pleasant or unpleasant.

5. Being fully vulnerable.

6. Knowing our personal history well enough to be able to recognize when old survival strategies have possessed us, along with the willingness to fully share and work with this.

7. Being empathetic without any loss of personal boundaries.

8. Keeping at least some connection to our core of self as we allow our emotions as open an expression as our situation warrants.

9. Cutting through any tendencies to play victim to our emotions so that we no longer blame them for our bad behavior.

10. Being able to wake up in the midst of our reactivity and not let it run the show, at least not for any significant length of time.

All of these factors, both alone and in conjunction with each other, are considered throughout this book. I suggest that you return to this list at least several times as you progress through the chapters, so as to reinforce your overview of emotional intimacy.

NAVIGATING THIS BOOK

This book has three parts. In part 1, I explore emotion, go deeply into what emotional intimacy is, and introduce what it means to work with our emotions in a more general context. In part 2, I take a comprehensive look at each emotion and provide practices for knowing and optimally working with each one. And last, in part 3, I explore material that helps deepen our understanding of emotion and emotional intimacy.

A note on the practices that you'll find throughout part 2: Read each one through before beginning it. Make sure that you have paper and pen handy, because some of the practices require a bit of writing. Also, make sure that you won't be disturbed during a practice and that you have adequate time to rest and reflect at the end (ten minutes minimum). I also ask that you consider doing at least some of the practices more than once, especially those that most deeply affect you. And learn the meditative practice described in the appendix; doing so will help ground and deepen your experience of the various practices.

Putting this book together has been a joy for me, a richly rewarding labor of love. In my uncommon bond with my wife, Diane, and in the healing/awakening work we do together, emotional intimacy plays a central role, whether we're working with a couple stalled at a relational crossroads or with those in the throes of their core wounding or are training a group of psychospiritual practitioners. We don't treat emotion as something to simply talk about and analyze but as something to directly explore, to be nonconceptually known from the deep inside, finding that once it is thus known, fitting insights and meaningful connections spontaneously emerge, often with equally spontaneous awakenings to one's true nature.

Everything in this book is rooted in the intuitive integrative work I've been doing with clients worldwide during the past thirty-five years—work that has, from the very beginning, been strongly focused on emotion and emotional well-being. Along the way, my personal path and the direction of my work became increasingly focused on developing intimacy with all that we are—high and low, dark and light, dying and undying—with a special emphasis on emotion. So throughout these pages, I speak from both direct experience and from an ever-fresh appreciation for the mystery that is emotion.

Cultivating intimacy with our emotions is a deeply rewarding odyssey, which we are invited to embark on by our circumstances. We don't have to enlist for emotional boot camp; life will do that for us! Whenever an emotion arises—an *extremely* common occurrence—we have an opportunity to deepen our intimacy with it and to respond to it in ways aligned with the highest good of all involved.

Emotion implicates us as a totality. This means that emotion is not just something stored somewhere in our body but is a vital process— more verb than noun—that includes all that we are. Emotion is feeling, but not just feeling; emotion includes cognition, conditioning, social factors, and arguably also spirituality in its more developed stages. So in emotion we have biology, biography, behavior, perspective, and bare awareness all coexisting and interacting for better or for worse. What complexity, what an exquisitely alive interplay always in motion—and yet such easily felt, rapidly registered immediacy! Becoming conscious in the midst of this without distancing ourselves from it is the essence of emotional intimacy.

Becoming intimate with our emotions is a challenge that we'd do best to wholeheartedly welcome. There's some risk involved—the risk of getting more vulnerable, more emotionally raw, more hurt—but the far greater risk is in not developing such intimacy. When we truly befriend and make wise use of our emotions, we benefit ourselves and all those with whom we are involved, directly and indirectly.

However uncomfortable they may be, our emotions are our guests. Let us treat them as such, neither rejecting them nor letting them run roughshod over us. Let us learn from them and learn deeply, for the benefit of one and all.

Part 1

Orientation

1

The Anatomy of Emotion

Emotion is far more verb than noun, being not some
entity or thing we can get out of our system but a
vital process always in some degree of flux.

GIVEN HOW FUNDAMENTAL our emotions are to our very
being and how frequently they arise in us, it is remarkable how little
intimacy we may have with them. We might, for example, feel shame
quite often and yet have almost no in-depth sense of its actual nature
and impact on us.

Why are our emotions fundamental to us? Because without them
our capacity to engage in meaningful communication would be all but
nonexistent. Emotions are evolutionary phenomena—present only in
warm-blooded animals—that make possible a greater complexity of
relational savvy and contextual sensitivity, as well as a more creative use
of both our outer and inner world.

It is common to take our emotions for granted, as if they are no
more than innate forces of nature that come with being human. Our
language often points to how these "natural" forces move through us:
we "storm" out of the room, we are "flooded" with sadness, we "erupt"
with rage. But just as we may not be students of weather, despite its
ubiquitous presence in our life, we may not be students of emotion.
We all get angry (whether or not we are conscious of it), but we might
know very little about anger, having spent no quality time in Emotional Literacy 101's classrooms.

Our only normal break from emotion is during deep dreamless sleep,
when consciousness is withdrawn not only from the senses but also

from the mind. During our dream states, emotion is just as present—and every bit as central—as it is during our waking times. Dreams are not just private motion pictures (do our dreams ever really hold still?), but also emotion pictures. In fact, much of our inner life—whether dreaming or waking—could be characterized as multidimensional emotion pictures (ranging from snapshots to feature dramas), with much of the framing provided courtesy of our conditioning. And our outer life is just as pervaded by emotion.

EMOTION IS MORE THAN FEELING

So what is emotion? Is it just another word for feeling? In the literature on emotion, the terms "emotion" and "feeling" (and the more academic "affect") are often used interchangeably. And even when they are not, there is not much agreement as to what they mean. Nevertheless, it's important to distinguish feeling from emotion.

Feeling means the registering of sensation (e.g., the feeling of a stone in our hand or hunger pangs in our stomach), and it also refers to the registering of a specific sort of sensation: an innate noncognitive evaluative sensing that's at the very core of emotion (e.g., the visceral feeling of fear or shame or joy).

"Noncognitive" means that no thinking processes are needed for the arising of feeling—even though thinking can certainly trigger feeling. When it comes to the pure speed of something arising in us, thought lags far behind feeling. Someone cuts us off in traffic—and we already were having a bad day!—and a rush of rage surges through us almost instantaneously, prior to any thought, let alone appraisal, of the situation. It is pure feeling in the adrenaline-saturated, raw, fierily coursing through us.

Feelings often burst forth before thoughts have even formed. The good news is that this ultraquick arousal readies us for instant action (like braking to avoid smashing into a car that just cut us off). The bad news is that such instant action gives us no time for any reevaluation of what's just happened (like considering that maybe the driver who just cut us off is making an emergency dash to the hospital).

And here's where *emotion* comes in, giving our feeling of rage at being cut off in traffic not just its *intrinsic* context of being thwarted or unjustly treated, but also a context that takes into account our entire history and relationship with anger, as well as other influences that may factor into the situation. We now have more options than just cutting loose or burning up with our rage; we have a choice, however conditioned our anger may be by our past.

Emotion includes not only feeling, cognition, social factors, and related action tendencies, but also the interplay between all four, making for a complex flux that eludes any neat mapping.

So to truly explore any emotion is to explore more than just the *feeling* of it. For example, we need to be familiar—and not just intellectually familiar—with the early-life dynamics that largely determine how we usually express a particular emotion under certain conditions. We also need to feel into and relate to those times with enough presence and care so that they have less say in how we now deal with the emotion in question.

If we're not aware of the actual perspective with which we tend to infuse or hold a certain emotion, we're likely to express it in ways established long ago, often by our parents. Not being sufficiently aware of the social factors (both current and past) affecting our emotional expression means we'll probably let them play a governing role in such expression.

Emotion is the dramatization of feeling. What constitutes this is ours to know, and know very well, if we are to become emotionally literate. We cannot be intimate with our emotions unless we're deeply acquainted with their storylines and shaping factors.

For example: If you hated a sibling who was unrelentingly cruel to you, and if your parents repeatedly told you it was wrong or a sin to hate thus, your hate might become internalized and self-directed, saddling you with an industrial-strength inner critic. If you don't explore and work through this part of your history, you'll be at the mercy of your hate-internalizing habit whenever others treat you badly, avoiding confronting them, turning your anger toward them back at yourself.

Where feeling is reaction, emotion is adaptation. So feeling is an instantaneous, nonreflective (there's no time for reflection!) arising, but emotion is all about how we handle that feeling.

For instance, the pure feeling of shame kicks in with body-slamming suddenness: we redden, our gaze drops, our head hangs, our mind goes fuzzy or blank, our awkwardness shoots into high gear with no brakes to be found. We have been stopped in our tracks and are excruciatingly uncomfortable, as if stripped naked in public. Then—usually within a few seconds—our customary way of being with shame shows up, perhaps accompanied by a memory or two of previous incidents akin to the one now happening.

This is where we make the move to emotion, to adaptation. Now our shame is on a *particular* stage; the drama is underway, with us as the ultrareluctant centerpiece, already automatically resorting to one of our preset strategies for dealing with our shame. So our initial shame reaction is yielding to already-established tactics, at least in intention, perhaps already morphing into other emotions, like anger or fear—or into states like withdrawal or dissociation. All this, dictated by our conditioning, may happen in a very short time.

Emotion can overwhelm us, especially when the feeling at its core is particularly intense or compelling, or has been suppressed for a long time. I say "compelling" because when our emotional state is sufficiently intense, we may find ourselves captivated by or even addicted to its point of view, however unrealistic that might be. We may be overrun by "uncaged" or "unleashed" feeling, which may "bring out the beast in us" or "drown us in sorrow." (These and other metaphors for emotion are, as we shall see, grounded in our sensory and motor experiences.) We may accuse another of being emotional—or perhaps unemotional, even though we are all emotional beings. We may be embarrassed by our overt emotional expression when it contrasts with our usual self-control (consider the "stiff upper lip" or "poker face" or "cool" countenance).

Many of us are inclined to view emotions as being lower or more primitive—less trustworthy—than reason. We may think of emotions as clouding the skies of rational thought or muddying our objectivity. And we often blame our emotions for this, saying for example, "My emotions got the better of me." The metaphor here is that of emotion as an *opponent*. When we "fight" or "wrestle" with our emotions, we are far from cultivating intimacy with them. Intimacy implies friendliness—and it is only by befriending our emotions that we can work with them in ways that allow us to benefit from what they offer.

EMOTION AND REASON

Emotional illiteracy—or lack of emotional sensitivity, understanding, and savvy—has much of its rooting in the historical devaluation of emotion relative to cognition. Thinking clearly thus gets overly associated with dispassion or a muting of our emotions. And moral decisions? They are—when we devalue emotion—supposedly best made when passion and feeling are kept out of the decision-making process, much in the way children are excluded from parental discussions. What we see here is the automatic identification of emotion with subjectivity, in the sense that subjectivity is a failure to be objective. In fact, our logical faculties tend to lag behind our emotional "knowing" when it comes to making good decisions. This lag primarily occurs because our emotionally based take on a topic employs more of the brain and draws from far more data—and thereby processes it more multidimensionally—than does our purely logical take.

Can we be objective and emotional at the same time? Yes. An example: You are crying deeply, at last letting go of a relationship that no longer serves you, a relationship that you desperately had tried to keep together for a long time. You now know, right to your core, that the relationship is done, and you're grieving its loss. Your uninhibited emotional release washes away what remains of your once stubbornly dug-in stance, leaving you not *in* a particular position, but rather *aware of* possible positions. You are far from lost in this grief; you are both hurt and lucidly present, clearly seeing what is going on, beyond any mental analysis.

Not surprisingly, research shows that the unrepressed presence of emotion significantly contributes to mental and social skills. Emotions only cloud the skies of rational thought when we lack intimacy with them. And rational thought muddies its own waters when it's cut off from emotion—slipping into, so to speak, an irrational rationality!

Distancing, dissociating, numbing, or otherwise estranging ourselves from our emotions hobbles our capacity to act wisely and compassionately. Research has shown that deteriorated emotional functioning—likely caused by damage to brain regions involved in emotional processing—can retard our ability to make sound decisions, even if our IQ remains intact. So if you want to make optimal decisions, do not leave your emotions out of the picture!

Another problem with viewing emotions as lower or less reliable than reason is that emotion is often associated with females, and rationality with males. This all-too-common gendering of emotion and rationality keeps us stranded from a state of wholeness, in which masculine and feminine work together. Complicating this are views that claim that the neocortex—the headquarters of rational thought—is "higher" than the older zones of the brain that "house" and deal with emotions. "You're being emotional!" carries far more critical heft than "You're being rational!"

When we criticize another for being emotional, we're essentially shaming them for something that's innate. Even if they respond by shutting down or going numb, they're still being emotional—as are we—but in a far less openly expressive way. As long as we associate being emotionally expressive more with being female than with being male, we will stunt our growth. We're all emotional beings; once we wholeheartedly accept this and deepen our emotional literacy, we make more room for meeting one another in ever-richer, more relationally rewarding ways.

CONTAINING AND EXPRESSING EMOTION

In this book you'll learn how to become intimate with each of your emotions and how to take into account the interplay of your emotions. Among the many factors you need to consider in examining a particular emotion is the *interrelatedness* of emotions. Fear expands, and anger often arises; anger contracts, and fear often arises. Anger might be covering sadness, or sadness might be covering anger. Rage can suddenly shift into joy—or grief. Infuse shame with fear, and guilt may arise. When hostility and disgust mingle, contempt shows up. And so on. This mixing and morphing of emotions happens because the boundaries between emotions are far from fixed, existing more as contextual constructs than actual things. For example, anger and fear are clearly different emotions, yet they're biochemically almost identical; what separates them is their operational context. As that context shifts, so too do the emotions; when we tighten up against the expression of our anger, we may start to feel more fearful than angry, or we may start to cry.

If we are to live a deeper, more vividly alive and awakened life, we need to know both our repressive and expressive tendencies regarding our emotions, along with the factors that can catalyze such tendencies. This means not only being more open with our emotions, but also being more aware of them in both their detailing and overall presence. So both an expansive *and* a finely tuned focus are needed.

We also need to know what we're feeling while we're feeling it. We may be conditioned in such a way that we can be feeling a particular emotion without even recognizing that it's happening. This can occur even with something as apparently obvious as anger. A sudden rise in pulse rate, excitation, jaw tension, and blood flow to the hands and torso may not be noticed or acknowledged as signaling any sort of agitation; our face may redden, our eyes glare, and our hands curl into fists, yet we still may not acknowledge that we are angry. For instance, a man may be angry at his wife and yet not consciously register that fact, as research on marital conflict has shown. When we don't register the presence of our anger—often because our attention is literally occupied with other things—we usually deny that it's there, even if our partner or friends insist that it is. This can be immensely damaging to our relationships.

En route to developing emotional intimacy, we must learn to find a fitting balance between *containment* (as when our anger is on the verge of turning into hostility) and *expression* (as when our held-back anger needs to be given emphatic voice). There's a lot of debate about the merits of expressing versus not expressing emotions, particularly those that are labeled "negative," but beyond the sniping between these two camps is another approach: we can make skillful room for both expression and nonexpression, so that expression ceases to be self-indulgent or harmful, and nonexpression ceases to be mere repression. Imagine emotional restraint and emotional uninhibitedness in savvy sync, coexisting consciously and compassionately.

Learning to infuse our emotional expression with compassion and discerning awareness asks much of us, but gives back even more, feeding and empowering our lives. Along the way, we deepen our capacity to guide and be guided by our emotions. Healthy emotional openness is not a submission to emotion per se—which would mean being enslaved or overridden by its imperatives—but rather a kind of awakened surrender to it, or a dynamic, conscious nonobstruction of its essential energies.

So we simultaneously "ride" and are "swept along" by our emotion in much the same spirit that we might successfully bodysurf a big wave. We are out of control and yet simultaneously are not, as encapsulated in Carlos Castaneda's phrase "controlled abandon." Instead of just fighting the wave or letting it overpower us—as in submitting to it—we blend with it, perhaps even to varying degrees "becoming" it. Yet however absorbed we may be in it, we do not lose touch with what really matters.

IDENTIFYING AN EMOTION

We also need to learn how to identify emotions, to clearly read the signs that ordinarily characterize them. This means paying close attention to the gestures, leanings, facial signals, vocal tone, and whatever else is expressive or indicative of particular emotions, sharpening our capacity to attune ourselves to such cues. The more we practice this, the more adept we become at reading whatever emotional dynamics may be at play. Though most emotions have a distinct vocal quality and cross-culturally validated facial expression, such identifying characteristics can be, in some cases, so suppressed or camouflaged that it may not be apparent to an untrained observer that a particular emotion is indeed occurring. Nevertheless, we can still often look to facial expression, body language (like shame's hanging head, fear's raised shoulders, or anger's forward lean), and vocal tone to identify a particular emotion.

So can we always identify a particular emotion through the observed presence of certain behaviors? Not necessarily. We can, for example, display none of the behaviors supposedly characteristic of anger and still be angry. Instead of pounding the table or cursing our misfortune in having such an uncaring partner, we may instead express our anger by trying even harder to please our partner or by withholding a piece of information that we know would help him or her. Or we could be simmering with rage, sporting a huge grin (a sublimated snarl!), and acting very considerately.

Similarly, can we identify an emotion through the observed presence of particular sensations? Not necessarily. Two emotions—like envy and jealousy—may feel very similar and have much the same physiological characteristics, yet they do differ. Intensely gripping excitation (imagine getting an injection of adrenaline) can signal either fear or anger, depending on the circumstances, but it doesn't reveal which emotion is occurring. We discriminate between emotions by attuning, however unknowingly, to the prevailing context of the situation. Shift the context, and we'll likely find ourselves experiencing a different emotion, even though we are physiologically in much the same place.

Because bodily sensations are usually so obviously involved in emotion, we may confuse them with emotion itself. There is, however, more to emotion than just the feel of it. Anger is an attitude, not just a feeling of ready-to-fight heatedness. We evaluate emotion, but not feeling—and I mean "feeling" in a very broad sense. We may speak of our anger as "justified" or "unjustified," but would we speak of our feeling like vomiting or yawning as "justified" or "unjustified"? Or we might speak of our shame as "ridiculous," but would we speak of our feeling like making some breakfast as "ridiculous"?

Also, we can cease being angry yet still feel the very same feelings that a moment ago we identified as anger. For example, I am furious at you for scratching my new car, and suddenly I find out from a deeply trustworthy friend that you are in fact innocent, and I am now no longer angry at you. My evaluation of the situation has radically and almost instantaneously changed, yet the very feelings I experienced just moments earlier—pounding heart, flushed face, knotted shoulders— are still clearly present, having diminished only slightly.

So can I now call these feelings "angry feelings"? No, because their evaluative framework—or emotional basis—has changed.

Given how easy it is to suppress, camouflage, or misunderstand emotion, it is crucial that we become very familiar with how we have done and still tend to do this, but without shaming ourselves for it. There are times when suppressing or camouflaging a feeling is entirely appropriate, but we need to be aware that we're doing so and also to be open to sharing this with those who are close to us.

Emotion is simultaneously very simple and very complex. The feeling of emotion, however difficult it might be to describe, is undeniable and simply present. But the anatomy of emotion is not something that can be neatly dissected and pinned down. An emotion is actually more verb than noun, because it isn't just some endogenous entity or thing we can get out of our system, but a vital process always in some degree of flux.

In some places, there's a saying that if you don't like the weather, just stick around for few minutes and it will change. Emotion is like that. Stay present with it for a few minutes and watch its changes; its directional tilting; its unfolding layers; its shifting colors and textures; its play of dark and light, cloudiness and clarity; its ever-evolving presence.

Emotion is the central station of communication, the connecting fabric of relationship, the currency of intimacy, the life blood of embodied sentience, both moving and motivating us, whatever our circumstances. There's no getting away from it, no matter how much we numb ourselves. So we might as well turn *toward* emotion, regardless of how unpleasant it might be, cultivating as much intimacy with it as possible.

2

Cultivating Intimacy
with Our Emotions

Invite your hurt close and closer
One inhalation after another
And the time—soon but space—
Between your thoughts will widen.
Invite in your hurt minus its dramatics
And there'll be an anchoring ease
More than enough room
To be and to unfreeze.
Room for sun, room for rain
Room for loss, room for pain
Cradled in the grace and vast care
Of what all of us
Cannot help but share

CULTIVATING INTIMACY WITH something means becoming sufficiently close to it to know it very, very well. When we don't get close enough—like scientists keeping themselves emotionally detached from their subject of study—we miss essential aspects. And if we get too close, to the point of *fusing* with it—like new lovers letting their boundaries collapse in a romantic swoon—we lose the ability to keep it in focus.

In intimacy, we are deeply relating to an "other"—a person, object, or state—and we become close to it in a manner that transcends mere proximity. When it comes to cultivating intimacy with something, connection with it and separation from it are not opposites but rather fluidly intertwined dance partners.

When we become intimate with a particular emotion, we no longer treat it as a bad thing, regardless of how uncomfortable it may be when it arises. We welcome the emotion, so to speak, into our living room, giving it enough space to breathe and flow and evolve without necessarily adopting its viewpoint or presenting context. Part of our chosen intimacy with it involves clearly seeing not only its energetic characteristics and somatic signs, but also its take on a given situation.

And in seeing this take—this evaluative framing—we also recognize how our personal history has shaped it. We are not seduced by this emotion's energy, feeling, viewpoint, or tendencies; we keep it close to us, listening attentively and giving it the benefit of our intuition.

Just as we can raise our IQ, so too can we raise our EQ (emotional intelligence). And how? Through developing intimacy with our emotions—both in their arising and in their expressive options—and through involving ourselves in practices that address the weaker or less developed areas of our emotional life.

Becoming intimate with our emotions requires no lowering of IQ, no intellectual slumming, no shunning of rationality, no devaluing of cognition. As our EQ (emotional intelligence) goes up—especially through our increasing capacity for emotional intimacy—our IQ may also go up. And why? Because we're broadening and deepening our scope, bringing more of us to whatever we are facing or dealing with. Put another way, we're operating from a fuller sense of self—after all, emotion includes not only feeling and social factors, but also cognition.

Emotion and rationality can, of course, function separately, but they function optimally when they work *together*.

FOUR STEPS TO DEVELOPING EMOTIONAL INTIMACY

The first step in developing emotional intimacy is to identify what you are feeling.

No details are needed—just the recognition of the emotion. If you are feeling fear, simply notice and acknowledge its presence, without getting absorbed in any accompanying dramatics. If you are feeling more than one emotion at the same time, acknowledge this.

If you are not sure what you are feeling, ask yourself as directly as possible: Am I feeling sad? Am I feeling shame? Am I feeling peaceful? Am I feeling disgust? Am I feeling happy? Am I feeling guilt? Am I feeling unhappy? Am I feeling angry? Am I feeling jealous? Am I feeling afraid? Am I feeling uncomfortable? And so on. Ask sincerely, and it's likely that you'll receive some kind of near-instant response to each question, usually in the form of a relatively visceral "yes," "no," or "maybe." Look for such a response not in your thoughts but in your body and intuitive knowingness. To locate a bodily response, notice where in your body you most clearly feel an increase or change in sensation when you ask any of the above questions. Then bring more attention to this place in your body, noticing what kind of answer—as to what you're feeling—emerges. This may be verbal, nonverbal, or a combination of both.

If after asking these questions and opening yourself to receiving a response, you still cannot identify your emotional state, examine the general tone of what you are feeling: Is it pleasant, unpleasant, or neutral? Is it a distant "hum" or is it more in the foreground? How steady is it? Don't overlook your possible numbness. Numbness is an absence of feeling—the feeling of no-feeling—beneath which there is usually an abundance of emotion. If identifying what you are feeling is still elusive, pay closer attention to your bodily sensations (how your neck, belly, forehead, chest, hands feel), noting their texture, intensity, depth, movements.

Place your attention—not your thinking mind but your bare attention or nonconceptual awareness—on whatever it is that you are feeling. (See the appendix for a meditative practice that grounds and clarifies this awareness.)

Implicit in this first step toward becoming more intimate with emotions is the need to be more emotionally literate. In order to recognize and name the arising emotion, it is incumbent on us to be better educated about the collective characteristics of each of our emotions, along with our personal history with each of them. Such education is a largely experiential undertaking, so it's helpful here to approach our emotions not only intellectually but also with embodied curiosity and the spirit of discovery, as if uncovering a continent of ourselves that has long been shrouded in fog and warnings to keep our distance. It is a far-from-predictable adventure; we may be surprised, for example, by how little we have known about the major role that a particular emotion has played in our development and relational choices.

The second step is to directly state what you're feeling.

Once you have identified what you're feeling, it's time to state this as simply and straightforwardly as you can. This means no fluff, no smoke-screens, no dramatics, no obfuscation—just the bare facts. I say the bare "facts" as opposed to more vague, debatable statements such as "I feel unheard" or "I feel like you're not here for me" or "I feel I'm wasting my time here"—which aren't actually expressing an emotional feeling. At such times what we're actually sharing is our perception—or opinion—of what is going on rather than the simple fact of what we are feeling. So the practice here is to simply state the data. Saying "I feel that you're not hearing me" is a perception, but saying, "I feel angry" is data. The former is debatable; the latter is not. And at this point you can refrain from stating what you are angry or fearful or sad or happy *about*. It's enough just to state the feeling itself.

Practice directly stating what you are feeling in your relationships as much as possible. After you've said what you're feeling, don't immediately follow it with the details. If you've just said that you're feeling angry, let the bare fact of that sink in, giving yourself—and your listener!—time to settle into and resonate with the reality of what you've just shared. Not jumping too quickly into the storyline of what you're feeling lowers the odds that you'll lose yourself in emotional dramatics—as does not letting your listener draw you into a debate, thereby making more room for you and your listener to simply be present with whatever you're feeling.

The third step is to make sure the other person is really hearing what you're saying.

He or she may be able to repeat back to you what you said—without truly having heard it—because they have not yet registered it at a feeling level. When they do, you will know it, sensing an emotional clicking-into-place between you and them, a palpable heightening of mutual empathy. Unfortunately, more than a few of us tend to give the cultivation of empathy and emotional resonance a backseat in our interchanges, including with our partner. Without a significant degree of empathetic attunement, our dialogue can easily degenerate into enervating argument, prolonged withdrawal, or heart-crushing distancing, in which what we are actually feeling becomes secondary to our interpretations of (and debates about) what is going on.

So if you are on the receiving end, let in the other's sharing of their emotional whereabouts until you can clearly feel it—whether or not you like what's being said! And if you are on the giving end? Keep it simple, resisting the temptation to cut loose with what you are angry or fearful or ashamed about. Don't lose touch with what you're feeling. Keep your mind out of it as much as possible, letting your empathy for your listener deepen as much as possible, without in any way diluting what you are sharing with him or her.

And if you are alone, breathe in what you know you are feeling, and keep opening to it. Stay with its rawness. Its storyline, however relevant, does not have to be given energy or attention at this point. Don't argue with yourself. Don't get into a debate with your inner critic about what you should be feeling. Stay consciously embodied, remaining aware of how you are breathing.

Many of us want a quick, feel-better resolution when we are upset. Notice your urge to make this happen, and keep your focus on your bare feeling, bringing into your heart whatever desperation for resolution may be there, as if you are holding in your arms a distraught child. Access as much compassion as possible for yourself when what you're feeling is far from comfortable.

The fourth step is to get into the details without losing touch.

The point of articulating the details is to flesh out the context of what you're feeling, to make sense of it with regard to both your current circumstances and your conditioning. Once what you're feeling is out in the open and acknowledged for what it is, then it's quite natural to give it more context.

This can be done both alone and in the company of others. If you are by yourself, resist getting into the details until your contact with what you're feeling is deep enough to prevent your being seduced by whatever dramatics accompanied the arising of your emotional state.

In the context of relationship, especially intimate relationship, it's essential to make feeling for, or emotionally resonating with, the other more important than whether they agree or disagree with the content of what you are saying. Make your connection with the other person primary, and the working out of relevant details secondary. Doing so is much more effective—and efficient—than attempting to work out the details when you are insufficiently connected with each other. Not taking care of whatever emotional disconnection is present greatly increases the odds of slipping into mutual reactivity—which only reinforces the disconnection.

If you're losing touch with the other person as you get into the details, admit this as soon as possible and *stop*. Then go back to steps one and two, and remain with them until you feel more connection happening with the other. No rush. The time this takes is well worth it! Simply sharing what's going on for you emotionally—in the simplest possible language—can shift things more quickly than getting wrapped up in the details.

If you find that you're still getting emotionally overwrought—somewhere between being "hot under the collar" and "about to blow your lid"—resist reducing what you're saying to courtroom dramatics. Back away from the content, doing nothing to fuel its contentiousness. Say that you can feel yourself getting reactive or overloaded, without justifying this. Notice if there's any underlying feeling occurring; you may, for example, be feeling a sadness that you are not sharing, going instead for the anger atop it. (And if you feel emotionally at a strongly reactive edge—whether you're alone or with another—consider having a *conscious rant,* as described in the next section of this chapter.)

These four steps—identifying, stating, sharing, and providing the relevant details of what you are feeling—are well worth making your own, along with your investigation of your emotions and emotional history. Be intuitive with these steps. Sometimes it will be enough to simply follow the first step only; at other times it will be fitting to follow the first two, three, or all four. This is your own Emotional Literacy 101 training program; treat yourself with compassion throughout, neither rushing nor putting off your engagement in it.

Practice

DEVELOPING INTIMACY WITH DIFFICULT EMOTIONS

Think of the emotion you are usually least comfortable with. (If there's more than one, pick the one that stands out most strongly right now.) Close your eyes and bring to mind a situation in which this emotion strongly emerged. Breathe a little deeper, letting yourself assume the body position you were in at the time. Remember how your face felt when this emotion was present; let your facial expression reflect this as much as possible. Now, instead of keeping your distance from this emotion, pay closer attention to it, bringing it more into focus, simultaneously feeling and observing it.

Next, start taking your attention (perhaps "wearing" it like a miner's headlamp) into the particulars of this emotion—however slightly or slowly—even though your aversion to it might pull you to move in the opposite direction. Bring as much precision as possible to your exploration of this emotion: take note of its texture, directionality, density, temperature, color, intensity, movements, and interactions with other emotions. As much as you can, match your discomfort with your curiosity.

If you stay with this practice long enough, you will become intimate with this emotion to the point where its arising is no longer such a concern for you. Instead, you'll see the arising of this emotion as one more opportunity to deepen your self-knowledge and your capacity for relational intimacy. It will be obvious to you, then, that our darker or "negative" emotions are not the problem; our aversion to them is.

HAVING A CONSCIOUS RANT

It is easy to get so charged up or upset about certain things that we lose perspective, and so it is crucial that we identify, name, and *stay with* the bare feelings that are arising while we're attempting to look—with at least some clarity—at the specifics of our situation. If we don't stay present with our emotional upset or intensity, we will easily get caught up in the surrounding details and dramatics. And if we find ourselves on emotional overwhelm or close to it, then a conscious rant may be called for. In this, you get to cut loose—and I mean loose!—with full-blooded emotional openness, exaggerating your sounds and gestures minus any editing or tiptoeing, taking risks you wouldn't be able to take in the situation that you are disturbed about, all within the confines of a well-boundaried context (the parameters of which you have thought out and clarified *beforehand*).

If you're with another person (your partner or a close friend), you will have already established with them the context and ground rules for having a conscious rant. This needs to be clearly preset, so that your rant—essentially an adult temper-tantrum—takes place in a manner that does no harm. It's as if you are in acting class and your assignment is to give volcanic vent to your emotional state, with a clear beginning and end. (Note: If you're upset with the other person, don't face them during your rant; and if your upset with them is particularly inflammatory, conduct your rant apart from them.)

Here's an example of a conscious rant done with another person present. You've had a rough day at work and arrive home fuming. Your partner greets you, and you snap at him. Even though you don't want to take out your frustration on him, you're starting to do so. He says that it feels like time for a conscious rant, something you've both already agreed to do under certain conditions. Grumbling, you say OK. You both go into the living room; he sits and tells you to go ahead. You stand in the middle of the room, deepening your breathing, seeing him sitting steady and still, holding space for you to cut loose. Now you *fully* express what you're feeling, perhaps shaking your fist, perhaps crying, perhaps melodramatically saying the things you wished you could have said earlier, letting yourself be outrageously alive. No longer can you contain yourself; the lid is off. You can feel your partner's encouraging steadiness of presence. When you get especially dramatic and begin to enjoy your sheer aliveness, you can feel his enjoyment of and appreciation of your performance. After a few minutes you start to wind down, and your partner lets you know that it's over. You lie or sit down comfortably for a while. Soon you're both proceeding with your evening, with far more ease than if you'd bypassed your conscious rant.

If you are by yourself or don't have someone to do this with, the process is still much the same. You proceed, knowing ahead of time that you will do no harm and will go full-out emotionally until you start to naturally unwind. If you find yourself holding back or feeling self-conscious, you simply *exaggerate* what you're doing, including physically—after all, it is a rant! Once you're done, sit or lie down, and close your eyes, resting for at least a few minutes, letting your body soften and settle.

In summary, the steps for a conscious rant are:

1. Name your prevailing emotion(s).
2. In an already established context (for suitable containment), cut loose with what you're feeling. Exaggerate your speech, your tone, your body movements. Be melodramatic!
3. Do this full-out until you naturally run out of steam (usually less than 10 minutes), then lie down or sit comfortably for a few minutes.

If you're a parent, you can teach your children the art of the conscious rant. You're not really introducing anything alien to your children; it's likely they're already adept at having temper tantrums and cutting loose emotionally with their entire being. So how to make this more conscious? First, make sure you are personally capable of having a conscious rant; if you feel inhibited doing this, you probably won't be sufficiently at ease teaching your child how to have a conscious rant. Second, proceed with this only if you and your child have a close, emotionally connected relationship. And third, teach this at least in part as an age-appropriate game, introducing it as naturally and playfully as possible.

For example, your seven-year-old daughter, with whom you're close, is upset about an exchange she had with a friend. She's not saying much, but you know she's really suffering. So you sit with her, perhaps holding her, and briefly tell her about when you've felt hurt but didn't want to keep all your feelings inside. You tell her about this without talking down to her, and to some degree you share this as if you were recounting a captivating story. Then you show her what it's like when you have a conscious rant to get those feelings out—and you invite her to join you.

Once this is underway and flowing naturally, you ask your daughter to imagine her friend standing right in front of her, and you give her permission to say whatever she wants, as openly as possible. You explain that she gets to say anything she wants while she's here with you, but that this is not necessarily what she would say directly to her friend. You help her, if necessary, to get her whole being into her self-expression. No pressure, just the exuberance of full-out expression. You exaggerate your movements, at least initially, to help her get going. You say things in the spirit of: "Show me how angry you are!" and "What do you wish you could have said if it wouldn't get you in trouble?" When your daughter is done, she rests in your lap; a little later, you and she talk about what happened and what might be the best thing to do with her friend.

BEING EMOTIONALLY VULNERABLE

Sometimes one emotion is secondary to another emotion. A common example is when sadness is about to surface and anger arises compellingly, obscuring the sadness. If this is our condition and a friend asks us what we're feeling, we'll probably say that we're angry. Given that we look and sound angry—maybe very angry—this seems like an obvious answer. It's true, but only partially. We're also sad, and in fact are primarily sad. But perhaps we're ashamed to show our sadness, and we feel safer operating from behind our anger. If we know we're sad, not just angry, and we're embarrassed to share this, we might begin by saying that we're having a hard time admitting what's going on emotionally (and we might even be angry that it's so damned hard!). And we might add that in challenging circumstances, we find it much easier to be angry than to directly show our sadness.

Being vulnerable—transparent, open, and unguarded—is immensely helpful when emotions begin to overlap or obscure each other, because it keeps an emotionally honest resonance going between us and the other, along with an amplified receptivity that invites more in-depth disclosure and sharing. Vulnerability can be scary, given that dropping our guard might seem dangerous (and perhaps once *was*). But without vulnerability, we maroon ourselves from our emotional riches and depths—and when that happens we block ourselves from authentic connection with others.

Vulnerability does not have to be a collapsing or caving-in or even disempowering. *It can be a source of strength,* especially as we learn to soften without losing touch with our core presence. There is an inherent dignity in such vulnerability, even when we are in degrading circumstances.

Being emotionally vulnerable means that we are in touch with—and transparent about—what we are feeling, sharing both its surface and its depths. And we are also honest about what we're doing with our emotions, blowing the whistle on ourselves when we're being defensive or aggressive, for instance, or when we're pursuing distraction from what we're feeling. So we are thus willing to share the difficult stuff with people we trust, knowing that the more openly we share the emotional states (and their roots) that we're fearful of revealing, the deeper and more fulfilling our relational connections can be.

EMPATHY AND EMOTIONAL INTIMACY

The capacity to feel or emotionally resonate with what others are feeling—known as empathy—is essential to emotional intimacy. Without it we remain isolated from others, cut off from any sort of intimacy. Our capacity for empathic arousal appears to be innate, but it can be suppressed or derailed through certain conditions, such as abusive or traumatic early-life circumstances. Yet whatever obstructs our empathy can, at least in most cases, be rendered permeable enough to allow us to reconnect with our empathic abilities.

If we score low in empathy, we need to do more than just say that's the way we are; it's important to realize that we're not doomed to occupy the lower rungs of empathetic capacity! Once we stop acting as if we're more empathetic than is actually the case—and also stop shaming ourselves for our lack of empathy—we're on our way to elevating our empathy score.

We might begin by taking a look at our history with empathy—an empathetic look! What situations stirred our empathy? When did we feel no empathy when it seemed that we should? When, if ever, did our empathy overwhelm us? (Having compassion for our shortcomings—including our lack of empathy for others who are suffering—is not license to leave them unaddressed, but a kind of sanctuary in which we can more deeply consider them.) Combining a study of empathy with some empathy-generating practices—like visualizing ourselves in an unliked other's shoes or doing meditative practices centered by wishing others well—will deepen our capacity for empathy.

An elevation in IQ may not mean an increase in MQ (moral intelligence)—we can be cognitive giants and moral midgets—but an elevation in EQ (emotional intelligence) can mean an increase in MQ.

Why? Because the more we are in touch with our emotions, the more in touch we'll likely be with the emotions of others—which greatly increases the likelihood that we'll have a relatively high level of empathy for them. And the more empathy we have for others—along with a capacity for well-functioning, emotionally based communication—the greater the odds are that we will not dehumanize others or treat them badly. Instead, we may take a moral approach to them that goes beyond narrow self-interest and ethnocentric stances, eventually embracing an "us" that includes everyone. (Through such an embrace we start to know, right to our marrow, that what we do to another we do to ourselves.)

And let's not forget cognition in considering empathy. The capacity for empathy is present within twenty-four hours after birth, but it is not a *chosen* empathy. To even *consider* standing in someone else's shoes requires some thinking, as does *recognizing* that we are in fact doing so.

If such recognition escapes our attention or simply does not emerge into consciousness, empathy may become problematic, especially when we overabsorb another's emotional state, taking in that person's feelings so deeply that we lose touch with ourselves. Once we're overwhelmed by another's emotions, we have a hard time telling where they begin and we end: our boundaries are washed away, dissolved, gone. When this occurs, we are of no more use to the other person than if we remained cut off from their emotional condition.

Without empathy, there is no intimacy. But intimacy requires more than empathy. We need to be able to get close enough to others to know them well and to openly feel their state—and at the same time, we need to keep just enough distance from others to maintain the focus needed to separate *their* state from ours.

Without empathy, there is no compassion, but more than empathy is necessary for the genesis of real compassion—including the capacity to set and maintain an *empathic wall* when it's called for, such as when we're feeling excessively absorbed in another's emotional condition. Such a wall can be the thinnest and most permeable of psychological membranes, or it can be much thicker and denser—whatever works to keep us and the other from fusing (or getting lost in each other).

Poet Robert Frost once wrote that good fences make good neighbors. Likewise, good boundaries make good connections, preventing empathetic overload. There are times to open our empathic gates wide, and there are times to close them. We need to have both capacities on tap. Good boundaries make this possible. Releasing, abandoning, or dissolving our boundaries so as to include the other is not the same as expanding our boundaries to include the other.

Through mutually sharing and exploring our emotions with another—which includes not only a transparent expression of them, but also a transparent exposure of the operational context for this—we generate a powerfully alive, emotionally rich "we space" for further relational exploration and deepening.

We exist through relationship, and the more intimate we are with our emotions, the deeper and more fulfilling our relationships—and therefore we—will be. So when you find yourself turning away or withdrawing from an emotion, take a deep breath and turn toward it, furthering your acquaintance with it, knowing it is a relationship worth cultivating.

Deepen, and continue to deepen, the relationship you have with each of your emotions; treat each one as a guest, regardless of how unbecoming or embarrassing its manners may be. Set firm but fair boundaries regarding their expression, regardless of whatever fuss they (with your permission!) might make. Study them closely, knowing that to really know them is, in part, to also know the "I" (or sense of self) behind them.

And let's not leave the investigation of feeling and emotion to the researchers—let's be both curious explorer and the very thing/process being explored. Developing more emotional intimacy is far from a tedious task; it's a remarkably challenging and rewarding adventure that beckons to us every day as our emotions, inevitably, arise.

3

There Are No Negative Emotions

Instead of turning away from your pain
Sit with it for a bit
Until you and it are on the same side
Ready for the needed ride

The pressure to be positive—and therefore not to be negative—strands us from our darkness and its riches, including what can be mined from becoming intimate with our difficult emotions and the negative states into which we may funnel or enlist them.

OUR PRIMARY, OR CORE, EMOTIONS—fear, anger, shame, joy, disgust, surprise, and sadness/grief—have four key features:

1. They are not combinations of other emotions. Sullenness (a mix of sadness and anger) and contempt (disgust infused with anger)—to take but two examples—are not primary emotions, regardless of their intensity of feeling. They're actually a combination of two primary emotions.
2. They are not extensions of other emotions. For example, hostility (something we allow anger to become) and anxiety (something we allow fear to become) are not primary emotions.
3. They can coexist with compassion.
4. Regardless of their degree of darkness or difficulty, they themselves are not negative. They simply are. What may be negative (or positive) is how we're handling them: what we're

allowing them to become, what context we're holding them in, what attitude in which we are enlisting them.

WORRY, HOSTILITY, HATE

Many of us conceive of worry as an emotion, but it is something that we do with an emotion, namely fear. Fear itself is neither negative nor positive; its adrenaline-infused contractedness can serve or stymie us, depending on what ends we employ it for. Worry is an emotion-based *state,* a particular direction in which we are taking—or are taken by— fear. Worry is a *framing* of fear in which we hold ourselves captive to a certain viewpoint. (And there are, of course, many viewpoints we can bring to the experience of fear.)

When we encapsulate the energy of fear in the context of worry, we find ourselves huddled in a "mind"-field of negative anticipation, a mood of nervous concern. A tempest in a "me-knot." In worry we keep ourselves spinning in darkened circles, held hostage by "what-if" mental loopings—so long as we continue to feed it our attention and life force.

This might not seem to be a choice, but it is. If we're habitual worriers, such fearful concern—or overconcern—may seem natural to us, to the point where we don't question it. But question it we must if we are to cease being bound up in it and its negative forecast of what might happen. Worry can easily be presented and accepted as concerned caring for another person, but it's actually little more than projected fearfulness in caring's garb—and who really wants that kind of energy and negative focus coming their way? (To project a quality of ours is to disown it and see it only in others.)

Cutting through worry doesn't necessarily end our fear, but it clears the air, allowing us to bring more lucid awareness to the actual source of our arising fear. That said, worry is worth penetrating and dismantling. Where we once caved in to its dire view, we can divest it of that very view—so that it simply is here-and-now fear—and instead invest our energy in more life-affirming activities, even if we are still feeling fear. In other words, worry does not have to be our default when a bad possibility crosses our mind.

So is worry really not an emotion? It certainly can pack an emotional wallop and get our guts churning. But however worry manifests—usually as a *mood*—it remains something we're doing with our fear, a negative emotional choice. And while emotions are almost always short-lived, moods are not—worry can go on relatively unabated for a long time, much like its darker cousin, depression.

Worry is but one of many emotional choices made from a feeling-state that isn't inherently negative. Other negative emotional choices include contempt, guilt, and hostility. Contempt is something we are choosing to do with disgust; guilt is something we are choosing to do with shame; and hostility is something we are choosing to do with anger.

If you look deeply into such endarkened emotional choices, you'll note that they are devoid of empathy; once empathy arises, such states quickly cease, not reemerging until our empathy wanes to nothing.

Consider contempt. In it, disgust and some degree of anger coalesce and are rigidly held in a context of superiority. Contempt is a particularly negative and dangerous emotional choice, given how strongly and readily we dehumanize others when we're in its grip. Like worry, contempt cannot coexist with compassion. But the emotional core of worry—fear—and the emotional core of contempt—disgust—*can* both coexist with compassion.

Guilt is another so-called negative emotion. Like contempt, it is a combination of emotions: shame and fear. Guilt certainly cannot coexist with compassion, given that its very nature involves turning away from compassion: one part of it, fixatedly childish or immature, acts out while the other part, fixatedly parental, punishes the first. No real caring—just a nastily stalemated parent-child conflict. Strip down guilt and what is left? A load of shame mixed with a significant dose of fear. And shame and fear, both primary emotions, are neither negative nor positive.

When we assume that an emotion is negative or unwholesome, we strand ourselves from the life-giving impact that it could have for us. For example, if we've saddled anger with a negative connotation (perhaps because it was handled badly in our childhood, or it is stamped as unwholesome in some way by our spiritual path), we likely will greet arising anger with aversion, muting its expression as much as possible and distancing ourselves from its raw power. Such distancing can be draining—we use up a significant amount of life energy when we cage, muzzle, or otherwise suppress an emotion. Not that anger has to be left to run free or take bites out of whoever offends us!

Anger has the power to fuel necessary changes for us and to back us up when we need to take a stand. When we make anger's power and fiery intensity wrong, we're simply shortchanging ourselves, estranging ourselves from a potentially empowering force. Getting openly angry because you have just been fired from your job may give you the energy to look for a better job. Similarly, getting openly angry about the affair your partner is having and is trying to blame you for can fuel your drive to draw firmer boundaries, providing the energy to either turn the relationship around for the better or to say goodbye to it.

When we get hostile, we're angry—perhaps very angry—but we're also operating in a harsh, mean-spirited context, channeling our anger into aggression toward our target. Repressed anger is implicated in disease, but so too is hostility. It's not expressed anger that makes heart disease or heart attacks more likely, but the act of directing it into hostility. It's easy to equate anger with hostility, ill will, aggression, and hatred, but these are things in the service of which we are enlisting our anger.

Hate is a particularly dark emotional state that's important to know very well. Its intensity and black-hearted focus can easily burn through any restraints we attempt. (And, as we shall see, there is something to be said about ceasing to restrain hate under certain conditions.) Where anger is fire, hatred is conflagration, regardless of how contained it might be. In hatred there is an abundance of anger along with deep-cutting hurt and perhaps some disgust, all darkly bunched together in the service of a context where an offending other has become the highlighted object of our hatred. Hatred is something we are doing with emotion; we are not just outraged and hurt and disgusted, but we are transmitting this in an extremely negative way.

Hate is a passion, however tightly contained or hidden its flames may be. By a passion, I mean any state that has the power to overwhelm us, to take us over, to really consume us. Passion can be positive or negative, but in either case it possesses us. Passion is not an emotion per se, but it always includes emotion. Passion is life force on the loose, a relinquishing of the reins, a full-blooded infusion of grippingly uninhibited intensity. Sadness is not a passion, but grief is. And so is rage/fury. And ecstasy, and sexual lust. Like any other passion, hatred can *completely* occupy us, perhaps even becoming our predominant state of being or emotional baseline rather than just an occasional reaction to unusually difficult or unpleasant circumstances.

However, hate is not necessarily something we should always try to get over as soon as possible. There are times when we truly need to openly feel and *fully* express our hatred—under suitable conditions, such as provided by quality psychotherapy—in order to properly heal and authentically move on. (I say "authentically" because many people prematurely move on, avoiding dealing with the full impact of what catalyzed their hatred.) For example, if we have been brutally assaulted, it may be quite natural, at least for a while, to hate the attacker and to want to violate that person. Such dark longings and fantasies can harm us if we house them very long, because they easily can eat away at us, solidifying our hatred and ossifying our heart. But if we let ourselves fully express such hate—again, under suitable conditions—we will cease rooting ourselves in our hatred, again and again breaking down until we break open, at which point our rage-initiated agony will flood through us unimpeded, making sufficient room for our woundedness without our being overrun or controlled by it.

Not surprisingly, this is no one-shot undertaking, yet the time it takes to work in such depth with hate is far, far less than the time consumed when we let out our hate superficially or in ways that reinforce it (as when we hold it so tightly that there is no room for our raw hurt to emerge). Hate that is stifled or bypassed (perhaps because we want to show that we are beyond it or we are ashamed that it is still present) only festers and feeds upon itself, slowly but surely metastasizing, encoding its dark will throughout us. When we make room for our hate—neither demonizing nor indulging in it, nor dissociating from it—and express it all-out without harming others or ourselves, we ready ourselves for real forgiveness. Hate does not go away just because we vacate its quarters or layer it over with feel-good practices and beliefs.

Forgiveness and hatred may seem like polar opposites, but they are strongly connected—the path to genuine forgiveness is often paved with hatred. As much as we might want to bypass hate en route to forgiveness, it is much more efficient and effective to go into and *through* our hate so that we fully face and take good care of our darkest reactions to what was done to us—opening up the core of our woundedness, releasing the darkness there, and letting in healing presence. This is not a gentle meditative process undertaken in low tones, but a full-bodied, full-throated, deeply vital undertaking.

Journey to the heart of hate and what will you find? Not more hate, but pure anger—which is actually a very vulnerable emotion—and gut-wrenching grief, a broken-open depth of being that's not only excruciatingly painful but also liberating. In many cases, it's through this primal passage, through hatred, that forgiveness becomes not some paint-by-numbers process that confers on us the spiritual status of being able to easily forgive, but that instead becomes a remarkably empowering practice. Can we call hatred an *entirely* negative emotion when it guides us toward such opening? No.

Practice

MAKING WISE USE OF HATE

Sit down in a place where you won't be disturbed, and think about a time when you felt hate. Breathe it in. Immerse yourself in it. Notice what is happening to your body and exaggerate it. How does your heart feel? Your mouth? The tissues around your eyes? Your hands? What do you want to say? Say it. Don't edit, don't be polite, don't be careful. Give yourself full permission to speak freely. Raise your volume. If this embarrasses you or otherwise makes you uncomfortable, note that and still proceed, doing your best not to let your view regarding hate get in your way. And if cutting loose vocally continues to feel too uncomfortable, hold a large, firm pillow against your face and say what you have to say into it, as powerfully as you can (knowing that no one will hear you, given how muffled your sounds will be). Do this full-out expressing for no more than a minute.

Now sit across from where you just were, imagining that you are not the aspect of you who hates but the aspect that sees and cares about the one expressing the hate. Talk to that one, spontaneously. Instead of making their hate wrong and instead of merely tolerating it, be with them, sensing not just the anger in their hate, but also the hurt. Imagine holding that hurt, bringing it close, simultaneously embracing and protecting it as if it were an extremely upset child. If your eyes aren't already closed, close them now, bringing more awareness to your heart and belly. Be silent. Feel yourself softly expanding, extending beyond your usual boundaries, both holding and being the one who hates, making more and more room for their hurt to be both expressed and healed. Stay with this for at least ten minutes.

THE SHADOW OF TRYING TO BE EMOTIONALLY POSITIVE

The more we label our difficult emotions as negative, the greater the odds are that we'll tend to overvalue our "positive" emotions, making too much of a virtue out of being happy, upbeat, optimistic. We may try extra hard to be nice; we may become driven about positive thinking—trying to affirm our way into a more abundant life. Or we may try to camouflage the lines on our face that indicate anything less than happiness. We may buy into sunny-side-up spirituality (leaving ourselves with egg on our face and a big bill). We may confuse emotional flatness with equanimity and emotional dissociation with transcendence; we may try to be nonjudgmental, forgetting that judging comes with having a mind. And we may get negative about our negativity!

The pressure to be positive cuts us off from our darkness and its riches, including what can be mined from becoming intimate with our difficult emotions and the negative states into which we may funnel or enlist them.

Telling someone to "lighten up" or be more positive can be shame inducing, however nicely we might do it. What if they need to stay with their hate or despair or depressiveness for a while? How can we be sure they'd be better off getting away from such states as soon as possible? Perhaps at such times we're starting to feel—through our contact with their endarkened condition—more in touch with such states in ourselves, and want the other person to get away from their "darkness" so that we don't have to feel our own to any significant depth.

We need to stop attaching "better" to up-ness, positivity, light, and expansion and "worse" to down-ness, negativity, darkness, and contraction. Doing so keeps us split, divided, cut off from our wholeness. Better to make compassionate room for both camps, developing an abiding intimacy for them without taking on their viewpoints or pleas to take their side. In such awakened spaciousness, our emotions can only serve us, attuning and connecting us to all the relational dynamics that are at play in our life.

~

By turning toward your painful emotions—especially those you tend to label as negative—you will start to feel a more embodied sense of wholeness, a sense of internalized reunion and communion. Instead of abandoning or trying to transcend what is unwanted, disowned, ostracized, or otherwise cast aside in you, you can include it in your being, intimately, until it is no longer a distant "it" but rather a reclaimed *you*.

4

Emotional Disconnection

> So much of what we do is but a strategy to escape painful
> emotion so as to not get significantly hurt, not get really
> vulnerable, not get rocked by relational demands—and
> to somehow become all but immune to suffering.

EMOTIONAL DISCONNECTION—being significantly removed
or dissociated from what we're feeling—is so commonplace that it
easily gets both overlooked and normalized, regardless of its obviousness. We may, for example, detect an emotional flatness or emptiness
in a friend we're speaking with, a disconnection from feeling, an
incongruity between what's being said and how it's being said, and
just let this pass, even when it's having a negative impact on us. Of
course we're not going to expect every conversation to be emotionally
alive and flowing, but when we over and over again leave unaddressed
a contact that lacks feeling where there clearly ought to be feeling—as
when a friend talks in an unwaveringly level voice about something
that disturbs him or her greatly—we're doing little more than deadening ourselves.

None of this, however, is to say that we should never engage in
emotional disconnection, for there are times when doing so is entirely
fitting. An example: We're with someone who is raging, right on the
edge of getting violent, and we're in no position to oppose this, regardless of our intense aversion to what they're doing. So we disconnect
emotionally and keep our voice very level and neutral, giving the raging
one as little as possible to react against. We have, in a sense, skillfully
disconnected so that we can connect at a deeper level, namely that of

pure survival, with our radar turned on high with no emotional turbulence clouding its moment-to-moment reading of the situation.

An extreme example is a person enduring heavy violation. When what they're being subjected to reaches a certain point, they'll very likely emotionally disconnect completely, being launched into full-blown dissociation (losing touch with their body). Such removal—which is not so much a choice as an organismic default—allows them to survive their hellish circumstances, with the bare reality of it encapsulated within, kept apart as much as possible from their daily reality and waking consciousness so that they can continue functioning. The trauma will of course affect them greatly, but it won't necessarily bring their life to a grinding halt. If, later on, they are in a sufficiently safe environment (like that of high-quality psychotherapy), what has been encapsulated can surface to the point where it can be fully faced and worked through, and whatever emotional disconnection was originally necessary can now shift into fully felt feeling and energetic mobilization.

Disconnecting from our feelings can sometimes serve us—even save our life—but this doesn't mean we need to keep it as our default whenever life gets difficult or "reminds" us of the original factors of our tendency to disconnect emotionally.

During relational conflict, many of us shut down, withdraw, go silent, or otherwise emotionally disconnect when there is nothing at all dangerous, abusive, or threatening occurring (though it may well feel dangerous or threatening to the child in us). Though such behavior initially arises automatically, we have the capacity to be aware of it right after its inception—and this capacity can be greatly deepened with practice—so that we can acknowledge that it is indeed happening. This helps us cut through any tendency to play victim to our emotional cutting-off during contentious times, knowing that it is not just something we cannot help but do.

Before our emotional shutting-down or disconnection gets solidified, we can counter it in various ways once we've admitted it's happening. For example, we can state what we feel like doing (withdrawing, going silent, and so on) but not act it out; we can breathe more deeply and deliberately; we can give a running description of what our internal workings are (physically, mentally, emotionally); we can give ourselves permission to openly feel and *express* what we long ago did not dare let ourselves express; and we can do whatever else helps us awaken in the midst of our reactivity.

Nondefensively admitting to someone that we're feeling emotionally disconnected from them can help us reconnect. Vulnerable self-disclosure ordinarily needs to be at the top of our list of options when we're stuck in the sticky stuff of relational discord. Instead of shaming ourselves for slipping into emotional disconnection, we can use the blatant obviousness of it to reestablish our intimacy with our significant other—all we have to do for starters is say that we're feeling disconnected—without blaming the other for our being in such a state.

It's not uncommon for emotional disconnection to be overlaid by a pseudo-equanimity, a steady-state pleasantness, an unperturbed demeanor, or whatever else helps provide a socially acceptable face or facade. This is epitomized by unrelentingly even-keeled television-news anchors who present all the news, from the horrifying to the trivial, in the same well-modulated, professionally confident tone of voice. Such "levelheadedness" and apparent composure doesn't indicate true stability but rather a photogenic distancing from real feeling and the possibility of losing face. Another example can be found in the realm of spiritual bypassing (using spiritual practices/beliefs to avoid dealing with painful feelings and unresolved wounds). Responding to a tragedy by stating that it's all perfect or that it's just the playing-out of karma merely disguises our emotional disconnection from the tragedy as spiritual transcendence.

Emotional disconnection—especially as a flight from vulnerability—isn't something only a few of us are stuck in. It's the prevailing operational status of many, camouflaged by periodic bouts of emotional intensity and/or sexualized vitality. We can, for example, flare up with rage and still be emotionally anemic, using our aggressive outbursts not only to give ourselves a power break from our usual reality but also to take the edge off our hurt, grief, fear, and shame so that their presence ebbs—at least for a while.

Another example: we might get overly absorbed in our sexuality, amplifying—and perhaps also advertising—it in all sorts of ways, eroticizing our desire to be wanted or to feel better or more secure, accessing enough excitation-centered "feeling" to appear to be far from emotionally numb, even though our erotic heatedness is far more about sensation than actual emotional feeling. When sex is employed as a means of distracting us from our suffering—including our emotional pain and disconnection—it leaves us out in the cold, no matter how hot it is.

So much of what we do, so much of what we are driven to do, so much of what we think we should do, is but a strategy to get away from painful feeling—especially from feeling fully and openly—so as to not get significantly hurt, not get really vulnerable, not get rocked by relational demands—and to somehow become all but immune to suffering. But the inevitable pains of life again and again let us know that such immunity is a fantasy, a bubble of consoling separation that the rude pricks of reality will easily and inevitably burst, exposing us to the very emotional material and challenges from which we so recently fled.

THE ANATOMY OF "COOL"

Let's consider a form of emotional disconnection—being "cool"—that still gets approval in many circles. The more emotionally cutoff we are, the less vulnerable we will be and—assuming that we are otherwise functional—the more likely able to stay "cool." The stylized invulnerability, the show of savvy ease, the engaging disengagement, the display of emotional immunity that underlie and animate the "coolest" versions of "coolness" are often taken as signs of "having it together" instead of dysfunction.

"Cool" is run by shame, and not just run but *driven*. Of course, "cool" doesn't look like it has anything to do with shame, other than perhaps to trigger shame in others when in the presence of someone apparently cooler than them. But "cool" is a byproduct of shame that's run about as far as you can get from shame. If we didn't *already* feel shame—the excruciatingly self-conscious sense of being seriously flawed in the eyes of a convincingly critical audience, outer or inner—we wouldn't have so much investment in being or acting cool. There are, of course, other directions that shame can take, such as when it morphs into aggression (whether self-directed or other-directed) or flat-out withdrawal, but "cool" looks a lot better—much cooler—than these.

"Cool" doesn't—mustn't—look ruffled, not because it's courageous or knows how to get centered when there's a crisis, but because it's attached to looking good in an in-the-know kind of way, and being ruffled just doesn't look so good. "Cool" does not, does not, does *not* want to lose face—and what is shame, but a painfully mortifying loss of face? Emotional disconnection keeps "cool" in business. And this starts at a young age. Consider the five-year-old boy who falls down and immediately says, blank faced and shrugging, "I meant to do that."

But now "cool" is starting to lose some of its cool. The less cool it is to be cool—so that it becomes cool not to be cool—the more that "cool" will fade. Behind its shades and costumes, "cool" is losing its cool. The lid is coming off, as it must. We've done our time with trying to be cool; the stakes are too high now to continue making such a cultural virtue out of disengagement and emotional disconnection, regardless of its edgy fashionableness.

Perhaps the biggest shortcoming of "cool" is not its lack of vulnerability but its tacit pride in such lack. "Cool" doesn't wear its feelings on its face, other than perhaps flickers of happiness or traces of contempt. Instead, it simultaneously buries its feelings and then projects them onto the uncool. Getting emotional usually is a sign of failure for "cool" (and for those overcommitted to rationality)—"blowing our cool" is a fundamental no-no. When "cool" is in the presence of real love, it gets very uncomfortable, for such love could, like shame, cause it to lose face or control, which of course is very uncool.

Strip "cool" of its outward appearance—after all, it's all about exteriors—and what is left? The debris of its unexamined interiority and absence of heart, constellated around shame, shakiness, insecurity, and fear—in other words, a trembling abundance of vulnerability.

To enter such states with openness and awakened attention requires that we let go of being cool, and start reembracing our bare humanity, our woundedness, our shamed selfhood and raw beauty of being, so that these get not just a token nod or some pharmaceutical help or the latest shades, but rather a depth of healing and integration that puts us back on our feet and in our hearts, unseducible by the siren call of "cool" or any other channel for emotional disconnection.

TURNING TOWARD EMOTIONAL DISCONNECTION

Once we really understand that there is no true escape from feeling, including unpleasant or distressing feeling, we may start, at last, to consciously and consistently turn *toward* such feeling, like a loving parent turning with full presence and compassion toward their just-hurt or badly frightened child.

The work here—a deep labor of love—is to compassionately relate to and connect with our zones of emotional numbness and estrangement.

It is crucial to make that connection without shaming ourselves for having been so out of touch. When we are in the throes of emotional disconnection and recognize that it is indeed happening, all we initially have to do is openly admit this. Then we can start turning toward it, drawing it out of the shadows, until we are reestablished in feeling fully.

Emotional disconnection doesn't necessarily disappear as we grow wiser; it happens to even the most mature of us. Our task is to acknowledge its presence as soon as possible after it shows up, and to then deeply attend to it, to the point of bringing it into our heart and deliberately cultivating intimacy with it, knowing it from the inside, being as open to its historical origins as we are to illuminating it.

We need to deeply value both our capacity for emotional connection and what it takes to establish, maintain, and deepen this capacity. Otherwise, we are in danger of letting emotional disconnection become the norm, thereby sentencing our relationships to a mere shadow of what they could be, keeping ourselves estranged from the emotional resonance and depth that make possible the kind of interrelatedness that our times so badly need.

5

Emotion and Language

Exploring the Use of Metaphor
for Emotional Experience

We usually don't "blow our stack" without first having gotten
"steamed up." If we can catch ourselves while our anger is
still "simmering," we have a better chance of not slipping into
aggression or violence than if we "keep the lid on" until we "erupt."

IN DESCRIBING OUR EMOTIONAL experience, we often
resort to metaphor, relying far more on its succinct, colorful shorthand
("I'm about to blow a fuse") than on more abstract or relatively disembodied descriptions ("I'm feeling that you're not hearing me").

To convey the felt reality of emotion, there is no more apt language
than that of metaphor. Its descriptive power lies in the visceral accuracy of its compact, streetwise utterances; it's not heard as abstraction
because it's rooted in our sensory and motor experience. (Research
shows that the very act of hearing metaphors can activate brain regions
involved in sensory experience.)

Using metaphors to describe emotional experience is not something
to be outgrown, but to be generously applied, ideally in timely conjunction with a capacity to more precisely detail what has just been
metaphorically conveyed. For example, we could say that we're about
to blow the proverbial gasket—which makes it clear that we're at the
edge of getting explosively angry—and then add as precisely as we can
where we actually feel such pressure (our jaw, upper chest, forearms,
hands), and what we're *doing* with the intensified sensations in these

places, hopefully along with the options we're considering. Such "doing" occurs along a continuum with suppression/containment at one end and full expression at the other.

By paying closer attention to the language we use to describe our emotions, we can become more intimate with our emotions and how they operate in our lives. Our words can cut us off from our emotions, but they also can be a gateway to emotional intimacy. So let us attend closely to how we describe our emotions, finding as fitting and full a language for our emotional experience as we can.

Our metaphors for emotions can provide a felt sense of how we are experiencing them, but we need to see this viscerally apt descriptive capacity for what it is, rather than as the full picture or core truth of what's happening emotionally for us. And, if at all possible, we need to factor in what we are doing with our emotions, letting the recognition of this coexist with our metaphoric captions for how our emotions feel. To say "My blood is boiling" or "I'm doing a slow burn" tells us more than saying "I am angry." The implied degree and quality of heatedness gives us valuable information in one short phrase, as does "I'm getting hot under the collar" or "I'm about to go through the roof." We can feel the pressure in each of these metaphors, along with a sense of rising in the second one ("eruption" is upward). So by verbalizing in this way, we feel a touch more intimate with the anger being described; we can sense its heat, pressure, directionality, and explosive capacity through the linguistic shorthand of metaphor.

What symbols are to the mind, metaphors are to the body and emotions. When we hear an emotion described metaphorically, we register it more deeply than when we hear it described in abstract terms. (And how ironic it is that most research on emotions articulated in scientific journals is written in the dry, disembodied language of academic discourse.)

THE "CONTAINER" METAPHOR FOR EMOTION

Let's begin with the container metaphor for emotion. It's so common, so entrenched in everyday conversation, that we may not realize we're using it. To say "I am overflowing with sadness" or "I am feeling bottled up" or "I stuff my feelings" suggests that our emotions are *inside* something. Of course, if we believe that we are inside our bodies—as if our body is a literal container for *us*—then we're likely to feel at home with the various container metaphors for emotion. "I feel contained" says it all.

There are two main container categories: emotion as a liquid in a container and emotion as a heated liquid in a container. "I am filled with sorrow" or "I feel drained" are examples of the first category, whether there's a surplus or shortage of fluid. The second category is, not surprisingly, dominated by anger: "I am getting steamed up" or "I am about to blow my lid" suggest different degrees of heatedness. There are also metaphors expressing a decrease in the temperature of that fluid: "My feelings for you are cooling."

If the container is not expandable and pressure increases due to the "heated liquid" in it, the situation intensifies. We shift from "simmering" to "boiling" to "blowing our stack," apparently unable to "contain" ourselves. When we are very angry, we do feel a very real pressure: our pulse jumps, our blood pressure rises, our sense of "bursting" shows in a reddened face, inflated upper torso, and perhaps bulging eyes. The more amplified the emotion, the experientially greater the pressure in the "container." We might "break into tears" or "pour out" our emotions, finding great difficulty in "keeping it in" any longer. The pressure hits a certain level, and we "lose it" or "explode," perhaps even going to the point where "all hell breaks loose."

When we "burst"—with rage, grief, exultation—we are, so to speak, no longer "walling ourselves in." With such decontainment, we're not necessarily freeing ourselves; we may feel looser as a result of our energetic discharge, but without any increase in our intimacy with the actual emotion being expressed. We have neither gotten "to the bottom" of the container nor gone "deeper" into it, but have simply taken a break from it.

MAKING "INNER" SYNONYMOUS WITH "MORE REAL"

The container metaphor for emotions is often used to convey emotional intensity or depth. If I say, "My feelings for you are getting deeper," then I am feeling more drawn to you, and if I say, "Deep down inside I know we are meant to be together," then I am underlining my sincerity, fueling it with the positive connotations of depth.

The closer our feelings are to the center of the container, the less superficial they apparently are. Saying, "From the bottom of my heart I love you," suggests that you really mean it. The more we can frame what we're feeling as our "innermost" feeling, the more we can—for better or for worse—present it as being especially authentic. It's easy and very common to make "inner" synonymous with "more real" or "most real." Given this, the "inner life" is often taken as something of unquestioned importance, including spiritually. It may be strongly recommended that we "look within" or at least "get to the bottom of things"—for that's where the truth apparently is. And we might have to "dig" for it. None of this is meant to devalue our interiority (feelings, thoughts, perceptions, sense of self) or the need to become as intimate with it as possible; it's meant to highlight the exaggerated relevance that the notion of "inner" may be granted.

If we overvalue the "inner," then the closer something is to the "surface," the less important or authentic we may take it to be. "Layers" of dubious selfhood may then have to be exposed and peeled until we get to the center or bottom of the "container," where the true self supposedly abides. This, of course, fits the belief that we are "in" our body, whether we view the body as a temple or prison or housing project. How could you "come out of your shell" if you were not already *inside* your body? And if we are "in" our body, so too must be our emotions—or so we think. (My intuition is that who and what we truly are is making an appearance not *in* a body, but *as* a body. In this sense, our body expresses rather than contains us.)

OTHER METAPHORS FOR EMOTION

In the container metaphor, emotion is conceived of as an indwelling entity or mass, a thing within us. If this is true, then emotions are things we can externalize, discharge, and empty ourselves of. There are plenty of metaphors for emotions that don't locate them within us ("He flew into a rage"), but still conceptualize them as things, nouns, masses. (It is important to note that conceiving of emotions as things residing within us is arguably culturally bound. In Japan, for example, emotion is often viewed not so much as a subjective phenomenon as an *intersubjective* phenomenon, existing as a kind of atmosphere associated with particular social circumstances.)

We can conceive of our emotions as not just something inside us, but as something *outside* us. For example, consider the metaphor that emotion is an opponent: "I fought my fear" or "I wrestled with my guilt" or "I was overcome by shame." It's hard to be intimate with something that is so interior that we can't quite see or reach it, and it's equally hard to be intimate with something that is so exterior that it remains distinctly "other" to us. If our anger "gets the best of us," how well are we going to know it? Probably no more than a defeated wrestler "knows" the one who has submitted or pinned him.

Or consider the metaphor that emotion is an overpowering natural force: "I was flooded with grief" or "She stormed out of the room" or "I was swept off my feet." Here, we are conveying not only a sense of being taken over, but of being unable to stop it. If we are—or play— the victim to something, how intimate can we be with it? Being "eaten" by jealousy does not give us a very clear view of it; if we are being "consumed" by envy or grief, we are unlikely to be focusing with much lucidity on their particulars.

And what about metaphors that depict emotion as an illness or infection? We can be "terror stricken" or "worried sick" or "sick with dread." Notice that these expressions are all fear based and that there is, again, an implied helplessness. If we are helpless before such emotions, how responsible can we be held for them?

Another common metaphor is emotion as an animal: "I unleashed my anger" or "Fear burrowed through me." Anger and lust share some common ground here: If she "brings out the beast in me" to the point where I have "mounting expectations," then I may feel justified in "pouncing" upon her. We can "bristle" with rage, "raise our hackles," and "bite someone's head off." Such animalistic metaphors convey the biological aspect of emotion (much of which we share with other mammals) and can lead to a devaluing of emotion into something primitive, in stark contrast to our species' capacity for rationality.

CONCEIVING OF EMOTIONS AS UNTRUSTWORTHY

Many of our emotion metaphors convey that we largely experience emotion as something that's being done *to* us. Fear can madden us ("crazy with fear"), anger can render us violent ("I saw red" or "I went ballistic"), shame can immolate us ("a burning shame"), disgust can make us sick ("I can't stomach you"), guilt can trap us ("caught with her hand in the cookie jar"), and jealousy can destroy us ("eaten alive by jealousy").

So emotion metaphors generally suggest that we are—or can be— run by our emotions. They can "rule" us, "sweep us away," or "drive" us. And trying to get away from our emotions is far from easy, if only because they are often "written all over our face." Such "takeovers" and hard-to-conceal facial displays (and body language) may make it seem that our emotions are not really under our control, and therefore should be. If they are not under our control (they may "intoxicate" us or "carry us away"), we may blame them for this, categorizing them as animalistic or uncivilized. How odd that the proverbial "stiff upper lip" is considered more of a sign of maturity than the outright vulnerable expression of emotion! Anger may seem primitive, but what we do with it is often far from civilized.

It's common not to trust our emotions, especially in contrast to our rational faculties. Not only can they apparently "rule" us and even reduce us to "animals," but they also can "mislead" or "deceive" us. We may speak of being "fooled" by our emotions, but can we talk of being fooled by our rationality? When we don't trust our emotions—and assume that this is a natural thing to do—we obstruct our capacity to become intimate with them, and vastly narrow our lives.

And here's the deeper danger: if we conceive of our emotions as untrustworthy and of being things inside us, we place ourselves in the difficult position of trying to keep a certain distance from our "inner" dimensions, given that our emotions apparently reside there. If we "let them out" or "unleash" them, they may behave badly—much like animals kept too long in a cage. If we keep them in, we have to keep a vigilant eye on them, which is impossible to maintain around the clock. So our emotions then pose both an "outer" and an "inner" threat to us. If we "stuff" or "swallow" our feelings, increased internal pressure will be required to keep them in. All this adds up to a heavy load of self-policing, which is inherently exhausting.

Being on guard against emotional uprisings or breakout attempts from "within" guarantees chronic tension. To keep from falling apart or "losing face," we overbudget for defense, treating our emotions—or at least our "negative" emotions (which we further endarken by keeping incarcerated)—as untrustworthy. The resulting disconnection from our emotions may help us "keep our cool," but it actually leaves us out in the cold.

This is exacerbated by not distinguishing between the "I" that wants to keep emotion under house arrest, the "I" that wants to give emotion occasional outings, the "I" that wants to "unleash" or "give free rein" to emotion, and the "I" that wants to both regulate and openly express emotion in a mindfully compassionate context. Our work is not to identify with any of these apparent selves, but to learn to embody a quality of awareness that can hold all of our "I's" with spacious compassion.

~

We need to liberate emotion from our confining notions of containment and decontainment—ceasing to burden emotion with excesses of control-from-within and control-from-without. This means not getting caught up in or investing in conceptualizations of emotion as untrustworthy or dangerous.

Whether we are "beside ourselves with fear" or "bursting with joy" or "getting steamed up," we have an opportunity not only to pay close attention to such experientially apt descriptions, but also to become more intimate with what they are pointing to—emotion. We can choose to relate to emotion not as a thing but as an ever-fluxing activity—a fluidly vital process that is the life blood of communication.

6

Emotional Intimacy
in Relationships

If we want more depth, connection, and joy in our relationships,
we're going to have to develop more emotional intimacy with
our significant others. It's that simple and that challenging.

ONE OF OUR DEEPEST AND most common longings is for a
genuinely intimate relationship, as attested to by the vast number of
books and courses about how to find such a relationship. Songs abound
about love found and love lost, replete with aching, breaking, and forsaken hearts. We may settle for less than deeply fulfilling relationship,
but this doesn't necessarily mean that we don't want more. It's just that
we may feel so reluctant to do what it takes (perhaps having given up
hope) to have such relationships that we stay put on the shore, unwill-
ing to take the leap into what will greatly increase the odds of us being
in the kind of relationship for which we yearn. And that leap, that
trust-infused departure from our shallows and day-to-day conditioning,
is none other than a conscious entry into the depths of our emotions.

Our dreams about this often feature going underwater, under-
ground, plunging beneath surfaces, opening doors, passing through
walls, and leaving the familiar behind. The feeling in these dreams is
typically a mix of fear and excitement, for the journey we're embarking
on is one of both promise and peril. It's a vividly emotional undertaking—and the more deeply we come to know our emotions and how to
best navigate them, the more successful our journey will be. There will
be dragons—every treasure has and needs its dragons—that we'll have

to face, requiring that we get close enough to our fearfulness to render it our ally. And so too with the rest of our emotions—the closer we are to them, the more capable we will find ourselves of being in genuinely fulfilling relationship.

Developing and deepening emotional intimacy in our relationships asks for courage and trust. Getting more vulnerable—which is absolutely essential to emotional intimacy—can be a frightening and shame-laced venture, but without taking the jump into such an unguarded openness of being, we will remain in the shallows of relationship. Hence the need for courage. And for trust. If we have to talk ourselves into trusting, we probably would do best to step back and explore our mistrust, rather than trying to override it. Part of the leap here would be to trust another (our partner or a close friend, assuming that they have proved themselves worthy of trust) with our mistrust, exposing it and the feelings with which it is associated.

> When we stop caring who's right
> We uncover enough shared heart to see
> What's right about what's wrong
> Finding enough mutuality to be
> More comfortable with our discomfort
> Including the fear of being so close,
> So removed from relational immunity,
> That even the tiniest unkindness
> Can pierce us

TURNING TOWARD OUR FEAR WITHIN RELATIONSHIP

An essential step to take, and keep taking, is to turn toward our fear within relationship. Courage doesn't mean that we're not afraid but that we're not letting fear dictate our course. And central to courage is trust in ourselves, especially in our intuition to proceed, even when we are shaking in our proverbial boots.

Such a resolute and inherently vulnerable turning-toward—a movement not so much of thought as of embodied attentiveness—is an essential step. This movement may feel unnatural at first, given that we are probably accustomed to sidestepping, turning away from, or otherwise distracting ourselves from the painful or uncomfortable. However small or halting this step may be—this facing of what we'd rather not face—it is hugely significant to our evolution. And it's a necessary step if we are to have truly authentic relationships.

Here's an example: John has been experiencing a nagging fear about what his partner, Mary, may be considering doing about her dissatisfaction with their relationship. He's reluctant to share this with her, for fear that such a revelation might drive her further away; she's been somewhat remote lately. And yet if he doesn't share his concern, he'll once again isolate himself, generating more distance between Mary and him. The temptation is, as usual, to keep this fear to himself while trying to find enough distraction from it so that he doesn't have to feel his fear or his shame about being fearful. Easier said than done, of course.

However, a niggling sense that he needs to share his fear with Mary keeps grabbing John's attention—along with the candy or the movie or the sexual possibility or whatever else is high on his list of potent distractions. He, of course, wishes it were easier. If he shares his fear with her, she might pull away or consider leaving; if he doesn't share this fear, it squats between them, taking up more and more space. So should he trust her with it or not?

Slowly and reluctantly, he turns toward his fear, responding less to its mental dimensions and more to its coursings through his chest and guts. He sees his shame over keeping his fearfulness to himself, along with his shame for being fearful. His intuition to take the leap intensifies. It's a hell of a risk, isn't it? But, he somehow reminds himself, it's even more of a risk to keep quiet. So he takes the jump.

Sharing our fears with a partner or a close friend is an act of uncommon trust. When we allow ourselves to thus share, memories might surface: memories of times when we didn't dare speak about our fear or when we were dismissed or shamed for speaking about it. We may have learned not to give voice to such fear, associating doing so with losing love or approval. But such sharing, such heroic vulnerability, builds courage and self-respect, creating bridges between us and our significant others—connection-makings that invite our mutual step and full presence, deepening the safety we feel with each other—and the intimacy.

It may be even more difficult for us to share our shame than our fear, especially when we've done something to our significant other that we not only feel bad about but also feel strongly compelled to keep secret. For some men, this might be a pornography habit that their partner knows nothing or very little about. For some women, it might be an eating disorder they've managed to keep hidden. To even consider bringing up such matters in front of one's partner or close friends can trigger massive shame, but not to talk about it keeps us isolated and may well reinforce the habit we're ashamed of. The increased stress of keeping our secret actually *amplifies* our excitation level—and therefore also our desire for a satisfying release or break from such stress—with our hidden habit being high on the list for such release/relief production.

Practice

SHARING WHAT WE'RE AFRAID TO SHARE

Do this with your partner or a close friend whom you trust. You already should have mutually agreed that you both will be sharing something that you are, to whatever degree, afraid or ashamed to share.

Sit facing each other, making sure you're comfortable. Gaze into each other's left eye, and do not break eye contact. (The left eye is recommended for this practice because it's usually the more receptive eye.) Bring your awareness to your breathing, noticing how your abdomen moves with each inhale and exhale. Stay with this in silence for a couple of minutes, keeping your gaze soft but steady.

Now decide nonverbally who will speak first. If you're the one listening, stay aware of the sensations generated in your abdomen by your breathing. At the same time, pay very close attention to the other person, opening yourself to them as much as possible.

If you're the one speaking, begin by saying how you feel. Be as precise as possible. Describe the qualities of the emotion or emotions you are experiencing. Keep eye contact. If you feel like looking away, say so, but don't act it out. Now begin sharing what it is that you're afraid or ashamed to say. No rush. Let your belly soften. Breathe a little deeper.

Be as transparent as possible. Report what is occurring for you as you share the details, doing your best not to pull away from what you're feeling as you do so. Have compassion for yourself. Feel—really feel—the other person listening to what you are saying and to how you are saying it. Notice what's happening to your fear or shame. Share that. Keep talking until you sense a natural completion. (There may be more to share, but you will intuit when you've said enough for now.) Ten or fifteen minutes should be plenty of time.

When you are done, let there be silence for a couple of minutes, then switch roles—unless it doesn't feel right to do so. Sometimes when the sharing has been emotionally intense, it feels better to stay with it and spend some time talking about it and winding down emotionally.

After you've both had your turn, stay in silence for as long as feels fitting, then talk about what happened during the practice, including how it felt to listen to the other. Take your time. Stay as soft as possible, appreciating each other's vulnerability.

GENDER DIFFERENCES
IN BEGINNING RELATIONAL WORK

In the relationship work that my wife, Diane, and I do, we often see quite a difference—at least initially—between men and women with regard to emotional literacy and expression. When we ask the men what they're feeling, many say something other than what they're in fact feeling—not to intentionally obstruct the process, but because they don't know better. They may look up and a bit sideways, as if the answer is on the ceiling or in their mind, and say that they don't know or that they "feel" that their partner doesn't give them enough credit for their efforts to communicate. They might also say that they "feel" that she doesn't want to have sex unless there's a lot of talking beforehand. Or they might say something inappropriately abstract, completely changing the topic, trying to keep the conversation from getting at all vulnerable. Or they might stay silent, avoiding eye contact, until we again ask them what they are feeling, at which point they may say "Fine" or "OK" or "I don't know."

Most men who do this aren't trying to be difficult, but they're clearly uncomfortable with things "emotional"—especially with their partner sitting across from them waiting for a feeling response. One of the first things we do at such times, other than making sure we don't shame the man for his expressive difficulty, is explain the difference between "I think" and "I feel." We point out that, "I feel like you're not appreciating what I do" or "I feel that you expect too much of me" are statements about what one is thinking or perceiving, rather than about what one is actually feeling. This usually goes well as soon as the man gets what is being asked of him: to simply state the data, such as "I feel angry." Nothing complicated, nothing that can debated—so long as he's being honest.

How do women fare in the beginning stages of couple's work? When we ask them how they're feeling, most are able to answer quickly and directly. If there's a problem for a woman initially, it's frequently one of overly intense expressiveness or emotional dramatics, which could overwhelm or emotionally flood her partner if allowed to go on for very long without any restraint.

Most women can usually say what they're feeling in a connected way—meaning what they're saying and how they're saying it are congruent—without avoiding eye contact, responding well to further questioning about their emotional state. Of course, as the work progresses and the key issues of the relationship are clarified, the woman's greater emotional fluency may contrast with what she is actually *doing* with her emotions—which is often no more life-giving or relationally supportive than what her partner is doing with *his* emotions. Even so, her capacity to quickly recognize, name, and accurately express what she's feeling usually places her ahead of her partner with regard to emotional literacy.

Not surprisingly, men who are discovering Emotional Literacy 101 have a varied response to their partner's more developed emotional literacy. Some are grateful for it, even inspired, and are determined to develop the same capacity. Others feel shamed by it—and not only when their partner criticizes them for lack of emotional savvy. Others are threatened by their partner's emotional literacy and will invest their attention and energy into finding fault with her delivery and turning the focus back on her—even when she is addressing something they know they have handled badly. If they can manage to redirect the conversation into a more "reasonable" discussion—with their partner having capitulated against her better judgment—all they have achieved is flattening or deadening the relationship.

~

Nothing brings a relationship really alive like emotional intimacy. When we are intimate with our emotions, they are not forces that lead us astray or interfere with reason or mess with us interpersonally. Instead, our emotions become psychoenergetic allies. By paying close attention to our emotions, we can read/intuit what's going on both externally and internally, evaluating our situation in a more comprehensive way than is possible through cognition alone—so long as the lens we're doing this through is nonreactive.

The deeper our relationship with a particular emotion, the more its arising can serve our relationships with others. The transparent sharing of our emotions—when done discerningly, compassionately, and consistently—helps deepen the trust and safety in our relationships. If truly fulfilling relationships with others is high on our list of priorities, then cultivating intimacy with our emotions is a must.

7

Gender and Emotional Intimacy

When we adopt a nonproblematic orientation toward
the differences between women and men, we position
ourselves to make wise use of these differences, seeing
both what is innate and socially constructed in them,
holding this in ways that equally respect both sexes.

See through biography and biology
To both expand and enter truer lands
No gender wars here, no polarizing fears
Just this primal grace, this everlasting wild
This uncommon embrace of male and female
That nothing in particular can replace
Since it wears every face

SOMEONE ONCE ASKED ME HOW we can understand the
dynamics of the opposite sex when we cannot even understand ourselves.
I remember suggesting that we begin by doing whatever's necessary to
deepen our understanding of ourselves—for in so doing we discover
that we are, in parallel, also deepening our understanding of the opposite sex. And in this we might also cease viewing male and female as
opposites and instead think of them as clearly different, yet comple-
mentary, dance partners who share an abundance of common ground.

As we become more intimate with what is essentially the same in
men and women, we find an increasing capacity to understand and
appreciate the differences between men and women. And what better
place to do this than on our emotional terrain? After all, emotion is

common to everyone, however unknown and unexplored its anatomy and operational dynamics may be.

The topic of gender tends to be touchy and often contentious, arranged as it mostly is around the contrasting notions of gender traits/identity being primarily either social constructions or biological givens. For the purposes of this chapter, I'll explore the relationship between gender and the capacity for emotional intimacy through the lens of both of these seemingly oppositional notions.

When it comes to gender itself, I'll view it as a male/female categorization independent of sexual orientation (with the caveat that gender itself is not always a clear classification, as exemplified by transgendered individuals). Whatever the differences between women and men, I question the value of claiming that certain traits or qualities are in fact masculine or feminine. For example, why say that being nurturing is feminine and being forceful is masculine? After all, men can be nurturing, and women can be forceful. One might argue that a man who's nurturing is simply accessing his feminine side and that a woman who's being forceful is simply accessing her masculine side—but assigning "masculine" or "feminine" labels to qualities like these unnecessarily narrows us. Why not just consider "nurturing" or "forceful" as traits common to us all?

"THE MASCULINE" AND "THE FEMININE"

To label certain qualities—like interpersonal directness or receptivity—as "the masculine" or "the feminine" is of questionable value. Being direct does not make a woman less of a woman any more than being receptive makes a man less of a man. Why genderize such qualities? If we tell a woman who is being direct—especially if she's fiery—that she's "in her masculine," we inadvertently or indirectly imply something about her femininity, perhaps to the point of shaming her for not being more feminine. By making such a comment, we may not be associating masculinity and femininity with being biologically male or female, yet for most of us the terms "masculine" and "feminine" do refer, to a very significant degree, to male-ness and female-ness.

We often speak of women's capacity to sense energy and read the emotional weather in relational contexts, but I have seen men demonstrate the same quality of attunement and vision—and these were not men who could be considered "effeminate." Were they manifesting "the feminine," or were they simply being highly attuned, in intimate communion with their intuitive capacities? When I'm "reading" others in my work, I don't feel particularly male or female but rather androgynous, dynamically androgynous. Intuition transcends gender. And so does intimacy.

Attributing qualities exclusively to "the masculine" or "the feminine" tends to generate more confusion than clarity. Nevertheless, there's still something to be said about what it means for a man to step more deeply into his quintessential maleness and for a woman to step more deeply into her quintessential femaleness. When I see a man embody his raw male-ness, he becomes more present, more alive, more radiant, more connected. When I see a woman embody her raw femaleness, she becomes more present, more alive, more radiant, more connected. He becomes his true size, and so too does she. She radiates presence and love and integrity, and so does he. He becomes more "he," and she becomes more "she"—and both become more fully human, without any dilution of their individuality. He is not trying to be masculine, and she is not trying to be feminine. Her warmth might be more out-front, and his steadiness might be more out-front, but *both* are warm and steady. Certain anatomical and hormonal differences aside, it's not that women have something men don't, or vice versa, but that both genders contain the same qualities in differing proportions and relevance. And such proportions and relevance are themselves far from fixed; they change according to shifts in context and circumstances.

Masculine/feminine classification is based on the assumption that male-ness and female-ness are opposites, like light and dark, high and low, introversion and extroversion. Part of the difficulty of categorizing various qualities and principles as belonging to either "the feminine" or "the masculine" is that femininity and masculinity aren't really opposites! As such, they don't offer the clear contrast that other oppositional pairings—like rising/falling, positive/negative—offer. There is enough overlap between them, enough common ground, to justify conceiving of them not as opposites, but as dance partners with sufficient differences to generate a mutual magnetism.

The point is not to discard the notions of masculine and feminine, but to limit their use to denoting male-ness and female-ness, however culturally conditioned that might be. Consider a woman who has had to adopt apparent masculine traits—like getting really competitive or emotionally hardened—to survive in her workplace. We might describe her as stepping into a masculine skin, but is this armoring really "masculine" or is it simply something that we, male or female, get inculcated with under various conditions? Just because more men than women are emotionally armored does not mean that their protective shell is "masculine." Instead of getting caught up in such labeling, we could instead openly investigate the structure, origins, catalyzing factors, and emotional makeup of our armoring.

To categorically genderize qualities that we all have in common leaves us out in the cold, abstracting us from our experience and overly emphasizing the differences (conditioned or not) between males and females.

GENDER DIFFERENCES IN EMOTIONAL INTIMACY

To the extent we associate rationality with maleness and emotionality with femaleness, we'll insufficiently value emotional intimacy and fail to grasp the power of a fully integrated self. The ways females and males do differ with regard to emotional intimacy need to be taken into account if the gap between the sexes is to be more fully and compassionately bridged.

In general, women tend to be more emotionally literate and empathetic than men, and they're more inclined toward emotional intimacy. Men are usually less invested in doing what it takes to develop and deepen emotional intimacy; a much higher percentage of women than men seek out psychotherapeutic help with their relationships. To what degree this is innate remains debatable; that there are considerable cultural pressures at play is *not* debatable. Brain research indicates plenty of gender differences; for example, women's brains have more white matter and less gray matter than mens'. But those who view gender roles only as social constructions can always claim that such differences have a lot more to do with cultural conditioning than with biology, citing how subject the brain is to environmental factors.

Given that relational intimacy tends to be a more central concern for women than men, and given that emotional resonance and empathy are crucial factors in the formation of healthy relationship, it's no surprise that women—especially women who have children—ordinarily place a higher value on emotional connection, depth, and well-being than do most men. Does this mean that women are innately more capable of emotional intimacy than men? Not necessarily.

Historically, women have had a far greater investment than men in having a bonded relationship, simply because without marriage women would have lacked the security needed to adequately function in their social milieu. Also, the very act of relating/bonding can be seen as an evolutionary adaptation for female survival, an adaptation with a strong biological component. (Women, for starters, have higher levels of oxytocin, a hormone centrally implicated in bonding.) The considerable gap between men's and women's rights in Western culture up until the last five or six decades also has greatly impacted and intensified women's need to have the stability, however unpleasant, of an established relationship. Women's well-being and survival—deeply entwined with the well-being and survival of their children—has depended on emotionally connected relationships far more than that of their male counterparts.

And that need still persists, despite the increased socioeconomic equality between women and men in the Western world, if only because of the fact that having and caring for children asks an enormous amount of a woman, more often than not amplifying her dependency on the man with whom she is in relationship. That dependency, that fundamental need for solid security, works best in relationships (including same-sex relationships) that feature a deeply loving mutuality and true peer-bond, in which emotional literacy, communion, and compassion are centrally and consistently featured.

It's also important to consider gender differences in the value given to emotional intimacy. Culturally many of us tend to value reason over emotion, associating rationality with maleness and emotionality with femaleness. In my work I've found that many men insufficiently value emotional intimacy, assigning a much more negative connotation to being emotional than to being rational. Fortunately, there is a growing knowingness in contemporary culture that emotionality and rationality work best when they work together. Emotionality and rationality can deeply inform each other when neither is forsaken or marginalized. The no-one's land between the two—generated by our viewing them in an oppositional context—is ours to explore and inhabit, both outwardly and inwardly, until we are equally comfortable with both reason and feeling, so that *together* they serve our highest good personally and collectively.

So are women *really* more emotional than men? Yes and no. Men who have broken relatively free from their conditioning are, in my experience, just as emotionally open and alive as women, just as vulnerable and empathetic, and just as emotionally intelligent and capable of deep connection. Men who are still stuck in their conditioning—including the shame-rooted pressure to avoid full vulnerability and transparency—are going to be far from emotional intimacy. And the same is true for women who are still stuck in *their* conditioning. Being emotionally intimate takes more than being able to openly express emotion. For example, we can rage or weep but not be responsibly connected to what we are expressing, being caught up in the drama of reacting to rather than responding to whatever is happening.

There's no inherent virtue in simply being emotional; what matters is how we handle our emotions. The fact that men suppress their sadness more than do women does not confer on women any sort of superior emotional status; free-flowing tears can be expressive of a variety of contexts, ranging from the manipulative to the liberating. Yes, men need to cry more—and especially be able to cry hard—but both women and men need to free their crying from reactive ruts. (Nonreactive crying does not support the conditioned dramatics that feature us in roles like "poor me" or "it's not fair." Instead, it allows us to openly express the core of whatever hurt we're feeling.)

Plenty of the gender differences regarding emotional intimacy are socially constructed. Take anger, for example: it remains a more culturally acceptable emotion for men, despite decreasing resistance to female anger during the last forty to fifty years. We still have less flattering labels for female anger than male anger. As a result, anger does not serve as a resource for many women, especially those ensnared in the kind of conditioning in which externalization of anger is considered to be negative and unfeminine. True, many men are also conditioned to repress, marginalize, or otherwise disown their healthy anger, but there's usually less stigma attached to their openly expressing it. (See chapter 11 for more on gender and anger.)

Little boys are less likely than little girls to be given the message that they shouldn't get angry. Little girls are more likely to receive niceness implants than little boys. Boys, of course, are often encouraged to engage in activities that reinforce their anger—and boys are, in general, more *naturally* drawn to such activities than are girls. In addition, boys are shamed more often than girls for crying or showing vulnerability and tenderness. (See chapter 12 for more on gender and sadness.) Girls generally are more inclined toward relationship and less inclined toward competitiveness. And the list goes on, seemingly making the case that emotional differences between males and females are socially constructed phenomena, as if biology had nothing to do with it.

But we can't sidestep genetics so easily. Consider a study done on twenty-five boys who were born without a penis. All were castrated and raised as girls, yet all behaved more like boys than girls in numerous ways. Half of them eventually came to believe that they were boys. If "behaving like a boy" were a matter of cultural shaping only, these children wouldn't have questioned their gender. What was hardwired in them regarding their sex kicked in despite their being raised as girls.

So we have to consider both biology and culture, along with the interplay between the two. One of the clearest ways to see male and female biological differences is in the makeup of the brain. Research indicates that men have much more gray matter than women, and that women have much more white matter than men. Gray matter, comprised of neurons, deals with information; white matter, made up of axons, deals with connections.

Is this generated by gender roles? Perhaps to some degree, because the brain is susceptible to environmental factors, but the contrast between male and female is too great to be explained away by social constructionist theories (brain differences between females and males start to show up in the twenty-sixth week of pregnancy). From our earliest human times, it has been essential to our survival that males gather and internally organize as much information as possible in a short time (so as to maximize awareness of their environment and its dangers) and that women make as many connections as possible in a short time, in order to attune to their social milieu and responsibilities, especially for their children's sake. These are not just gender roles, but species-centered survival strategies dating a long, long way back. In our times, these very strategies are shifting—especially in the Western world—leaving us in a kind of gender-role limbo, which itself arguably could be altering us biologically.

In females, the corpus callosum—the bundle of nerve fibers that divides and facilitates contact between the brain's left and right hemispheres—may be richer in connecting nerve fibers, according to some preliminary studies. What this arguably means is that in women there is more communication—more relating—between hemispheres, and less of a tendency to get overly absorbed in one hemisphere. Men's common tendency to "be in their head" means, among other things, that they are operating too much from their left hemisphere (logic and abstraction having their *headquarters* here), so that right-hemispheric input (creativity, intuition, holistic perception) is not being adequately attended to.

It appears that men in general are wired—and also culturally conditioned—to compartmentalize things more and to be less holistically inclined than women. And women are wired—and also culturally conditioned—to operate in relational contexts more than are men. Women's generally greater verbal fluency supports this. And the good news? None of this is set in stone. No left- or right-hemispheric bias here—what really matters is having both function optimally, *together,* leaving us not with a split brain, but a truly whole one. Though we are born with certain traits, some of these can become overdeveloped and some can become underdeveloped, depending on various environmental factors. What really matters is how we relate to them.

Men are, with very few exceptions, stronger and more muscular than women and therefore are not only better able to perform tasks that require considerable physical strength, but also are in a dominant position to women when relational discord turns physical. Most women are aware that when push comes to shove and worse, the man they are with could, if he wished, do them great bodily harm, and they likely could not stop him. This, of course, points to an extreme, but the very fact of a man's physical dominance generates in most women a desire to be with a man who would unquestionably protect her and who also is incapable of such dark aggression toward her.

Women can be violent toward men—my wife, Diane, and I have worked with men who were battered by their wives—but male violence toward women is far, far more common and physically threatening. Not so long ago, violence against women was even more common and brutal *and* culturally permitted. My sense is that most contemporary women carry some of this collective memory, however far away in their psyches it may be stored. Centuries ago, women in general understandably looked more for security than love, so that relationship for them was a potential bastion of safety, even if they were little more than a slave to their husbands. As hard as life was for men in the past—and as enslaved as they were to those with greater status—life was likely even harder for the women they took as "partners."

DEEPENING EMOTIONAL INTIMACY REGARDLESS OF GENDER DIFFERENCES

In healthy peer-bonds, there is deep respect between the genders and between partners in same-sex relationships. This means, in part, no diminishing of the other, however unintentionally, including in our ways of conceptualizing and talking about/to each other. For instance:

> Man in his fifties: "I'm dating a really nice girl. She's 51 and has her own business."
> Woman in her fifties: "I'm dating a really nice boy. He's 51 and has his own business."

Does the word "boy" here feel less fitting than "girl"? If so, why? I've heard men in their sixties describe the woman they were involved with as a "girl"—and these men were not chauvinists, womanizers, or any other sort of female belittler. Yet they would probably be uncomfortable if they had been referred to as a "boy." Gender-based conditioning, however explicit or subtle, is so common that it seems all but normal; the more we free ourselves from its programming, the more respect we'll have for the other gender. Respect also means no shaming or devaluing of each other, regardless of how adeptly it might be excused as nothing more than teasing or everyday relational humor.

Emotional intimacy is the lifeblood of good relationships. Those who want to live in vibrant, thriving relationships don't just value emotional intimacy, but do what it takes to make it a living reality. They take action. Unfortunately, far more women are thus inclined than are men. More women than men go for psychological and emotional healing work, and in couples who come for relationship counseling, it is usually the woman who initiates the process. I have found that in same-sex relationships, more female couples are likely to come for psychotherapy than male couples.

It appears that women have an advantage over men when it comes to emotional intimacy, being not only more hardwired for it but also more culturally supported in it. Men have a biological and cultural advantage over women when it comes to aggression, but the disadvantage is enormous: aggression militates against emotional intimacy. This is partly due to its lack of vulnerability and partly due to its dehumanizing operational tendency. It would be an understatement to say that emotional intimacy tends to be more of a stretch for men than women. But men who work at it become, in my experience (both personally and clinically), just as adept as women. Furthermore, to reach the more mature levels of emotional intimacy, women have to work at it too; it doesn't just come with being female. For both men and women, emotional intimacy is a labor of love, birthing truly fulfilling relationship.

I have said elsewhere that intimate relationship is the ashram of the twenty-first century, meaning that men and women now have an opportunity to use committed relationship as both a crucible and sanctuary for the deepest sort of healing, awakening, and integration. But this is possible only if they are—and consistently meet as—true peers, empowering rather than overpowering each other. Implicit in this is a deeply shared trust, anchored by mutual transparency, wakefulness, integrity, and emotional intimacy.

When a relationship reaches this stage, gender differences don't make enough of a difference to make a significant difference.

Part 2

Meeting the Emotions

AS YOU'VE BEEN READING, EACH emotion is a potential gateway to a deeper intimacy, both with yourself and with others, especially when you turn toward whatever you're experiencing emotionally and approach it in the spirit of exploration. So far, we've looked at emotion in general, getting better acquainted with its anatomy and terrain, finding enough footing there for a comprehensive exploration of specific emotions and emotional states.

And so we come to part 2. It begins with primary emotions—emotions that are not combinations or extensions of other emotions—then follows with combination emotions (like contempt) and emotional states (like self-doubt). Each chapter delves deep and is detailed; each is best absorbed by carefully reading and rereading, along with doing the practices.

About the practices: Take your time with them. Repeat them at least once, so as to get more out of them. Before beginning a practice, make sure that you won't be disturbed while doing it and that you have adequate time afterward to properly digest what you experience. Keep paper and pen handy, as some practices require writing. If at any point you want to stop while doing a practice, do so. Make haste slowly. And do the meditative practice described in the appendix as often as possible.

What you will meet in the upcoming chapters may seem new, but it is none other than you in emotion's fascinating, ever-changing garb, with one hand on a mirror and the other on a walking stick.

Greetings to the you who has already arrived, and greetings to the you who is still arriving. Both are equally welcome. Your emotions await.

8

Fear

Stepping into the Dragon's Cave

The more we try to remove ourselves from fear,
the more we remain entrapped within it.

If you are truly looking for genuine transformation,
you need look no further than your fear. For in it
there exists not only an abundance of trapped energy,
but also the very testing and challenge that we need
in order to live a deeper, more authentic life.

IT WOULD BE AN understatement to say that fear is one of our least favorite guests. When it shows up—and fear shows up for all of us—we're rarely in a position to greet it, let alone be a warm host. In fact, we may be trying to get away from fear before it arrives, even if we have to vacate the premises: our body.

Yet the more we try to escape or evict our fear, the stronger it gets, occupying more and more of us—especially as we inhabit less and less of ourselves. Eventually, it may seem that our fear is not in us, but that we are in it. Our "unwelcome" guest goes where we go, regardless of how much we may medicate, mute, or deny it.

This sounds like bad news, carrying the unpleasant, contracted feeling of a dream in which we are entrapped—but it is actually good news *if* we learn to work with our fear rather than fleeing it. And this begins with turning toward it, and not just intellectually.

The dragon of fear is there for a very good reason, which we'll discover firsthand as we get significantly acquainted with it. We are, quite understandably, not inclined to turn toward our fear, given how unpleasant it feels and how threatening its message may be. That part of us that does not want to go near fear is worth getting to know very well.

It is crucial not to make a problem out of our resistance to facing our fear. There is enormous energy bound up in resistance, energy that can be freed up for more life-giving purposes if we will but approach our resistance with clarity and compassion, moving at a pace that neither rushes us nor proceeds too slowly.

There's no point saying to ourselves that we shouldn't be afraid—doing so just shames us for being afraid, driving the fear-ridden us into more and more compensatory activity, anything to get away from fear. So treat your resistance to working with fear with care and respect, without, however, allowing it to run the show.

If you truly desire genuine transformation, look no further than your fear. In fear there exists an abundance of trapped energy and also the very testing and challenge that we need in order to live a deeper, more authentic life.

Fear pervades our culture, along with our "solutions" for it, which mostly only numb us to it. Anxiety, to take but one kind of fear, is so commonplace as to seem intrinsic to us, even when we try to offset its impact through a variety of means, including many forms of medication. These are tough times for many of us, times in which it is easy to slide into chronic fear, both personally and collectively. So what are we to do with our fear? Giving in to it only further entraps us in it, and avoiding it simply keeps us in the shallows, overly absorbed in distraction.

But fear itself is not the problem! What really matters is what we *do* with our fear, be it personal or collective.

MEETING THE DRAGON: GETTING ACQUAINTED WITH YOUR FEAR

Plenty of fear has preverbal origins and needs to be approached as such. And plenty of fear manifests not only as a physical/physiological phenomenon, but also as a mental phenomenon, most commonly illustrated by worry and self-doubt. However it manifests, fear easily eviscerates our rationality. Fear that's allowed to infiltrate and occupy our mind doesn't waste time generating thoughts that support and amplify it, thoughts that make it seem even more real than it first appeared to be.

Fear goes way back, having its origins in the contractile capacity of single-celled organisms, growing in complexity along the evolutionary trail, especially with the development of brains. In mammals, fear is not just a reflex but an actual feeling; consider how different a frightened dog seems as compared to a beetle that finds itself in sudden danger. Mammals become fearful—clearly demonstrating the physiology and characteristic behaviors of fear—when actual danger is present and is registered by them. The electrifying biochemistry of fear—increasing the blood flow to the legs—immediately enables them to take fitting action, whether it is to flee or freeze.

We humans, however, are usually far less practically inclined than other mammals. We become afraid not only in the present (in the face of real or imagined danger), but we also project fearfulness into the past (as exemplified by guilt, which is shame infused with at least some degree of fear) and into the future (as exemplified by worry or anxiety). All too often, we keep ourselves chronically afraid and overcommitted—or even addicted—to whatever most reliably keeps us distanced or disconnected from our fear.

Because fear is so often disempowering or crippling, we generally view it in a negative light, usually adopting a problematic orientation to it. But fear is not really the problem—what matters is how consciously and deeply we relate to it, how we choose to view it, how thoroughly we explore our personal history with it, how intimate we become with it.

The arising of fear is, among other things, one hell of an opportunity. We can feel the dragon's breath and heat, can see the icy fire of its gaze, can sense its capacity to eat us alive, and can intuit the presence of what it is guarding. Facing the dragon—engaging with it step by step, breath by breath—forces us to take stands that make us more alive and more conscious, readying us to make optimal use of the treasure once we have cultivated enough intimacy with what is guarding it.

Fear can show up in many forms: worry, anxiety, panic, paranoia, fright, angst, terror, dread, doubt. But fundamentally fear is apprehensive self-contraction, centered by a mild to extreme constricting feeling that announces: *I am not safe* or *I am threatened* or *I am in danger* or *Others about whom I care are in danger.*

Fear easily undercuts our rationality. We cannot just think it away. We might repeatedly tell ourselves that there's nothing to be afraid of, but the very fact that this does not significantly ease the churning in our guts and the knot in our solar plexus usually only gives our fear more solidity, more authority, more free rein to occupy us.

Our fear often points us to core wounds—from childhood or later—that need our care, understanding, and healing attention. Consider the following example: Charlene is frequently anxious, sometimes even panicked, about her partner, Tim, leaving her for another person, despite a complete lack of evidence. She tells herself that she is being silly, shaming herself for such unwarranted suspicion, trying hard to not be "negative." But her anxiety persists, intensifying when she tries to get away from it. When she was five, her mother suddenly left to be with another man, and she didn't see her for over a year. Her father wouldn't say anything about this and emotionally withdrew. When Charlene saw her mother again, things didn't improve; her mother showed little interest in her, which she interpreted (as young children do) as being a result of something she had done. So now Charlene gets very anxious about being abandoned by Tim, no matter how much he reassures her. Until she faces and works through her original fear of abandonment—which is far more than a merely cognitive undertaking—she won't be able to have a truly fulfilling relationship, given that she won't sufficiently trust her partner, even if he clearly deserves it.

Another example: If we were physically violated when we were very young—to the point that our biological survival was clearly at stake, we probably didn't analytically consider our situation (since our brain was not developmentally capable of doing so), but automatically reacted by "doing" what most rapidly and effectively reduced the danger—like "depressing" our vital signs—dissociating from our body and the stark reality of the abuse we were suffering. In short, we *had* to shut down; necessity demanded it. This shutting down, however, does not go away as we get older, showing up in a variety of circumstances. In the presence of danger (whether real or imagined), we not only get afraid but also tend to revert, beyond any cognitive countereffort, to what originally had saved our life—dissociating, closing down, turning off, or getting depressed. Shutting down or "depressing" our vital signs both "saves" and debilitates us, rendering us all but incapable of relational intimacy. When our significant others show anger at us, we usually retreat, saturated with both fear and numbness to that fear (and perhaps also some shame about it).

This is not necessarily a life sentence—for such primal fearfulness can be worked through—but it doesn't go away just because we've gotten older.

These examples illustrate the fact that fear can easily infiltrate us and that its messages can occupy and run us. When we have a *disproportionate,* fear-centered reaction to someone or something, we are literally in the grip of an unresolved issue *from* our past, an issue that will direct what we do in certain circumstances until we face and work through the fearfulness that centers it.

FEAR IS EXCITEMENT IN DRAG

Fear is basically just excitement in endarkened disguise, tightly knotted and turned in on itself—like a wide-open hand compressed into a fist or a snail pulling back into the innermost coils of its shell, squeezed into thick-walled darkness.

Pay attention next time you feel excitement, noticing the similarities between how it and fear feel; in fear, the sensations usually register as unpleasant, and in excitement they register as pleasant. Of course, in many situations we may feel fear and excitement at the same time. For example, when beginning psychotherapy, many people will say that they feel scared/excited. If you're excited—energetically aroused—and then contract, fear arises. Similarly, if you are fearful and then expand, excitement arises. Why? Because there is now room for it. Same energy, different context. When the fist relaxes and opens, it is no longer a fist.

Visualize fear as a chilled fist. Slowly uncurl this fist—your fist—letting your fingers spread wide, breathing deeply as you do so. Just as your fist represents fear, your open hand represents excitement. Notice that you don't have to force your hand open; simply relax the clenching that's making and maintaining the fist.

That clenching will relax, however slightly, when whatever is around it starts to *expand.* This means you are giving your fear more space in which to be, inviting it into a larger container. Instead of giving it a higher fence, you're giving it a larger pasture.

There is plenty of energy in fear: tightly contained excitation, an abundance of life force squeezed into a cramped space. So do whatever you can to expand—thereby giving your fear more room to breathe. Don't pressure yourself to have big results—for such pressure only reinforces contractedness—but simply keep intending and generating a certain expansiveness, however subtly. A millimeter more space may be more than enough.

Practice

FEAR AND EXCITEMENT

1. Write about how fear and excitement each feels in different parts of your body, especially your lower belly, solar plexus, chest, thighs, arms, jaw, eyes, throat, and shoulders.

2. Imagine a frightening situation, and then imagine converting the fearfulness you feel into excitement (perhaps in part by breathing more deeply). Notice what actions—or intentions to act—then arise in you. Imagine taking such action, and taking it fully. What happens then?

FEAR AND ITS RELATIONSHIP TO ANGER

One form that excitement can take (or be channeled into) is anger. This is especially relevant when considering the nature of fear, given how closely related fear and anger are. Research shows that they are biochemically all but identical. Same adrenaline, different directionality: fear retreats; anger moves forward. Same adrenaline, different intentionality: fear avoids, anger engages. Both ready us for action, whether we freeze or erupt, run or fight, implode or explode.

When the fearful get truly angry, they're not significantly afraid any more—just angry. Not that getting angry is the solution for fearfulness, but the arising of anger can really empower us, for better or for worse—in contrast to the arising of fear. When those who are suffering from abuse-generated, debilitating fear do healing work with Diane and me, we find that the *mobilizing* of what they'd had to shut down during their original trauma—showing, for example, any opposition to their abuser—is not only radically freeing and healing, but almost invariably involves the full-out expression of anger.

The more intimate we are with our anger, and the more at ease we are with both its containment and expression, the less fearful we will tend to be, if only because we won't be letting the energy of our anger contract into fearfulness.

Practice

FEAR AND ANGER

1. Become more aware of the difference between anger and aggression: aggression attacks, but healthy anger does not, no matter how fiery it may be or may need to be. Aggression is not so much an outcome of anger as an avoidance/ mutation of it and its underlying feelings of woundedness. When you find yourself being aggressive, acknowledge as soon as you can that this is indeed happening. Then as much as possible get vulnerable and transparent, letting your aggression lose its armor until it is just anger. (For more on this, see chapter 11 on anger.)

2. The next few times you feel fear, inflate your torso, breathe more deeply, and squeeze your fists and jaw as if really angry, and see what happens. There are times when it is entirely fitting to get angry when we are fearful; because of this, it's crucial that we have the capacity to fully express our anger (non-injuriously, of course).

ADAPTIVE AND MALADAPTIVE FEAR

Sometimes fear is adaptive, sometimes maladaptive. The sudden rush of fear we feel when we're too close to the cliff's edge or to a large carnivore is extremely useful; it immediately alerts and readies us for action, such as stepping back to safety or fleeing. Such fear catalyzes instant situational adaptation, bypassing any thinking processes that could cause us to hesitate in such conditions. Trouble usually begins when we let our fear go to our mind. A classic example is worry, which is maladaptive and far from useful. When we permit worry to infiltrate and occupy our mind, we keep ourselves unpleasantly bound, Velcro-ed to a calamitous "what if" kind of view. Worry—socially acceptable anxiety—keeps us bouncing to and fro in a cranial cramp, so preoccupied with thoughts of bad possibility that we have little room for anything else.

As challenging as our maladaptive fears might be, and as much as we might be convinced that we're stuck with them, their hold on us can be broken so that we are no longer bound to their imperatives. To journey into, unguardedly feel, and directly relate *to* our fear (instead of from it) requires that our usual distancing strategies, cognitive and otherwise, be exposed and disarmed—assuming, of course, that it's timely to do so. Our fear can then be touched and known from the deep inside and eventually divested of its power to shrink, misguide, or intimidate us. Then, instead of getting a temporary respite from worry because we've had a few drinks or have "worried our head off," we cut off our tendency to worry at the pass, rejecting its application to set up camp in our mind.

There can be an odd, irritable comfort in our smaller fears, despite their inherent discomfort. As unpleasant as worry or doubt may be, they're not usually all that hard to take breaks from. They're like old friends we don't particularly like but nonetheless remain attached to because of our long history with them. They're ordinarily not that overwhelming and they are familiar, so they perhaps provide us with a certain security through their very predictability. And the various strategies we use to take the edge off such fearfulness—narcotic, erotic, electronic, and so on—give us at least some sense of control.

By clinging to our everyday fearfulness—and our "solutions" for it—focusing on its mental content much more than the raw feeling of it, we keep some distance from our deeper fears (including those that don't have a clear-cut object). And we also leave the nature of fear out of our inquiry, settling instead for explanations about why we are afraid. But no matter how strong our reasoning powers and capacity for distraction are, we do not remain far from our core fears. They will continue to knock on our door, regardless of what we do with our lesser fears; we can wait until they break in, or we can, however slightly, let them in—at which point we realize that the door was never really locked. Until we turn toward and enter our fear, we will be bound by it.

Practice

GETTING TO KNOW YOUR FEAR

Find a comfortable place to sit, and keep a notebook and pen handy. Make sure you will not be interrupted in the next ten minutes or so (remember to turn off your phone and electronic devices) and wear clothing that's loose enough to allow easy, unrestricted breathing.

Sitting comfortably, bring your attention to your breathing. Without trying to change it in any way, simply notice it, allowing your belly to soften.

Below is a list of incomplete sentences. Complete them as spontaneously as possible, out loud, and write down your response to each immediately after voicing it. Don't edit. Words may not immediately emerge, but more often than not they will. Let yourself speak as freely and sincerely as possible, doing so in any tone or volume or intensity that feels fitting. When you're done, take some deep breaths, soften your belly, and rest for a few minutes.

When I feel afraid, what I usually do is _____.

And I've been doing this since _____.

For me, fear is _____.

I felt most afraid as a child when _____.

And how I dealt then with that fear was _____.

The image I now have of myself as a child when I was afraid is _____.

The position my body usually was in at that time was _____.

My breathing feels _____.

If I could say anything to that child, I'd say _____.

And if that child could respond, he or she would say _____.

As I let myself feel that child's fear, I notice that I am _____.

Where I now feel that fear in my body is _____.

And if that fear could speak, it would say _____.

As I stay open to that fear, I notice that I am _____.

As an adult I still deal with my fear the same way I did as a young child when _____.

The kind of situations that most easily increase my fear are _____.

My breathing feels _____.

When I look at my fear, I see _____.

When I let myself get a bit closer to my fear, I see _____.

As I make more room for my fear, I notice that I am _____.

Follow-Up

1. Write out your history with fear, including times of fearfulness that particularly stand out. Be as specific as you can. Also briefly include your "solution(s)" to such fear and your historic and current degree of attachment to them.

2. In the next few days, whenever you feel fear, even slightly, say "fear" or "fear's here" in a voice only you can hear. Then take three full breaths, emphasizing the exhale, and bring your attention to softening your belly.

GETTING UNDER THE DRAGON'S SKIN: WORKING WITH FEAR

Our usual—and entirely understandable—reaction to fear is to get away from it, to somehow be outside it, far from it, untouched by it. But the key to working effectively with fear is to get *inside* it. And getting inside it—getting to where we can witness its inner workings—begins with giving it our full attention and directly facing it, however counterintuitive this might seem.

However small this step may be, it is actually enormous, indicating that we have begun to make our longing to be truly free more central than our habit of distracting ourselves from our pain. Once we have taken this step a few times, we generate a momentum to keep going through our fear—regardless of whatever obstacles might appear.

Getting inside fear does not mean that fear is a literal container that we enter; it means that we cease keeping our distance from it, getting close enough to its constituent elements to see them clearly. One could call this *radical subjectivity*—we are very close to our subject of study, maintaining just enough distance from it so as to keep it in focus. If we were to pull back, we would see less, feel less, know less. Approaching our fear in this spirit keeps us on track, breathing both courage and curiosity into our stride.

When you explore the somatic nooks, crannies, and grottos of your fear, paying close attention to its anatomical peculiarities, you will sooner or later recognize that your fear is not a noun, not a "something" inhabiting you, but rather a verb: a process, a flow, always on the move. Here's an example of getting inside fear:

> I awaken from a dream of being in great danger. My guts are churning, my breath is shallow. Anxiety fills me. My mind is steadily grinding out frightening thoughts. Fear is jaggedly burrowing around between my navel and throat. Interpretations of what's happening keep clamoring for my attention, but I'm starting to focus primarily on the feelings in my body.
>
> A minute or two passes. Anxiety still occupies me, but so too does my awareness of it. Though I feel very shaky, I have no significant desire to change my state. There's no panic, but there is a pulsing fearfulness without an obvious object. No clear threat, no dire events ahead as far as I can see, but still the contractedness of fear continues, tunneling through my guts like a mole on amphetamines.
>
> Letting my attention drop more deeply into my fear, I notice its texture, movements, coloring, and intensity. At the same time, I begin allowing the areas around the hub of my

fearfulness to start to soften: my upper chest, my pelvis, my back, my jaw and tongue, my shoulders and neck. So I am both penetrating my fear and giving it more room in which to be. As I do so, and as I continue to soften, my fear lessens, my breathing eases, and my excitement grows in conjunction with an increasing sense of peace. My alertness is starting to relax me. Now I don't mind my fear. I have room for it; exploration has become more central than escape.

Getting inside fear means, in part, that we are going to experience it more directly and fully, feeling it as openly as possible, detaching from it only to the degree needed to keep from getting lost in it. We need to make haste slowly, getting inside our fear at a pace that keeps us from being blown away or consumed by it. In so doing, we *ground* our exploration of our fear, closely tracking its energetics without taking on its viewpoint, perhaps losing our footing here and there, but not seriously slipping.

Essential to this process is becoming well acquainted with our history with fear so we can clearly recognize the various ways in which we've learned to get away from it. When one of these strategies shows up, we can then look at it—rather than through its eyes—and, to whatever degree, say an undeniable "no" to it. Knowing our historic strategies around fear (ideally explored with a skilled guide, like an emotionally literate psychotherapist) allows us to stand our ground, however quivery our legs and resolve might be. And the more energy and focus we put into grounding ourselves, into wholeheartedly rooting ourselves in our core of being, the more skillfully we will be able to face fear, be it personal or collective.

As I mentioned in the beginning of this chapter, fear increases blood flow to the legs, readying us to run, and run hard, if necessary. But we can channel this surplus energy, this sudden surge of excitation, in a very different direction: further anchoring ourselves as we step forward, moving *past* our problematic orientation to fear.

Now we can start deepening our acquaintance with its basic features, namely the feelings, sensations, beliefs, and energetic structuring that together make it into something we label "fear." The more closely we approach it, the more clearly we can see it. Again, we need to move slowly and carefully—as if walking through a dark house—step by conscious step, with our senses extra alert, feeling our way bit by bit, anchoring ourselves with each step. (Again, this is ideally done with a skilled guide.) Our awareness is not just on what is in front of us, but also on what is all around us, steadily scanning it all. In this, we keep some sense of connection to the "outside world," a thread of remembrance that we lightly but firmly hold. We are in the dragon's cave. No maps.

As we proceed, we can ask questions to orient us, answering not with speculation but with data. Regardless of what we're feeling—and it can be intense—we are getting more intimate with the details of our fear. Some body-centered questions might be: "What sensations am I experiencing in my guts, my solar plexus, my throat, my jaw, my forehead, my hands, my eyes? And how are these changing? What is their texture, tone, temperature, directionality, color, shape?" Such questions ask not for general answers, but for specifics; the very act of going for the details brings our body into sharper focus.

Some mind-oriented questions might also help, so long as we maintain some body awareness: "What is my fear telling me right now? And how seriously am I taking it? How much energy am I giving my thoughts right now? How much space is there between my thoughts? What happens to my mind when I stay focused on my body?"

Given how easily fear can spread through and even colonize our mind, it is crucial that we keep a steady eye on our mind and thinking processes, not allowing fear to take root there. We are on guard, but not rigidly armored, literally not minding our fear and its storyline.

In this process, do not lose heart. Even if your heart is closed down or tightly contracted, keep your sense of compassion as alive as possible. Try personifying fear—and not only yours!—as a very scared child aching for your touch, your care, your presence, your protection, your *love*. Though that child may initially pull back from us, it is only for as long as we forget or avoid our compassion. Bringing that child, that innocent and exquisitely vulnerable place in us, into our heart cuts through our fear, both illuminating and softening it, until it cannot help but expand into life-giving excitement and connection.

As we *decentralize* our fear by becoming increasingly intimate with it, by witnessing its particulars, by holding it more tenderly, amazing things can happen. Yes, we still get afraid, but we don't panic or run like we used to. We hear what our fear is telling us, and we recognize how much of this is just our conditioning giving us a piece of its mind. What a relief it is when we stop automatically adopting a problematic orientation to the arising of fear! Though fear will continue to show up, its presence won't matter like it once did.

There is no freedom from fear as long as we keep identifying with it, losing ourselves in the "I" who is afraid. That "I"—personified fearfulness—needs to become the *object* of our awareness, not the subject. When fear arises, both own it ("my fear") and relate to it ("the fear"). And also feel it fully. Instead of revolving around our fear or fleeing it, we need to keep it in a fittingly peripheral position in our psyche, so that what's happening is but a fluxing play of phenomena that we typically label "fear," along with the raw feeling and awareness of it.

Practice

WORKING WITH YOUR FEAR

Find a comfortable place to sit, and keep a notebook and pen handy. Make sure that you won't be interrupted during the next ten minutes or so. Complete the following incomplete sentences as spontaneously as possible, out loud, and write down your response to each immediately after voicing it. When you're done, rest for a few minutes, letting your belly soften as much as possible.

What brings up fear in me most easily is _____.

This is at its most intense when _____.

What I notice about my fear at such times is _____.

The feeling of this fear in my chest is _____.

The feeling of this fear in my belly is _____.

If this fear had a shape, it would be _____.

This fear's coloring is _____.

This fear's texture is _____.

What I notice about this fear's movement is _____.

Now this fear's shape is _____.

Now this fear's coloring is _____.

I would describe this fear's density as _____.

I would describe this fear's temperature as _____.

As I move more closely toward this fear, what happens is _____.

When I penetrate this fear, what I notice is _____.

The thickness of my fear seems to be _____.

When I get inside my fear, I see _____.

What seems to be surrounding my fear is _____.

The edges of my fear appear to be _____.

Now my fear is _____.

What I notice about my mind right now is _____.

My breathing feels _____.

I would now describe my fear as _____.

Being present like this with my fear is _____.

If my fear could now speak, it would say _____.

And my response to that is _____.

The more deeply I pay attention to my fear, the more that I am _____.

As I relate *to* my fear, rather than *from* it, I feel _____.

Follow-Up

1. When you notice any fear arising in you, acknowledge its presence immediately, then let your belly soften and your breathing deepen a little, as if to make more room for whatever fear is there. Do this before you let yourself start thinking about your fear. For the next minute or two, pay as close attention as possible to the various sensations of your fear, particularly in your chest, solar plexus, and belly.

2. Feel into the contractedness of your fear; as soon as possible soften around it. That is, don't try to undo such contractedness, but instead allow the areas around it (e.g., the small of your back, the sides of your chest, the tissues right below your collarbones, and so on) to soften and settle. Do so by bringing focused attentiveness into these places, then letting that attentiveness relax, as if you were sighing.

3. If you're starting to think—or are getting focused on—fearful thoughts, acknowledge that this is happening by simply saying "fearful thinking" once or twice in a voice that only you can hear. Then count five conscious breaths (counting at the end of each exhale), letting your body ease as you do so.

EMBRACING THE DRAGON: BRINGING YOUR FEAR INTO YOUR HEART

> *And still I await the great night shining wild*
> *The great night so vastly ripe with child*
> *An undreaming love inviting me to meet my fear*
> *Inviting me to give the night my hand*

Until I cannot help but look through the eyes
Of every face no matter how dark the place

When fear arises, shift your attention from your head to your heart with as little delay as possible, softening your gut and relaxing your pelvic floor (the perineum and anal sphincter). As you do this, you give your fear more room to breathe.

Approach your fear with care and undivided attention, letting the feeling at its center start to penetrate you. Keep thus deepening your intimacy with your fearfulness, slowly bringing it into your heart, no longer treating it like an enemy or disease.

When we consistently meet our fearfulness with compassion and understanding, something marvelous happens: our very fear, unchained from its usual routine, helps catalyze our entry into a depth of openness wherein we do not—cannot—feel threatened to any significant degree. We might still be afraid, but now we don't mind—our heart has room for our fear.

When fearfulness infiltrates your mind, give its contents a quick, once-through reading, as though they belonged to a supermarket tabloid's front page. Notice which headlines most catch your eye. Next, immediately shift your attention to how your fear feels in your body, especially your heart; don't give in to the temptation to start thinking about it again.

When fear reaches a certain intensity, it can scare us scriptless. At this point—which may last for only a few seconds—we are so divested of our usual dramatics and mental scurrying that we're close to a truly deep openness, even though we are feeling quite the opposite. All we have to do is *not* flee to the surface—like a dreamer desperately trying to exit a nightmare—but remain right where we are. Though this is far from easy, it is doable with practice, as is turning to face whatever is pursuing us in a nightmare. We may be quaking in our dream boots, but we brave-heart our way toward what we are dreading—more often than not then connecting so deeply with our pursuer that we experience a powerfully healing integration.

Fear met with an open heart does not usually take long to transmute into excitement, passion, available life energy. By bringing some caring to our fearfulness, we cannot help but expand its containment, its contractedness, giving it all the pasture it needs with just enough fencing to keep it from running amok.

FEAR IN INTIMATE RELATIONSHIP

The fear of being left, the fear of being vulnerable, the fear of not being enough, the fear of not being wanted, the fear of being overly wanted, the fear of being controlled, the fear of displeasing, the fear of disconnection, the fear of being overlooked: there are so many fears that can infect, colonize, and otherwise obstruct relational intimacy.

The deeper our attachment to another person, the stronger our fears may become. Given this, we need to hold two aims at once in intimate relationship: (1) not to avoid attachment—which would only keep relational intimacy in the shallows—but to keep it from straying into addiction, and (2) to cut through the futurizing tendencies of such fearfulness, not allowing dire expectation or calamitous "what-ifs" to take root. Instead of getting caught up in the potentiality of bad possibility, we can face and move through the raw feeling underlying such worrisome cognition.

Fear does not have to be a relational obstacle. If we can share our fear with our intimate other without overdramatizing or identifying with it, we may find that our relational closeness has deepened, if only because of our vulnerability and courage. This doesn't mean dissociating from or numbing ourselves to our fear—so as not to appear fearful—but feeling it fully and doing nothing to camouflage or downplay it, while at the same time compassionately relating *to* it. Such courageous transparency invites our partner to meet us with an equivalent openness.

Identifying what we're most fearful of in intimate relationship is essential, as is being clear and self-disclosing about what we tend to do when we are thus afraid. For example, if we chronically fear that the other may leave, whether there is evidence or not for this, we may lose—or leave—ourselves in our efforts to make sure they stay, even as we sense that these very efforts increase the odds that we will indeed be left. The closer partners are, the more readily they share their fears with each other, treating such self-revelation with respect, curiosity, and compassion.

Among partners who have done little or no work on their relationship, fear doesn't get the kind of attention it needs. Such partners don't tend to share their fear—other than as worry that's frequently allowed to run wild—and may shame each other for showing worry. More mature partners take better care of their fear and are less prone to shaming themselves and each other for being afraid. In the best relationships, partners mutually explore their fear, mining its depths for gems of insight and revelation, opening themselves to what lies prior to and beyond all fear, without trying to eradicate their fear. However strong their fear might be, they choose to work with it together.

When we don't openly address our fears in relationship, we isolate ourselves from each other, clinging to a no-one's-land somewhere between our inner and outer fears, infecting our relationship with our various strategies to get away from our fears. Fear does not go away as we mature; we simply learn to work with it more and more effectively, minding its presence less and less.

Practice

WORKING WITH FEAR IN RELATIONSHIP

Sit facing your partner or a close friend whom you trust. Think of something that usually generates fear in you and that you're uncomfortable talking about. Holding steady eye contact with the other, begin talking about this particular fear. Say why you are not comfortable sharing it and what you fear might happen from doing so. Breathe a little deeper. Keep talking about your fear, fleshing it out as much as you can. If you feel shaky, let it show. Sense the other person feeling you as you speak. As much as you can, rest in his or her gaze and compassion.

Now start speaking only on the exhale (this means consciously inhaling, and then letting the words come as you exhale), letting yourself slow down, becoming even more aware of the other's caring for you. Let that caring, that heartfulness, get under your skin; breathe it in. After another minute or two, stop speaking, and imagine that you are holding the fearful you with great tenderness and care, putting your hands on your heart as if cradling that one.

If it feels natural, repeat this process with you as the listener and your partner or friend as the sharer of fear.

As long as we remain *outside* our fear, we remain trapped *within* it, bound by its viewpoint. However, when we consciously approach and enter our fear, it loses its grip on us. Once the contractedness, the darkly knotted inwardness that centers fear, ceases to be fueled, fear unravels, dissipates, ceasing to occupy us.

Journeying to the core of our fear is a challenging and remarkably rewarding adventure. Distractions will abound, not only testing us, but also honing and deepening our resolve. As we become more intimate with our fear, our problematic orientation to it dissipates, until it is no longer a foe but an ally.

Entering our fear ends our fear of it.

Wallflowers suddenly in bloom
Pain and joy arm in arm
So much room here
Where love cradles fear

9

Collective Fear

Letting Others' Fear Break Open Our Heart

When we really open to collective fear, we're hit in both the gut and the heart. We then feel not only our own fear, but also that of so many others, often in conjunction with a rising care for them, so that our capacity for compassion kicks into high gear.

TO WORK IN SIGNIFICANT DEPTH with fear we need to take into account not only personal fear but also collective fear—the kind of fear that could be called "our" fear and "the" fear, infiltrating us with its energies and core message: *we are threatened, we are in danger, we are at the mercy of far-from-benign forces.*

Although we might like to think we are immune to this, we are affected, we are impacted, in much the same way that a polluted atmosphere gets to us no matter how clean the air is in our home or how correctly we breathe. Collective fear is natural, at least to some degree, for any group that is at the mercy of "outside" forces, like unfriendly factions or dangerous weather. Such fear can, of course, be amplified by media outlets and political/religious leaders or other cultural influences, yet it remains an inevitable phenomenon, just like individual fear. In current times, collective fear is not just concentrated in scattered political and religious enclaves but has blanketed the entire planet, bringing us all together in a worldwide web of fearfulness.

You might question the value of opening to collective fear, perhaps thinking that doing so would only add to our already-present fear, but— as I explain later in this chapter—such openness doesn't necessarily amplify our fear. Instead, it cuts through our usual fearfulness, if only by shifting us into a sense of caring for and connection with others, both met and unmet.

PSYCHOEMOTIONAL NUMBING

One of the most prominent signs of our current collective fearfulness is psychoemotional numbing. This manifests as a muting and flattening of feeling, a depression of sorts—a *pressing-down* of fearfulness—that masks itself with whatever stimulation can be found, along with a big enough dose of denial to keep the lid on, generating a mix of apathy and nihilism that squats behind the label "coping."

Such mass numbing shifted into high gear in the decades following World War II. Knowing that we now had the capability to annihilate ourselves through nuclear war, an event that could definitely happen, hooked us up to enough fearfulness to successfully overwhelm us. (It's easy to forget that during the Cold War there used to be a lot of dead-serious huddling in bomb shelters.) So, quite understandably, we got busy fleeing such collective dread by investing enormous amounts of energy into finding various means that would keep us "safely" removed from it. Various fascinations—ranging from the narcotic to the erotic to the spiritually captivating—capable of potently distracting us from our dread occupied increasingly central places in our lives, and continue to do so.

As people became increasingly numb to their numbness, all too many adapted to it to the point of normalizing it. Pharmaceutical "solutions" ("magic bullets" for the psyche) became second nature. Being "cool" became more popular. Hypomania (meaning "mildly manic")—especially in the context of achieving at a high level—became mainstream and was increasingly believed to be admirable, if only vicariously. Revving up one's nervous system built up enough charge to necessitate—and perhaps also legitimize—some sort of energetic release, which took some of the edge off the fear. Nowadays we spend much less time fearing nuclear war than terrorism or global warming or random shootings, yet we continue to seek and market ways to numb our collective fears.

Today, like during the Cold War, if we really want to feel what we suppress, we can tap into it now and then by immersing ourselves in secondhand fears via such means as horror movies. The cinematic terrors that evoke our screams and fear are basically sensationalized surrogates and exaggerations of what we *already* have covered up in ourselves, rising from their subterranean holding tanks to confront us briefly. When the movie is over, we can sit back, relieved and somewhat sated by our plunge into "safe" fear in much the same way we can awaken from a nightmare so as to remain relatively unaware of what was actually animating it.

Such false or unawake "awakenings" only reinforce our slumber regarding our actual situation. We are, in short, not taking advantage of the shock that our nightmare delivers—the shock that could jolt us awake and propel us into life-enhancing action. Instead, we settle for the chills and thrills and eventual relief afforded by our immersion in secondhand fears.

We may have the best seats in the coziest section of the ecological and political nightmare that infests our planet, and we may have more than enough comfort and status to relegate this to the outskirts of our consciousness, but there fear resides, gnawing at our gates, sliding under our doors, finding more and more ways to get to us. In our heart of hearts we know we must face this nightmare with our whole being. It may be very late to be taking such a stand, but take it we must, doing our very best to align ourselves with it.

This begins with seeing collective fear for what it is and learning to recognize when we are susceptible to it—such as when we are feeling overwhelmed by various demands and we let ourselves spin off into the kind of functioning that only makes things worse. None of us are immune to collective fear. So let us turn to face it, with as little numbing as we can.

OUR "SOLUTIONS" TO COLLECTIVE FEAR

Numbing ourselves is not our only "solution" to collective fear. Another is *avoidance,* which overlaps with numbing. Collective fear insinuates its way into us—emotionally, psychologically, physically, electronically— and we may find ourselves sidestepping it, rising above it, withdrawing from it, and dissociating from it as much as we can. Whereas numbing is a freezing or congealing, avoidance is flight. So there's more movement in avoidance; it chooses not inertia, but removal. Its legs do not turn leaden in a nightmare but rather to wings—whatever helps us get away. For example, instead of numbly reading about a local tragedy, we shut ourselves off from any incoming information, refusing to learn or talk about it.

Aggression is another "solution" to collective fear. Instead of fleeing or freezing, we fight. We transmute the energy of fear into the energy of unhealthy anger—anger that is out to attack. Now we're not afraid, but pissed off and looking for someone or something to go after aggressively. However, we're still not relating *to* our fear, but are, as is the case with freezing and fleeing, only relating *from* it, moving not into healthy anger—nonblaming, nonshaming, nonattacking anger—but into modes in which offending others become our focus. Righteously targeting them and/or their shortcomings—those damned politicians!—distracts us from the very fear that is motivating us to behave with aggression in the first place.

The fourth "f"—the first three solutions being fleeing, fighting, and freezing—is obsession with sexuality. In laboratory studies, the more afraid an overcrowded collection of rats is, the more hypersexual and sexually aberrant they become. Humans are similar: under stress, we may overuse sex to provide a quick, potent, energetic release from tension or to act out our unresolved wounds and unmet needs. As collective fear spreads wider and deeper, so does the reliance on sex as a means of making us feel better or more secure. Modern culture is so hypersexualized, so obsessively eroticized—is there a more ubiquitous adjective than "sexy"?—that we generally treat such excess as all but normal. We are acclimatized to it.

There's often the promise of a certain liberating power in sex, however crude, and that promise becomes especially seductive and magnetically appealing when collective fear grips us. But only when we release sex (and everything else!) from the obligation to make us feel better—or at least less fearful—do we really start to free ourselves, if only to at last face our fear, both in its personal and collective forms.

Practice

MEETING COLLECTIVE FEAR

(Note: If you are experiencing paranoia or extreme anxiety in your daily life, do not do the following practice.)

Find a comfortable place to sit, with a notebook and pen handy. Make sure you will not be interrupted in the next ten minutes or so, and wear clothing that's loose enough to allow easy, unrestricted breathing.

Below is a list of incomplete sentences. Complete them as spontaneously as possible, out loud, writing down your response to each immediately after voicing it. When you're done, rest for a few minutes.

For me, collective fear is _____.

I'm most aware of collective fear when _____.

My usual way of dealing with collective fear is _____.

How this is similar to my usual way of dealing with my own fear is _____.

What scares me the most about our ecological and political situation is _____.

As I feel this, my guts are _____.

As I feel this, my heart is _____.

If my heart could speak right now, it would say _____.

My breathing feels _____.

My usual way of numbing myself is _____.

What scares me the most about not numbing myself is _____.

What happens to my suffering when I let myself openly feel the suffering of others is _____.

What happens to my fear when I let myself openly feel the fear of others is _____.

When I stop trying to get away from collective fear, what happens is _____.

The edge that humankind is fast approaching is _____.

If I could say anything to all of us, I'd say _____.

What we need to do with our collective fear is _____.

What I am going to do with it is _____.

Follow-Up

1. Watch (or read) the headline news for twenty or thirty minutes and observe your breathing the whole time without detaching from your feelings, reminding yourself to keep your belly as soft as possible throughout. Feel underneath the words and presentation, naming your emotions out loud as they arise.

2. Imagine that the worst has happened. Breathe it in, sit in it, stay present in it, breathe it in some more—and open as you breathe out. Feel yourself still present, right here, in the midst of it all, whether you are calm or angry or scared or weeping or taking some sort of action. Stay present. Finish with the practice described in the appendix.

3. As soon as you sense the presence of collective fear, name it out loud. As soon as you feel yourself pulling back or distracting yourself from collective fear, stop and stay put, breathing more deeply and grounding yourself for a few minutes (softening your belly, planting your feet, rooting yourself in solid ground).

WORKING WITH COLLECTIVE FEAR

Collective fear carries a lot of weight—a globe-encircling oppressiveness—so instead of being burdened only by our own fear, we also may be burdened by a general sense of chronic fearfulness coming at us from all directions. There is a felt density to this, an unpleasantly pervasive contractedness that is so common that it has become all but normalized. When we let this invade us, our personal fears are amplified and our resources for taking good care of ourselves dwindle.

Working with our collective fear in skillful ways is much the same as what we're learning to do with our personal fear: name it, turn toward it, take our wholehearted attention into it, and start cultivating intimacy with it, giving it a more expanded container and liberating its energies from their prevailing viewpoint. But now we're not just opening our heart to our own fearfulness; we're also opening our heart to our collective fearfulness.

It is essential that we allow ourselves to openly feel the forces of collective fear without letting ourselves collapse, dissociate, or indulge in worrying. This may sound counterintuitive, but it actually reduces the impact of collective fear, partly because we've expanded ourselves through the very act of such opening, and partly because we're allowing other emotions—like anger, grief, shame—to arise in conjunction with fear so that it ceases to dominate our emotional landscape.

When we really open to collective fear, we are hit not only in the gut and solar plexus, but also in the heart. We feel our own fear along with that of so many others, often in conjunction with a rising care for them. We more deeply feel everyone's sorrow and the enormity of all the grief, all the unaddressed wounding and dehumanization.

Through our rawness of heart and widening awareness, we start to shift into a vitally alive, far-reaching intersubjectivity or *we-centeredness*, letting the general fearfulness of humankind penetrate us in such a way that our capacity for compassion—and for compassionate action—kicks into high gear.

Then we're not so much afraid as we are undefendedly feeling great hurt, being touched by a depth and expanse of collective woundedness and pain that breaks our heart. We naturally now breathe *in* fear—not just my fear or our fear but also *the* fear—and breathe *out* care. Such caring for others is not done in some effort to be a compassionate or spiritual somebody, but simply because we've reached the point where there is nothing else to do.

The broken heart can go into endarkened contraction, a myopic curling-in—or it can break open. When this happens, there's great expansion, a sense of vast and deep roominess, however raw, however painful. In such radical stretching, we simultaneously bleed and soar. This makes it possible for grief—my grief and your grief and our grief and *the* grief—to pour through us until we are but an exquisitely vulnerable presence serving the good of one and all. Letting ourselves be thus opened by fear reduces our fear level and increases our capacity to live vital, loving lives.

So let collective fear into your heart—not all at once, but enough so that you feel your heart starting to crack and stretch. As you let it break open, you will discover that it has room for all. Then fearfulness will not be a problem for you, but simply one more arising, one more quality showing up, already seeded with its own transformation—and the catalyst for this is your willingness to enter such fear and to let it enter you, at a pace that doesn't overwhelm you. The point is not to become an undiscerning vessel for fear, but to make more room in our heart for fear, holding it the way we'd hold a frightened child.

When dealing with collective fear, it's of central importance that we ground ourselves. Letting our heart break open does not mean that we should turn to mush or let ourselves be passively blown around by circumstances. Stand as solid as possible, no matter how transparent or vulnerable you are. Feel the earth beneath your feet. Make and keep making real contact with the ground, as if becoming a kind of lightning rod for fearfulness.

Opening yourself to collective fearfulness does not mean that you should open yourself indiscriminately to fear-reinforcing material. Cut through whatever information is before you and feel what underlies it. If you watch the news, don't just watch it—feel it! Bad news should not be a spectator sport or just more info-tainment, but rather an occasion to cut through fearfulness so that our energies are mobilized for something more beneficial than merely distracting ourselves from fear. Of course, it's important to take in only as much disturbing news as you can hold and digest; if you take in too much, you'll simply get overwhelmed.

Another aspect of dealing skillfully with collective fear is that of maintaining and deepening our individuality—not our egoity, but our individuality or personalized essence—doing all that we can not to give in to groupthink or groupfeel or any sort of ethnocentric or nationalistic certainties. It is easy to lose touch with our autonomy when we're surrounded by others' fear and panic.

Our work is not to become hyperautonomous, keeping ourselves "safely" apart from whatever is happening with others, but to simultaneously embody autonomy and we-centeredness, honoring both individual and group needs.

In this, we have enough separation to stay clearly focused and enough connection to be deeply in touch with what is occurring. In short, we are enhancing our capacity for intimacy, both with others and with all that we are.

Essential to maintaining healthy separation and healthy connection is the ongoing presence of conscious, well-functioning boundaries. Fear either obliterates our boundaries or shrinks and calcifies them. A snail without its shell is too vulnerable, and a snail that won't leave the innermost spirals of its shell is cut off from life; one gets squashed, the other atrophies. Just like us. With effective boundaries, we can venture out without having to abandon our softness and vulnerability, and we can stay put without turning ourselves into a fortress of solitude or isolation.

And what is the primary guardian, emotionally speaking, of our boundaries? Anger. As we've seen, anger and fear are very closely related, being all but identical biochemically. If we're angry and shut it down (as we may have learned to do long ago for survival reasons), our fear level tends to increase. So it's crucial that we not convert our anger into fear or aggression, but give it space to breathe and unfold and find expression in life-giving ways.

Get as intimate as possible with your anger; keep it close by, and don't deny yourself your fully felt outrage over things you see and hear. If you suppress your anger over such things, the energy of that anger will become worry, anxiety, dread, along with varying degrees of numbness. There are things that we need to get angry about, but it's crucial that we not let such anger run away with us, as is the case in the frenzied aggression of a hyperstimulated mob. Similarly, if you suppress your hurt and grief over things you see and hear, the energy of that insufficiently expressed hurt and grief will become apathy, depression, dullness, dispiritedness.

Collective fear flattens and wastes and deadens us, if we leave it unchallenged. By contrast, our anger can enliven us, fueling us in more life-giving directions. Fear puts out the fire; anger flames it bright. And the fire of anger—if nonblaming and nonaggressive—provides both heat and light.

Once again, stay vulnerable, and do so without abandoning or neglecting your boundaries. Let your heart break open, again and again and again. Doing so will only enlarge it, without any dilution of your capacity to love. And don't confine your love to meekness. Give it room to be fierce, to be vitally alive, to make a fuss! Your unleashed voice is needed. Let it arise from your core so that by the time it's on the tip of your tongue, it is already passionately alive.

Practice

WORKING WITH COLLECTIVE FEAR

(Note: If you are experiencing paranoia or extreme anxiety in your daily life, do not do the following practice.)

Complete the following incomplete sentences as spontaneously as possible, out loud, and write down your response to each sentence immediately after voicing it. When you're finished, rest for a few minutes.

What is most obvious about collective fear is _____.

Knowing that many, many others are also experiencing such fear makes me feel _____.

What I wish I could do for others is _____.

What I can do for others is _____.

My heart has room for _____.

What's happening to my fear right now is _____.

No matter what happens, I am _____.

When I stop turning away from my fear and our fear, I am _____.

My vulnerability becomes a source of strength when _____.

Follow-Up

1. Do a one-week news fast: nothing from newspapers or magazines or television, nothing online. When you have the urge to see or hear "the news," count ten conscious breaths, then take your attention inside that urge, noticing what you're feeling emotionally. Stay with that feeling for a few minutes, letting yourself get as close to it as possible.

2. Notice when your compassion is low or nonexistent, and without delay breathe some life into it, letting yourself open to feeling the pain and fear of others, while at the same time wishing them well.

Fear separates us, but only if we let it. Shared fear—fear that is openly faced and discussed and felt with others—can draw us into an unusually potent intimacy, breaking us open to what matters most of all. (I'm not talking here about worry-fests, the "sharings" of which are all about absorbing ourselves in socially acceptable anxiety without any impetus to go deeper.) In such openness, we are not bypassing our fear but entering it so deeply and so fully that its energies unravel, burst, and dissipate, expanding beyond themselves.

Collective fear contains the very energy we need to fuel our leap to more fitting levels of being. Our work is to free up that energy, but we cannot do so if we remain distant from it. So both together and alone, let us face this planetary dragon, getting closer to it, learning to breathe it in right down to our toes without losing our ground. The treasure that it guards is the treasure we were born to find.

Collective fear is vast, but love is vaster. So are we.

10

Shame

From Toxic Collapse to Healing Exposure

Shame may be the emotion we fear the most.

Where healthy shame triggers our conscience (our
innate moral sense), unhealthy shame triggers our inner
critic, which often masquerades as our conscience.

WHEN PEOPLE FIRST RECOGNIZE THE part that shame has
played in their lives, many are amazed at and sobered by how influen-
tial that part has been—and what a gift it has been, in some ways. It is
as if a lost continent of themselves has surfaced. Shame kept in the dark
keeps us in the dark.

Shame may be our most hidden or submerged emotion; it also may
be the one we shun the most. I recall a poll that asked what people most
feared. Dying didn't top the list, but speaking in public did. (Speaking
naked in public was not one of the choices in this poll, but it should
have been.) The fear of speaking in public is a fear of being shamed in
public. Our aversion to directly feeling and staying with our shame is
highlighted by the common description of the experience as *mortifying*.

Shame is the painfully self-conscious sense of our behavior—or self—
being *exposed* as defective, with the immediate result that we are halted
in our tracks, for better or for worse. The felt sense of shame is that of
public condemnation, even if our only audience is our inner critic.

In healthy shame, the voice of our conscience picks up volume, and
the expression of appropriate remorse becomes a very real option for us,
which we act on as soon as possible. In unhealthy or toxic shame, which

is much more common than healthy shame, our very self is under attack, whether from outside ourselves or from within by our inner critic.

Implicit in shame is the fear of being humiliated. A burning loss of face, an excruciatingly contracted squirming, a crushingly negative exposure with nowhere to hide—and all in front of a hypercritical audience. The language of shame can be relatively benign ("I'm disappointed in you" or "You can do better than this"), cruel ("*This* is the best you can do?" or "I've shown you a hundred times how to do this, and you *still* can't?"), or toxic ("You'll never amount to anything" or "You're such a loser!").

To add to shame's impact, the preceding parenthetical statements can also be *self-directed,* giving them an added emphasis, before which we more often than not literally hang our heads, slipping into the characteristic sag of shame. As mean as others can be to us, we can be even meaner to ourselves, as is epitomized by having or being occupied by an unrelentingly harsh inner critic, in the presence of which our default— our automatic go-to habit—is to shrink, cower, regress, or please.

Furthermore, we tend to be conflicted around shame, attaching a negative connotation both to having it ("You're pathetic!") and to not having it ("You're shameless!"). Parents may accuse their child, whom they have just shamed, of being shifty-eyed, making the child wrong (more shame!) for having a downward gaze and squirming demeanor, yet they may get angry at the same child for not showing shame when he or she fails to measure up to a particular standard. When we have an early history of being shamed—being told in so many words that we are defective—we're very likely as adults to have little tolerance for simply being present with our shame, given how paralyzing it originally was for us.

There's a danger here: if we assign a totally negative connotation to shame, we will insufficiently attend to situations in which shame is entirely appropriate, such as when we've hurt another and need to openly admit this and access enough remorse to voice a heartfelt "I'm sorry," along with a sincere attempt to make fitting amends. Under such conditions we need to stay with our shame. If we're a parent, we need to help our child stay with his or her shame over being mean to a friend or sibling, for example, rather than "getting away with it."

Even the most well-meaning of us can slip into shaming others in damaging ways, without even knowing that we're doing so. For example, we may unfavorably compare one of our children to another with the intention of motivating him or her to do better at a particular task. Too few of us realize that shaming another to get the results *we* want or expect can backfire. Why? Because when we feel shamed, our capacity to function well plummets; we feel discombobulated, awkward, small, unable to focus very clearly. When shame is aimed at our very *being*, our disorientation or fuzzy-mindedness is compounded by feeling debilitated and flattened, as if our self-sense has been run over by heavy machinery, leaving us incapable of functioning the way our shamer thinks we should. At the same time, the intention to do what he or she wants us to do becomes hugely central to us. When our shame wanes, we'll probably act out that intention as best we can, so as to lower the odds that our shamer will come after us again. (Shaming dynamics are very common not only in families, but also in all kinds of organizations.)

Imagine a child who is shamed for not being able to figure out a math problem. She's told that she's a disappointment, that she should be able to do the math, that she is stupid. The more she is put down for her failure, the more she fails, and the more she fails, the more she is shamed. And the more forcefully the child is criticized, the more driven she is to dissociate from the whole scene, giving the impression that she is not paying attention to what is being said to her.

Giving others the impression that they are defective is an ineffective approach to encouragement, yet this strategy remains the operational preference for many of us when we're faced with someone falling short of our expectations. This is where many relationships founder: One partner is trying to measure up to the other's standards—often with the threat (voiced or tacit) that if they don't, they'll be abandoned. That partner, not surprisingly, is often on the verge of failing—that is, not measuring up—and the other partner is busy being disappointed, saying in so many words that the other is abandoning *them* by not showing up enough, by not making a full effort to meet them, et cetera after painful et cetera.

We are so pervaded, both personally and collectively, by shame that we have shame about how much shame we have. To even talk about shame is, in most circles, more than a little embarrassing, unless it is clearly not about us. Shame painfully exposes us, with our reddening face or suddenly awkward speech or stumbling stance that attracts even more unwanted attention. This can be helpful when we're in the midst of doing something harmful to another (like speaking cruelly to them), but in many cases it's just something we endure.

I remember being strapped by the school principal when I was nine (this was the mid 1950s), and making a huge effort not to cry when— less than a minute after my punishment in the principal's office—I had to walk back into the classroom, where the other students gleefully pointed out my red face, which was crimson with both shame and the struggle not to weep. Getting to my desk was one of the longest journeys I ever took. And what did I do with this shame? Kept it to myself, as there would have been even more shame if I'd told my parents about it.

A less dramatic but more damaging feeling of shame occurs when we're consistently put down by those who have authority over us, especially when they clearly have some distaste for us. If this characterized how one of our parents treated us when we were little, it's likely we felt demoralized by such ongoing censure, shrinking with toxic shame so often that we defined ourselves by it, perhaps finding ourselves in the grip of excessive shyness as if trying to literally shrink away from others' scrutiny. Such agonizing exposure—usually accompanied by megadoses of self-reproach—is at the core of the kind of shame that does no one any good. In its presence, our urge to disappear can be overwhelming.

Practice

STAYING WITH OUR SHAME

Recall a time during your childhood when you felt shamed by your parents, siblings, teachers, or other children. Close your eyes, letting your head hang down and your body slump. Remember what you did with that shame. Did you fight back, put yourself down, collapse, withdraw? Whatever it was, feel it as much as possible now. Stay with this for a couple of minutes, then finish this sentence: "I still handle my shame this way when _____."

Remember a recent time when you did this with your shame. Look at this situation without defending yourself. Simply feel it. Now imagine that you're back in that circumstance and that your shame has just started. Instead of doing your habitual practice with shame, stay with it, paying close attention to it, no matter how uncomfortable it is. You may feel the intention to escape it, but do not act this out. Now imagine that you can see the whole shaming scene. Zero in on the "you" in that scene—circling yourself with compassion, sensing how old that "you" seems—so that you are holding both the scene and the shamed you. What happens?

THE NATURE OF SHAME

Much of shame is about failing to meet others' values—or our own, which are mostly just an internalization of the values of those who originally shamed us. Whether our shame is the result of external or internal pressures, the experience of it is often disempowering.

When we feel shame or are being shamed, we may sense we should be taking action. Yet in its initial arising, shame readies us not for action but for on-the-spot stoppage. It strongly interrupts us, halting us in our tracks. We may also feel a sudden sense of self-shrinkage, perhaps further tightened by our full-bodied, painfully obvious self-consciousness. We may feel a loss of lift in our neck and upper torso, so that our head slumps forward and our chest caves in as if we've just been slugged in the solar plexus. We look down and very likely do not want to look up. We may feel increased heat in our face, and to our consternation we may blush. And we may experience a brief but unpleasantly intense period of confusion, mental blankness, and disorganization. Body and mind brake to a halt, however much they be spinning internally. Once these initial signs of shame start to recede, intentions to take certain actions appear, ranging from making ourselves as small as possible, to saying we're sorry, to getting angry at whoever put us in this position.

The slump and sag of shame show up at an early age. The upper bodies of many adults resemble a question-mark shape when viewed in profile, as if they're bent before a powerful force. Shame has that much power—enough to shape us for life. Other people might hold themselves extra erect, as if on guard against displaying anything that might resemble shame. Excessive pride is another camouflage against shame; it reddens us with effort instead of embarrassment, leaving us ever vigilant to not drop our eyes, holding the proof of our achievements unnaturally high, as if to offset the downward pull of shame.

Shame reduces our coordination, which only adds to its power to stop us in our tracks. This deposits us in a position where it's hard not to contrast where we were right before our shame arrived and where we are now. At best, this sudden contrast sobers us so that we rethink what we were about to do—like scorning another, overpursuing a particular pleasure, taking an ill-advised gamble, preparing to lash another with our rage, and so on. The interruption of shame can halt us so that we don't do harm—or don't do *more* harm—and it can also give us a timely time-out to clean up whatever mess we have made, to make amends, to clarify our focus on what was motivating us before we were braked by the feeling of shame.

When shame shows up, it can crush us, and it can also serve us, as when it makes us less immune to remorse or less full of ourselves. In the latter case, shame is not an enemy, but an ally.

One of the reasons we have such an aversion to shame is that it immediately takes us away from a pleasurable or positive experience. Shame is to positive feeling as disgust is to hunger. Disgust emphatically interrupts hunger when something for which we hunger—and not just food!—simply doesn't "smell" right or makes us feel "sick" or is distasteful. Shame does the same thing for upbeat or pleasure-driven feelings. For example, we're having a positive experience—but when this experience doesn't register as "right" to our core value system or innate moral sense, our pleasure-seeking usually gets decisively interrupted. This is one of the many ways that shame serves us: it can protect us from getting overly attached to our feel-good urges, especially when it's not safe or socially appropriate to thus indulge.

For example, a man on a date is showing signs of wanting to get sexual, even though the woman shows some reluctance to proceed. She's much younger than him and clearly has a hard time saying "no" without smiling, so it's easy for the man not to believe her. He keeps overriding her hesitation, feeling an increasingly strong desire to have sex with her. Suddenly he sees the woman's fear, innocence, and urge to please, and shame arises in him. He sees too much to proceed; his desire to go ahead has been strongly interrupted, with his conscience quickly taking up a lot of space. The man stops his sexual advances and soon is grateful that he did.

Without shame, there is no conscience, no moral time-out. Of course, we can override or bypass our shame, letting it morph into aggression, withdrawal, dissociation, or guilt, but its presence can serve us if we stay with it.

It is often a fine line between how shame can serve us and how it can debilitate us. Shame's presence can be toxic, such as when it's delivered or received in ways that crush or obliterate our self-esteem, making us feel like crawling into a hole or disappearing or even killing ourselves. When shame's focus shifts from our behavior to *us*, we're in dangerous territory. Once we're ashamed of and/or shamed for our very being (as in "feeling worthless") and we have no alternative view of ourselves to contrast this with—as frequently happens in childhood—we start to live as though we truly *are* defective. The more defective or unworthy we picture ourselves to be, the more driven we will be to seek some sort of compensatory "solution," some sort of strategy to distance ourselves from the raw feeling of our shame as much as possible.

STRATEGIES TO EVADE SHAME

Because of our aversion to the felt experience of shame, we rarely let it stay as it is. We may dissociate from it by getting emotionally numb or absorb ourselves in abstraction or energetically consuming fixes like pornography or long hours in front of the television. We may infuse shame with fear, which usually generates guilt, or we may push it into the background, letting other emotions—especially anger—take center stage. For example, if we're in a situation that triggers shame, we may get angry to such a righteously convincing degree that we genuinely believe that we are *only* angry, regardless of whether our anger is directed at another person or at ourselves. In either case, our anger—especially if it is allowed to mutate into aggression—distracts us from our shame and also amplifies it when we step back enough to see the damage our "attack other" and "attack self" activity has done.

So much of what we do is a "solution" to our shame—be it in the form of aggression, withdrawal, inflated pride, hyperachievement, spiritual escapism, or excessive interest in sex—a means of escaping or covering up our shame to the point of not even knowing we're feeling shame. When these "solutions" wane, our shame reemerges and reasserts itself, undigested and unresolved, ever inviting us to cease avoiding it.

Even if we can evade others' scrutiny when we're feeling shame or being shamed—a difficult task, given how noticeable and transparent our self-involvement may be—we cannot so easily evade our inner scrutiny. Long after our face has lost its blush, and long after the shaming episode, we may still be cringing or wincing internally, replaying the shame-inducing event and thinking, "How could I?" Eventually, we'll likely invest some energy into distancing ourselves from it, often by fantasizing about retaliation—after all, it's a short distance from shame to aggression.

If retaliation or revenge isn't possible, we might simply withdraw, finding solace in emotional dissociation, exaggerated privacy, or distracting activities (mental or otherwise). And if we can't successfully remove ourselves from our shaming—as commonly happens in young children—we may find ourselves burdened with debilitating shyness. Unfortunately, the shame "solutions" we used during our childhood and teen years don't necessarily go away as we grow into adulthood; they often continue in more sophisticated forms. For example, we might have achieved respite from shame by defeating other children academically or athletically; now as an adult we might be driven to intellectually overpower others who trigger our shame.

SHAME DEFLATES US

Not only does shame expose us, stripping us down in a second or two, but it also *deflates* us rapidly and emphatically, regardless of how much it might heat us up. In anger, such heatedness inflates our upper torso, seemingly enlarging us, but in shame it burns away our sense of internal structure so that we tend to collapse. This, so to speak, takes the wind out of our sails, halting our forward momentum, giving us a timely break to reconsider what we were doing right before our shame arrived.

It's tempting to compensate for shame's deflationary impact by investing in inflated pride in an effort to place ourselves beyond the reach of shame. Such pride holds us artificially aloft, leaving us nowhere to go but down, particularly when the intrusions of reality do their thankless job. When our pride bubble bursts and we fall, shame awaits us—including the shame of having fallen. Then more pride may ensue, or we might not be so quick to flee our shame.

We may also find respite from shame's deflationary power by indulging in anger's capacity to pump us up: think of the hugely bulked-up mesomorphic marvels of comic books seemingly about to burst with anger, getting increasingly thin-skinned as their upper torso expands. But once our anger passes, shame reasserts itself, however subtly, giving us an opportunity to stay with it without losing spine or heart. Doing so is an act of what could be called heroic vulnerability.

AGGRESSION, SHAME, AND THE INNER CRITIC

Shame easily, quickly, and commonly mutates into aggression against others or ourselves. In fact, it may so rapidly shift into aggression that we may not even notice there was any shame there to begin with. And if our shame is sufficiently strong to really humiliate us, our resulting aggression might manifest not just as ill will or hostility, but as outright violence.

The myth of the humiliated one seeking violent revenge upon his or her perpetrators gets a big dose of cultural justification in many films and among audiences, for whom there is a vicarious thrill in witnessing (and cheering on) such primal aggression. After all, there are few of us who don't enjoy seeing the underdog rise up and strike back, especially if he or she endured extreme humiliation.

Aggression against those who humiliate us is a potent distraction from such shaming, even if all we do is act out such aggression by mentally delivering biting thoughts and cutting comebacks. Aggression turned against ourselves is much more insidious, for it may be so well hidden that no one except us really knows the torture we're enduring through such internalized attacks.

The epitome and key agent of aggression against ourselves is our inner critic, a composite of the main critical/shaming voices we heard as a child. It provides a heartlessly negative appraisal of us, reinforcing our sense of ourselves as defective; we can never measure up. What was done to us by those who most successfully shamed us is what we are now doing to ourselves through our inner critic when we let it assume an authoritative position in our psyche.

As solid as it might seem, our inner critic is more verb than noun. It is not an entity, however much we have personalized it. The inner critic is a "doing," an activity, a cognicentric arising that feeds on our attention and energy, carrying a "should"-infested authority that few of us question, just as young children don't question their parents' authority.

We all have an inner critic, but not all of us are controlled by it. For a few, it's a mildly irritating voice emanating from a back corner of the

mind; for some it's an unrelenting nagging; for others it's a tyranni-
cal voice broadcasting with such force that they can't hear much else.
The inner critic can be so relentless, so viciously shaming, and so powerful that some are driven to suicidal thoughts. There are those who
believe the inner critic is always right, that it is none other than their
conscience, and that they have no more right to question it than a
child does his or her parents. These people believe their inner critic is
a clear-sighted, fully adult version of themselves. Their freedom starts
when they realize that *they* are not their inner critic, and that it loses its
power when they cease taking its content seriously and stop letting it
masquerade as their conscience.

HEALTHY AND UNHEALTHY SHAME

Since shame has such a negative impact on so many of us, it has become
commonplace to condemn shame itself. But shame is not inherently a
problem! Again, the issue is how we handle our shame. Toxic shame,
unhealthy shame, shame that dehumanizes and crushes, is not an
innate emotion but the result of choices with which we have saddled
shame. As with fear, we can become intimate with our shame so that it
serves rather than hinders us. This begins with learning the difference
between healthy and unhealthy shame.

First of all, healthy shame is directed primarily at a particular action,
whereas unhealthy shame is directed primarily at the *doer* of that
action. For example, if our partner has repeatedly lied about something
important to our relationship, it's fitting that they feel shame for what
they've done. It's not appropriate, however, that they go into shame for
who they are. In the former case, remorse and atonement are probably
close at hand, but in the latter case, they are out of reach. We certainly
need to hold a partner accountable, and we're under no obligation to
excuse their behavior, but we don't need to attack or vilify their being,
however tempted we might be to do so. We can rage at them for lying
to us, we can cry hard over their betrayal of us, and we can accept our
decreased trust in them, but we have no right to dehumanize them,
which would happen if we were to shame them for their very being.

Both healthy and unhealthy shame interrupt, expose, and deflate us,
but then the two diverge: in healthy shame we empower ourselves to
take healing action, but in unhealthy shame we disempower ourselves,
doing little more than looking for some sort of escape or compensatory

activity. In healthy shame we are stirred to set things right and to sincerely express our remorse, whereas in unhealthy shame we tend to freeze, rendering ourselves incapable of making reparations because we're so busy flagellating ourselves that we don't see what's needed right now.

In other words, healthy shame mobilizes us and unhealthy shame immobilizes us. Healthy shame triggers our conscience, whereas unhealthy shame triggers our inner critic, which often masquerades as our conscience.

And what is conscience? It can be defined, aside from whatever lens we pass it through, as the activated presence of our innate moral sense. Its core of compassion arises from a mix of empathy and shame-informed—but not shame-dominated!—consideration. It is moral intelligence in the raw.

Healthy shame opens our heart—after initially contracting it—but unhealthy shame closes our heart, and keeps it closed. In healthy shame, we feel for the one we have hurt (including ourselves), however painful that might be; in unhealthy shame, we're so swamped by our own contractedness that we don't feel for the one we've hurt (including ourselves) and our empathic wall becomes as thick as it is impermeable.

Healthy shame brings us to our knees temporarily; if we take fitting action, it then restores our dignity. Unhealthy shame doesn't just bring us to our knees, it *flattens* us, obliterating our dignity. Healthy shame features humility, unhealthy shame humiliation.

Compassion and healthy shame can coexist, but unhealthy shame and compassion cannot, simply because our empathy has been sealed off or crushed or become irrelevant to us—and without empathy, there's no compassion.

Practice

TAKING SHAME TO HEART

Recall a situation in which you felt strong shame over how you treated someone. Close your eyes, letting yourself open to the shame of that time. What were you doing right before your shame surfaced, and what did you do once it had surfaced? Did you apologize for what you did, and if so, when? Imagine that the person you mistreated is sitting before you, and notice how you feel as you imagine this. Speak to them as you did at that time, and then speak to them as you wish you had. As much as possible, speak from your heart.

Be generous in your remorse, noticing how this affects you. Stay with this for a few minutes, then ask for their forgiveness—even if you think you don't deserve it. And finally, step back from the original scene so you can see yourself doing whatever brought on your shame. Look upon your past self with caring, opening yourself to forgiveness. By doing so, you are not condoning what you did, but you are offering that younger version of yourself your heart's pardon.

WORKING WITH SHAME

Shame flattens our perspective and narrows our view, leaving us floundering in exaggerated self-consciousness—which is a misnomer, because when we're self-conscious, we're not so much conscious of our self as we are of others watching us. Becoming conscious of our self-consciousness—that is, letting it be the object rather than the subject of our attention—helps free us from shame's grip. The point is not to flee shame, but to step back from it just far enough so we can see it—and its hold on us—more clearly.

In shame, our privacy is usually undressed; there's an almost immediate sense of being disturbingly exposed, as if our clothes have just been removed in a public, well-lit place where people are watching intently. Imagine this scene, with you as the naked one on stage before a critical, unsympathetic audience. Notice if you feel any of the telltale signs of shame: hanging head; rounded upper back; hot, contracting face; cringing body. Now imagine there's no escape from this scene, and notice how hard it is to lift your head, gaze directly at your audience, and rest in your innate dignity.

Essential to working with shame is meeting it with compassion. This gives shame room to breathe, room to openly be itself without fear of being looked down upon. Bringing our shame into our heart is not easy but utterly necessary if we are to cease being diminished or run by it. The closer we get to our shame, the more clearly we can see it and our history with it.

We also need to differentiate shame from the fear, anger, hurt, or disgust that may arise from and camouflage it. Does the felt presence of shame drive us into compensatory emotional activity? What do we tend to do emotionally when shame is catalyzed in us? Addressing these and related questions is an essential aspect of working with shame. And to do this, we need to stop shaming ourselves for having shame.

Practice

WORKING WITH SHAME

Recall a time when you felt intense shame. What did you do with it? Let yourself feel that shame now, assuming the posture you were in at that time. Sink into this for a minute or two, then imagine that you're starting to feel angry at the person(s) or circumstances that catalyzed your shame then, whether you were the target or instigator of what happened. Stand up and inflate your chest, letting your face be angry. Allow your anger to amplify and speak it spontaneously. (If you don't feel any anger, act it out as if you were in drama class.) Exaggerate the anger. Get aggressive, as if you have been wronged. Get really righteous. Stay with this for a minute or so.

Now redirect your anger at yourself. Maintain its intensity and posture. Be aggressive, giving your inner critic a green light to really go after you. Do this for no more than a minute. Now let yourself sink back into the slump of shame, bringing your attention to your solar plexus. Again recall the original incident of shame. Stay with this for at least a minute.

Now imagine that you are pulling back more, withdrawing internally. Make no effort to keep your attention on your body. Keep pulling back, allowing your mind to drift. It's as if the shame-centered time you are recalling is fading, receding in the distance. You still don't feel good, but you don't mind as much, because you're becoming more numb, "safely" removed from your pain to not care much about what was hurting you. You may not be comfortably numb, but the edge has been taken off your pain.

Notice what you're being pulled into. Is it some sort of fantasy, or a book, or something electronic, or a physical activity? Remember where you went internally when you were most unhappy as a child. Immerse yourself there for a few minutes, as if you were behind a closed door in a room by yourself and that the shame you felt a short time ago is far, far in the distance.

Now let this go, sitting up straight and breathing deeply. Imagine you're now holding the you who was in that room, breathing in his or her hurt and emotional withdrawal, and breathing out your care for him or her. Let your body sway slightly, as if rocking a young child to sleep. As you do so, let your heart open, softening and expanding with each exhale. Now imagine you are holding the one who was aggressive, feeling his or her underlying shame. Stay with this for a few minutes, knowing that what you are holding is simply your shame.

The more room you make in your heart for your shame, the more you'll be able to stay with your shame, separating what's healthy in it from what's unhealthy and making space for whatever action needs to be taken, such as to express remorse or to set a clear boundary with someone who's putting you down.

EVICTING THE INNER CRITIC

Our inner critic can only keep us captive so long as we don't question it or argue with it the way children or adolescents argue with their parents. If we allow it, the inner critic plays parent. If we let it shame us—degrading us for not making the grade—we lose our power, either scrambling to meet its standards or losing ourselves in a favorite distraction. Even when our inner critic cannot find fault with us, as when we've done extraordinarily well with something, it lets us know that we have to maintain this standard, the implication being that we will slip sooner or later, at which point the inner critic will step in to "help" us. Many of us believe that our inner critic has our best interests at heart, forgetting that it is what it is partially because it has no heart.

Are we victims of our inner critic? No. It is no more than a pip-squeak in the back bleachers of our mind, but we still tend to give it a front-row seat and megaphone, letting it again and again trumpet our flaws and failures. Even when we have seen the inner critic for what it is, we might still submit to its shaming of us, perhaps as a way of keeping our long-ago parents "close" to us—especially if they were most attentive to us when they were shaming us.

The inner critic is one hell of a judge, even in people who claim to be nonjudgmental. Not being under our inner critic's thumb doesn't mean we'll never be judgmental again, for being judgmental comes with having a mind. Instead, it means we no longer take our inner critic's pronouncements seriously. We've heard them thousands of times before, so why hear them again? It's always the same old message. Better to give our attention not to the content of what our inner critic is saying but to the energetic feel of our inner critic, so that we don't sink in shame but rise in dignity, letting our imperfections have their place in us without allowing them to govern us.

We need to learn to relate *to* our inner critic rather than *from* it. So we speak to it without glorifying or looking up to it, keeping it in healthy perspective, no more going to it for advice than we would go to our toaster. In becoming intimate with our inner critic, we get to know it so well that when it arises—as signaled by its telltale signs of self-shaming, contracted breathing, and clamped-down heart—we can name it very quickly.

Developing such intimacy does not mean that we get rid of our inner critic, but that we are no longer at its mercy. We now have clear options beyond just trying to think positively or be nonjudgmental. We may, for example, withdraw our attention from it—reducing its know-it-all voice to less than an echo—or we may explore it, examining its terrain, perhaps sifting through it for nuggets of insight.

When we're initially learning to work with our inner critic, we will probably entertain hopes of getting rid of it, but as we realize that we're not going to get rid of it any more than we're going to get rid of our ego, we begin to change our relationship to it. In this process, we let it take its place in our psyche, knowing that it will, from time to time, speak up loudly, indicating that some old shame has been triggered. Then we can compassionately face that old loss of face, breathing love and integrity into it and holding the shamed us in steady embrace, while the voice of our inner critic remains so far in the background that its presence doesn't really matter.

The inner critic's grail is perfection; that's its nature. There is a more life-giving direction for us: to cultivate intimacy with all that we are, embracing our perfectly imperfect unfolding and holding it all—including our inner critic—with lucid caring, guided by the authority native to us.

Practice

EVICTING YOUR INNER CRITIC

Sit comfortably in a place where you won't be disturbed. Place a pillow across from you if you're sitting on the floor, or a chair if you're sitting on a sofa or chair. Imagine that your inner critic sits facing you. Close your eyes. Think of a name for your inner critic; it could be the name of whoever shamed you the most or whoever's vocal qualities most closely resemble those of your inner critic—or anything else that fits for you. If nothing comes to you, just name it "inner critic."

Now speak to your inner critic as spontaneously as possible. Notice your posture, your tone of voice. Every time you ask it a question like "Why are you doing this to me?" change the question to a statement (such as "I hate what you are doing to me"). After a minute or so of this, switch seats so you're now sitting in your inner critic's position. Start speaking as though you are your inner critic, using its tone of voice. Don't be careful! Tell the one you are facing exactly what you think of her or him. Raise your volume a bit, point your finger, lean forward—whatever helps you really get into being your inner critic.

After a few minutes of this, switch back to your original position, immediately responding to what your inner critic just said. Don't edit. If your voice is weak or subdued, amplify it as if you are standing up for a hurt child desperately in need of protection. Throughout this, call your inner critic by the name you came up with. If you feel self-conscious, get more dramatic. If you feel angry, squeeze your hands into fists and express your anger as fully as you can.

Go back and forth between the pillows (or chairs) a few more times, then come to rest in your original seat, still having the sense that you are sitting across from your inner critic. It is nearby but is not occupying you. Become conscious of your breathing, counting at the end of each exhale until you reach the number five, then start at one again. (See the appendix for detailed instructions on this.) While you do this, bring to mind and heart who you were when your inner critic began showing up, and hold that young one close to you, both embracing and protecting him or her.

Follow-Up

If you have a strong inner critic, do this practice daily for two weeks. Also—and this is especially important—every time you notice that your inner critic is holding forth, immediately name it and withdraw your attention from its tirades, bringing your awareness to your belly and counting at least five conscious breaths. This may be challenging at first, but doing it steadily, day after day, will help you break free of the dynamic you've had with your inner critic.

SHAME IN INTIMATE RELATIONSHIP

Shame that is not worked with skillfully pollutes relational intimacy. If both partners don't know their history with shame and shaming, including what they tend to do when it arises, then their relationship will suffer. For example, if we get aggressive when we feel shame—even when we've done something that warrants shame, like mistreating our partner—and this pattern is left unaddressed, we'll continue damaging our relationship, especially if our partner doesn't challenge our aggression. Or, we may habitually shame our partner for not measuring up instead of simply sharing our hurt over what he or she is doing.

The bottom line here: don't disrespect your partner. You have every right to disrespect what they have done or are doing, but you have no right to disrespect *them*. If you're frustrated that your partner is chronically tentative around you or overly compliant and you then say to him, "I wish you'd be more of a man" or "Why don't you grow up?" you're only making things worse. Whether he fights back, caves in, scrambles to please you, or withdraws into abstraction, he is reacting to your having shamed him. If he's afraid of losing you and thinks your disapproval or disappointment in him is a prelude for your exit, he may resolve to "be more of a man" but will inevitably fall short again and again. He may become even more tentative around you, which only spurs you into more frustration and probably more shaming of him.

So what to do? Recognize what it means to disrespect your partner, and when you're moving in the direction of shaming him, say out loud that you are tempted to put him down, and then share with him what you're feeling underneath your intention to shame him. If you're angry, state that without the details; if you're feeling hurt, state that again without the details. Be vulnerable. In this, you're tacitly inviting him to empathize with you, to be with you in your core feelings, and to be with himself in the same way.

Here's another example: Ingrid is very upset with Vince over his flirting with a coworker, and he's busy defending himself. Vince knows he's crossed a line, but he's not about to admit it. He's feeling some shame but has distracted himself from it by getting defensive and increasingly aggressive as Ingrid shows more anger. The more he tells her that she's overreacting and shouldn't be so possessive, the angrier she gets, even though she is still crying. The angrier Ingrid gets, the angrier Vince gets, feeling justified in doing so. Soon the couple is at an angry standoff: neither will back down.

Vince has already shamed Ingrid by telling her she's overreacting and shouldn't be so possessive, which has distracted him from the original issue. Now he starts to feel some remorse, but instead of aligning himself with it—which he knows would remedy the situation—he gets even more aggressive, taking flight from his shame, getting sarcastic with Ingrid and rolling his eyes, and giving her a lower-face smile. She screams at him and runs out of the room. Vince stands there, half-frozen, fighting his urge to go to her and straighten things out.

This scenario illustrates the need to do whatever is necessary not to disrespect or shame your partner. If he is upset and you roll your eyes at him or get sarcastic, you are not respecting him. In fact, you're a short step away from feeling outright contempt for him, which often marks the beginning of the end for a couple. (See chapter 18 on contempt.) If you tolerate disrespect from your partner—as you probably did from others when you were little, as a coping mechanism—you may appear to be the victim in the exchange, but you're not.

Both partners need to get clear about the difference between healthy and unhealthy shame. If you've hurt your partner, you will probably feel some shame about it. Share that shame without delay, and say you're sorry from your undefended heart, resisting the temptation to make excuses for yourself. This is healthy shame.

Practice

SHAME IN INTIMATE RELATIONSHIP

Sit facing your partner. Take turns describing something you did to the other that you were ashamed of. Keep steady eye contact as you do so. Sit tall, and be as vulnerable as possible. If this is difficult, imagine yourself in the other's position, and not just intellectually! If you are the listener, stay soft and open. If you are the speaker and find yourself getting flat or emotionally disconnected, share that feeling and also some times in your early history when you behaved similarly.

When you have both finished, sit closer, joining hands, and close your eyes for a few minutes, breathing consciously. Then open your eyes, gazing at each other for another minute or two. Finish by each sharing several things you appreciate about the other.

There's no real escape from shame, though we may live in a way that keeps us removed from it. In fact, shame may be our most hidden emotion. Bringing it out of the shadows is a deeply healing undertaking, a journey that we must take sooner or later if we are to truly live. When we have become intimate with our shame, we don't let it mutate into aggression or relational disengagement. Instead, we openly confess it as it arises, recognizing that it is simply the herald of conscience and needs to be related to as such.

11

Anger

Moral Fire

Anger and aggression are not synonymous.

The fiery intensity at the heart of anger asks neither for
smothering nor mere discharge, but for a mindful embrace
that does not require any dilution of passion, any lowering of
the heat, nor any muting of the essential voice in the flames.

THERE IS AN ABUNDANCE OF confusion about anger: confusion about what it is, about its value or lack thereof, about whether or not to express it and how, about its function in relationship. Anger can be a loaded or inflammatory topic that's likely to irritate, irk, rile, piss off, frustrate, annoy, and even infuriate more than a few of us. And as ubiquitous as anger is, it still remains largely unexplored.

Anger probably gets more bad press than any other emotion. It is one of Christianity's Seven Deadly Sins, one of Buddhism's key hindrances (categorized as an unwholesome or afflictive state synonymous with ill will and aggression), a core New Age no-no because it's "negative." More often than not, anger takes the heat for causing ugly behavior of the aggressive or violent sort. It's easy to blame anger ("I don't know what got into me") for what might seem like or actually be irresponsible or mean-spirited behavior. But holding anger accountable for our violence is akin to holding our sex drive accountable for rape.

It is true that when anger "possesses" us we are more likely to indulge in ill will and violence. And even when we can counteract such inflammatory occupying forces, we may be doing no more than curbing the beast, which requires us to remain on guard against anger breakouts. But there's much more to effectively handling anger than muzzling, muting, or playing zookeeper to it.

Some say that to hold anger in—to wait until we are calm before we say anything about it—is unhealthy, increasing our odds of getting ill, including to the point of having cancer. Others say that to let anger out—to openly express or vent it—is unhealthy, increasing our odds of getting heart disease. So we have two warring camps, one (Anger-In) focused on the dangers of expressed anger, the other (Anger-Out) focused on the dangers of unexpressed anger. Both make moral real estate out of their positions. Who is right?

The answer is both, but only partially. There are plenty of problems with Anger-In, and plenty of problems with Anger-Out, as we shall see. There are more ways to approach and work with anger than Anger-In and Anger-Out. We can, for example, mindfully attend to our anger, neither repressing nor indulging it, letting it be the object of meditative focus without any outward expression of it. We can also be mindfully present with our anger and still outwardly and fierily express it, letting such expression coexist with a significant degree of compassion.

Once we are angry—the raw feeling that almost instanteously arises—we may feel that we cannot help but be swept along by it, but we nonetheless do have options for handling it. Consider the following internal dialogue:

> I'm angry at you, really angry. A little more, and I'll erupt. My mind is now a courtroom and I've got you on the stand, my hands trembling with a list of things I can't stand about you. Now you're rolling your eyes, and I'm seeing red. Damn, this is happening so fast! My heart is pounding. I have an urge to move toward you, but not out of affection. A few moments ago you were my friend; now you are my enemy. Such reflection vanishes in a millisecond as I get closer to raging.
>
> Later today or tomorrow I'll very likely remember that my heart was closed, my jaw tightly protruding, my hands curled into fists. But now all I know is that I am about to yell at you, not giving a damn how harsh my words will be. You—you whom I have done so much for, I melodramatically remind

myself—have wronged me and I'm about to right that, or so it seems . . .

One option: I can simply let you have it, giving my anger full-throated expression. My outburst might actually serve us if I can (1) remember to do this without shaming or blaming or bad-naming you, and (2) remember to keep my volume and intensity at a level that doesn't overwhelm you. If I can do this, my strongly expressed anger will only momentarily shake things up, quickly clearing the air, leaving no smoldering residue of resentment. But if I don't remember—or don't choose to remember—my outburst will be aggression in righteous indignation's robes. All heat and no light, as sloppy as it is mean-spirited. In the face of that, you will either attack back, withdraw, or collapse.

Another option: I can take a couple of long, slow breaths and remember that you are my friend, and that I can and need to take a look at how I'm thinking right now. Not so easy, but I can do it. My assumptions about you are clamoring for my undivided attention, but I tell myself over and over to cool it, to turn down the heat, to step back, to recontextualize things. So I stop in my tracks, seeing more than just red. This doesn't change things much, but it does give me a much-needed breather.

I'm still churning, but I'm seeing you from more of a distance now. I won't express any of this anger; doing so won't do any good, I keep telling myself. Getting it out of my system, like some of my more impulsive friends advocate, just feels like indulgence to me. Now I feel a little more calm. I can see that you are a bit more relaxed, even though you feel far away. Maybe I'm still angry at you, but I'm not going to show you that. When I cool off my anger like this, it works best when I stay connected to you. But it's not easy to stay connected when I do this with my anger; in pulling it back, I pull myself back. I may be more peaceful but I'm too level, too detached. Flat.

Still another option: I tell myself that anger has arisen, and I step back from it enough to see it with at least some clarity, resuming my meditative practice of simply observing whatever is showing up internally and externally. So anger is here. I watch it surging through my body and mind, carefully tracking it. I often shut my eyes to facilitate this. I am aware of you watching me detach from my anger, and I imagine that you are eased by this. I still feel the sensations of anger, but I can't really say now that I am angry at you. The container (my body) has been depressurized. Later I'll nonangrily share my anger with you. Another potential disaster averted. You say that things feel flat between us, and I thank you for sharing that, for being honest with me, not noticing that I feel subtly deadened. Other times this practice of mindfully holding my anger has brought us closer, but not lately. Am I perhaps overrelying on it? Maybe so, but at least I'm not endangering us. And I am present with my anger.

And one more option: I recognize that my anger—which is particularly intense—doesn't feel all that appropriate to the situation. I realize that I'm being triggered—and occupied—by the memory of my parents harshly shaming me when I was a child, many, many times. But this doesn't let you off the hook. You roll your eyes again, and I know I have to say an emphatic "no" to what you are doing. I can feel my reactive urge to blast you for your sarcasm, but I remember that I love you. I feel some compassion for you, along with my anger.

With enough intensity to really grab your attention, I tell you to stop the sarcasm. There's no hostility in my voice, but there is force. I do not put you down or point an accusing finger or fist at you, though I'm tempted to. I'm heated and far from smiling, but there's nothing in my anger that is aggressive. I see that you realize I'm not attacking you. And I am vulnerable. You sense this and soften, apologizing for your sarcasm; suddenly we are gazing at each other with considerable care and relief.

It doesn't happen often, but when anger comes from my heart—at least to some degree—it usually cuts through our reactive bouts very quickly. Why doesn't this happen more often? Because it's damned hard to remember what really matters in the heat of rising conflict and to then take fitting action. Nevertheless, openly expressed anger that is not disconnected from caring is a viable option.

Whether we stuff our anger, cut loose with it, sit meditatively with it, or express it with both fieriness and care, we are doing something with it. It is common to confuse what we do with anger with anger itself. Hostility, aggression, hatred, violence, ill will, sarcasm, mean-spiritedness—these are *choices*, avenues we steer our anger into, even though we may feel as though we are being driven to do so. Such choices give anger a bad name. Working skillfully with anger is just as hard as working skillfully with fear, but it is essential if we are to live truly healthy lives and have thriving relationships.

Our task is not to cease having anger, but to develop the capacity for clean anger, anger that is free of shaming, blaming, and aggression. Such anger is simultaneously vulnerable and powerful.

THE NATURE OF ANGER

There isn't anything inherently wrong with anger. Yet because we so often handle it badly—regardless of how developed we may think we are and because we may feel some shame for slipping—we can easily blame our anger for our failures to meet our standards of behavior. Think of how simple it is to blame our anger for clouding our reason, for obstructing our vision, for propelling us into treating our partner like dirt. The shame we might feel about this, the shame about being so immature or reactive, can itself easily mutate into potential aggression, which of course further fuels our anger. So it is crucial that we learn to *wake up* in the midst of our anger, ideally as close to its inception as possible, so that we have at least some space in which to consider our options.

It is easy and common to turn our anger into a weapon, blasting away or sniping from behind its "pumped-up" front. But it's not so simple to keep our anger transparent and vulnerable, staying non-blaming even as we allow it as a full-blooded passion that the situation calls for. We can use our anger to get even or to overpower; we can also use it to revive intimacy, to level the playing field, to empower, to potently address and burn though barriers to love.

It's easy to condemn, reject, or lock away our anger, so that it—like a beast confined too long in a cage—behaves savagely when it does get out, confirming our belief that it needs to be treated like a large carnivore loose in our home. It's also easy to glamorize anger, with equally harmful results. Encouraging those who are inhibited to freely vent their anger may generate some relief for them, but doesn't bring them any closer to knowing their anger; in fact, it might lead them to overrely on such simplistic cathartic processes. (See chapter 29 on connected catharsis.)

What is not so easy is cultivating intimacy with our anger. Getting close to its heatedness, its intensity, its righteousness, as well as to our habitual ways of handling it asks for far more than just quieting it down or emptying ourselves of its energies. Anger can be destructive or constructive, depending on the kind of relationship with anger we choose to develop.

Anger is a heatedly aroused state combining a sense of being wronged or thwarted with a strongly energized impetus to do something about it. In our anger we typically feel compelled to lean into whatever situation is angering us, whether that is acted on or not.

Here's a quick study in anger: Let your eyes glare, your nostrils flare, your jaw tighten and thrust forward, your upper and lower molars press together, your shoulders bunch and tighten, your chest emphatically inflate, your breathing become forceful, and your hands curl into fists. Do all these things at the same time, holding this position for a half-minute or so. The odds are that you will start to feel some anger.

Anger is fiery, volatile, sometimes explosive ("I'm about to blow my stack")—even if it is not allowed any external expression. The message we need to hear when we're being infiltrated by such righteous heatedness is: Handle with Care. Otherwise, anger will very likely handle *us,* and not necessarily with care! It's important not to underestimate how readily we can slip into automatic when anger roars into us in high gear, already intensely sure of itself and its target.

"Handle with Care" might mean not letting our anger-related thoughts turn into kerosene, or it might mean stepping back a bit, or it might mean relating to our anger as we would to a furious child who is having a fit about not getting something he or she wants. There are a lot of options with anger, some healthy, some not so healthy, but we are going to have a very short list of options—or maybe only one—if we don't know our anger well.

ANGER AND AGGRESSION ARE NOT SYNONYMOUS

If we are to know anger well, we need to clearly distinguish it from aggression. Many of us equate anger and aggression, but they do differ. Anger does not attack; aggression does. Aggression is something we *do* with anger, using its energy to fuel us in going after our target. In aggression, we're closed off, whereas in anger we're vulnerable. If we're angry and want to get away from anger's innate vulnerability, we might turn to aggression, which can take many forms ranging from the smiling ploys of passive aggressiveness to sarcasm to outright violence.

Aggression is anger stripped of its heart, anger that has turned the offending person into an "it." Once we've let ourselves become aggressive, we're in danger of sliding into violent behavior. We've lost touch with our caring for others, so we feel more at home with treating them badly—which we will likely interpret as "giving them what they deserve."

When anger morphs into aggression, it can take forms that may not appear aggressive, such as the "niceties" of passive aggression or the "playful" jabs of sarcasm. When we are being sarcastic with a significant other, we may be smiling with the lower half of our face and speaking at a normal volume, but we are not vulnerable, not transparent, not in any sort of intimate contact. Our anger has fused with shaming, so that our recipient is, however subtly, being put down by us. We are, in our sarcasm, disrespecting them.

Even if our sarcasm is short lived, it does create some distance, so some time later we may find that our partner or friend has erected a barrier against us, even if they're being loving toward us. They may not be doing this as any sort of retaliation but because they're simply feeling on guard around us, especially if we haven't genuinely apologized for our sarcasm toward them.

Aggression can, of course, be far more overt, as exemplified by violent behavior. Violence, the brass knuckles of unchecked aggression, is not a result of anger, but an abuse of anger. Where violence ignores or trashes personal boundaries, healthy anger protects and guards them, fueling the taking of needed stands.

Aggression is devoid of compassion, whereas anger and compassion can coexist. Aggression stays on its endarkened track by continuing to dehumanize others. If any caring for them somehow arises in us, we will likely find ourselves starting to shift, at least to some degree, from being aggressive to simply being angry.

Implicit in this shift is a potential healing of remarkable magnitude: to reverse the direction and convert aggression back into anger. Such conversion is not about draining the energy out of our aggression, but about liberating it from its viewpoint, so that its passion and forcefulness can coexist with a compassionately present attentiveness. In this context, the world needs not less anger, but *more* anger—and I mean clean anger, anger that to a significant degree comes from the heart.

Aggression may seem to be an inevitable outcome of anger, but in fact it is an *avoidance* of anger, and the hurt and vulnerability that are part of it. Seeing anger as aggression or as the cause of aggression gives us an excuse to classify it as a "lower" or "primitive" emotion, something far, far from spiritual. Though anger does have a primitive side—shared with every mammal—it is more than just primitive, though what we tend to do with it is often far from civilized.

Anger can be very intense and still not become aggression. In the face of injustice, personal or collective, anger rouses us to take action. Its heat is activist, however much we might keep it under wraps. Anger is not just fire but *moral* fire; its nature is to protect what is weak or vulnerable or broken in us. It helps us take fierce-as-necessary stands to guard the sanctity of our being. Our job is to make sure that this does not become an overly zealous undertaking armed with us-versus-them invective and other modes of aggression.

Practice

GETTING TO KNOW YOUR ANGER

Find a comfortable place to sit with a notebook and pen handy. Make sure you will not be interrupted in the next ten minutes or so, and wear clothing that's loose enough to allow easy, unrestricted breathing.

Below is a list of incomplete sentences. Complete them as spontaneously as possible, out loud, writing down your response to each immediately after voicing it. When you've finished, do the meditation described in the appendix.

When I feel angry, what I usually do is _____.

I hold back my anger when _____.

I get really angry when _____.

How my parents dealt with anger when I was a child was _____.

And my response to that was _____.

When I'm angry my belly feels _____.

Anger scares me when _____.

I'm afraid that if I strongly express my anger I might _____.

My anger turns to aggression when _____.

When I can tell my anger is reactive, what I usually do is _____.

Without my anger I would be _____.

The child in me reacts to anger as if it is _____.

When I'm angry, my basic message usually is _____.

My ability to be vulnerable while I am angry is _____.

I turn my anger back on myself when _____.

When I'm angry, what happens to my breathing is _____.

When I'm angry, what happens to my hands is _____.

When I let myself get closer to my anger, I see _____.

Follow-Up

1. Write your history with anger and aggression, including times that particularly stand out. Be as specific as you can. Include what you tend to do when you are feeling not just anger, but aggression.

2. In the next few days, whenever you feel anger, even slightly, say "anger" in a voice only you can hear and take three full breaths, emphasizing the exhale. Then consider your options

as to how you might handle the anger, noting how strongly you are pulled to each one.

FOUR APPROACHES TO WORKING WITH ANGER

The two most common approaches to working with anger, mentioned early in this chapter, are Anger-In and Anger-Out. A third approach to working with anger, Mindfully Held Anger, is not nearly so well known, and a fourth approach, Heart-Anger, is even less well known.

1. **Anger-In** is all about restraining and redirecting anger, without directly expressing it. Anger-In advocates equate the expressing of anger with "venting," aggression, and poor self-control. Anger-In can simply be the stuffing down or unreflective muting of anger, but it also can be more sophisticated, cooling us down through a reinterpretation of what provoked our anger, which might reduce our perception of being under attack and therefore lessen the likelihood of our anger being openly expressed.

   Though Anger-In overvalues controlling and nonangrily "expressing" anger, we should give ample weight to its insistence on stepping back from anger so that its darker and clearly irrational impulses can be reappraised. Nevertheless, Anger-In has a thorny question before it: How effective can an approach to working with anger be that does not incorporate openly expressing the actual feelings of anger? In analogous fashion, how effective would a grief therapy be that did not include the actual expression of grief?

2. **Anger-Out** is centered around the importance of directly and fully expressing the energies and intentions of anger. A foundational claim of advocates of Anger-Out is that suppressed anger is not healthy—it is much better to bring it into the open (or "dig it up" if it's not surfacing enough) and release/express it. Advocates argue that keeping our anger bottled up is not good for us. Such down-to-earth logic may seem quite commonsensical and medically apt, but it can be used to justify hostility and other forms of unhealthy anger, as if simply cutting loose with them is inherently good for us.

Also, Anger-Out tends to overemphasize a merely physical approach to anger, as if anger were just something to "get out of our system" or eliminate from the body. The emotional-release work central to Anger-Out practices ranges from misguided exhortations to simply "cut loose" to profoundly healing release, illumination, and integration.

3. **Mindfully Held Anger** is a meditative approach in which anger is consciously contained and not emotionally expressed. In its emphasis on neither repressing nor acting out anger, this approach may seem to offer a solution to the Anger-In/Anger-Out standoff. In being mindful of our anger—nonconceptually observing the actual process of it, in its feeling, cognitive, perceptual, and social dimensions—we also become aware of the very "I" (or sense of self) that is busy being angry.

   Our perspective thus shifts from how angry we feel to *who it is* who feels it. At its best, the mindful holding of anger is both a containing of and intimate embracing of anger, a willingness to be with it without outwardly expressing it. This practice has its own dangers, as implied by the more negative connotations of the term "holding," and exemplified by those times when we are not so much sitting *with* our anger as *on* it.

4. **Heart-Anger** is the result of fully expressed anger coexisting with some degree of compassion. Bring together the virtues of Anger-In, Anger-Out, and Mindfully Held Anger—including healthy restraint, emotional openness, compassionate mindfulness—and minimize the difficulties associated with each, and Heart-Anger becomes a reality (albeit a far from common one). Heart-Anger is energetically vital, passionate, and ours to embody if we can bring together our capacities for full-blooded anger and caring. In the midst of it we may not look loving or compassionate, but we do retain some contact with our heart even at our most fiery.

   As fierce as Heart-Anger can sometimes be, it is but wrathful compassion in the raw. It is not simply anger given free rein in conjunction with the notion that we're doing good for the other—it remains attuned to what the situation is calling for, beyond our conditioned way of dealing with anger. It is infused with awakened attentiveness without any dilution or separation from its passion. It is clean anger at its best: nonblaming, nonshaming, nonaggressive, contextually sensitive, heated yet illuminating. Heart-Anger has enough faith in life to stand tall in its fierce caring—and it has the guts to carry this out.

Practice

FOUR APPROACHES TO WORKING WITH ANGER

Do the following practice in a place where you have enough privacy to be noisy. Imagine a situation that really angered you, and perhaps still does. Let yourself feel this situation as much as possible. Breathe more deeply, especially on the exhale. Tighten and thrust your jaw; intensify your bite. Make fists, hard fists. Glare.

Now imagine that you are a practitioner of Anger-In. Look at the situation that angered you and reinterpret it in a way that diminishes your anger. Take a minute or so to do this. Let your breathing soften. Open your hands and mouth, reminding yourself that getting angry will only make things worse. Recall the angry situation again and look at it as if from a distance, keeping your breathing as level as possible. Stay with this for a minute or two.

Now imagine that you are an advocate of Anger-Out. Squeeze your fists hard, stretch your mouth wide, keeping your teeth together, and focus on how badly or unfairly you were treated. Breathe more vigorously. Now pound your fists down on some pillows or a sofa over and over—without hurting yourself— yelling as hard and fiercely as you can, keeping your voice deep and your throat open so you don't hurt or strain it. If you get distracted or start laughing, pound and yell harder. You might also stomp fiercely; shake; or use your knees and elbows, staying focused on the situation that angered you. Do this all so intensely that there's no room for embarrassment. A minute of this will be plenty! Rest for a minute or two when you are done.

Next, imagine you are a devotee of Mindfully Held Anger. Let your belly soften and your breath slow, even as you feel the sensations of anger moving through you. Notice the agitation of your mind, keeping most of your attention on your breath. When aggressive, vengeful, or otherwise endarkened thoughts show up, disregard their content while letting their energy run unshackled through you, but with no outward expression. All the expression is interior. Feel the you who is angry, and hold that one with compassion, cradling him or her for a few minutes as you would an upset child.

And last, imagine you are a trainee in Heart-Anger. Feel the passion of your anger, reining it in as you would a horse that needs just a touch of restraint before shifting into a full gallop. At the same time, open yourself to the humanness of the person who has angered you, feeling some degree of caring toward him or her as you begin expressing your anger. Be loud if you need to be, but not so loud that you drown out your caring. Be fierce if doing so feels called for, but not so fierce that you bypass your compassion. Stay vulnerable. Stay rooted.

CLEAN AND UNCLEAN ANGER

Clean anger, as mentioned earlier, is anger that is handled skillfully; it does not shame, blame, or slip into aggression. However heated it is, it does not disrespect the other. Clean anger does not attack; unclean anger does. Once aggression arises, however indirectly or quietly, we are in the realm of unclean anger, swept along by our affirmation of our aggression.

Clean anger may start out reactive, but it soon becomes nonreactive. And unclean anger? It begins reactive and stays reactive, getting reactive to any suggestion that it is reactive. Unclean anger blames, righteously zooming in on whomever or whatever we are faulting, all but ensuring that we don't have to take a real look at ourselves. On the other hand, clean anger does not blame; instead it seeks accountability and takes a much deeper, more nuanced look at what is occurring.

Clean anger delivers heat—sometimes a real blast of fire—but in a responsible way, taking into account the particulars of the situation, including the capacity of the other to receive such anger. Unclean anger also delivers heat, sometimes to the extreme, but in an irresponsible manner, letting the other know that if they're upset it's their problem. Unclean anger shames, with little or no restraint, enlarging itself by belittling its target. Clean anger does not shame.

There is some degree of caring in clean anger, but none in unclean anger. Not surprisingly, unclean anger tends to dehumanize the offending person; unclean anger doesn't.

In clean anger we allow for and show our vulnerability—or something close to it. In unclean anger we wall ourselves off from our vulnerability; if any vulnerability threatens to surface, there is usually some amplification of the aggression, as if to obscure any sign of softness or tenderness.

We don't lose respect for the other when our anger is clean; we may be furious about what they've done, disrespecting *that,* but we don't slip into disrespect for *them.* In unclean anger, we readily and unquestioningly shift into disrespect for the other, perhaps rolling our eyes or getting sarcastic or contemptuous, talking to them as if they were trash, indulging in our disdain for them.

Unclean anger fights dirty—and usually feels justified in doing so. It's me against you, my tribe versus yours, my religion against yours, my country versus yours. There's no room for caring, no tenderness, no place to rest and review what's happening. Unclean anger is out for blood, even in the most erudite, emotionally stifled settings. And it's not always hot anger but sometimes a cold anger (an icy stare or "turning white with rage"), a calculated aggressiveness that is the stuff of the darkest sort of vengeance.

Clean anger, on the other hand, doesn't fight dirty—but it's not always 100 percent squeaky clean. Every now and then, especially at the inception of a relational hassle, clean anger may briefly stray into less-than-clean territory. Some might expect clean anger to be blemish free and consistently impeccable, but it just isn't.

We can call it "clean" only if we stay in a reactive mode for a very short time, do no harm, and quickly take care of whatever mess we've made. When anger kicks in, we often feel an instant surge of high-octane reactivity, the expression of which gets our anger flowing. So we might start to swear, start to blame our partner, or start to shame him or her—and then shift gears into clean anger, having caught ourselves in the midst of such sloppiness.

This by no means constitutes an excuse for reactive anger transmission, nor an expectation that the recipient of our anger should be OK with us starting off sharing our anger like this. But we do nonetheless need to learn to make at least *some* room for reactive anger; otherwise its transition to clean anger may not happen so quickly, which usually then strands us in an extended reactive bout with each other.

Accessing clean anger sometimes requires that we make room—conscious and compassionate room—for our reactive anger (especially when we've stockpiled it for too long), giving it at least some space for expression, so long as we *only* do this to get our anger out in the open. The point is not to force our reactive anger into submission, but to provide it with conditions through which it can be liberated without squelching its passion.

Practice

TOWARD CLEAN ANGER

Is anyone impeccable with their anger? Probably not, myself included. I say this so that you'll know that you have a massive amount of company when it comes to having handled anger in unclean ways.

Make a list of the ways in which you have handled—and still tend to handle—your anger uncleanly. Then briefly describe the specific circumstances that draw forth the various aspects of your unclean anger. For example, if you list sarcasm or scornful looks or passive aggression, give the details of what conditions catalyze these in you. Over the next week or two, notice when the intention arises to express your anger in any of these ways, and do your best to simply stay with such intention without acting it out.

In truly intimate relationships, there is usually at least some degree of tolerance for an initially messy (but nonviolent) delivery of anger—assuming that there is enough safety and trust for this to happen. If we expect our partner to always be clean in his or her anger delivery right from the start, we may get so focused on their initial sloppiness in expressing their anger that we short-circuit the full flow of their anger.

So how can we best work with this? Shutting down the other because their anger is emerging reactively doesn't help (unless they are being abusive), and allowing them to stay reactive doesn't help. Part of the answer involves knowing our own and our partner's anger so well that when it shows up in its reactive mode, there is no mistaking this. It also helps to have a previously established commitment to name such anger for what it is—and then to shift into clean anger as soon as possible.

Another part of the answer is to mutually create a context for having a conscious rant (as described in chapter 2), meaning a safe, boundaried space wherein the angrily reactive person can really cut loose with no effort to be clean, other than to do no harm. The other person simply bears witness to this, perhaps even doing some cheerleading. This is very different than simply acting out our angry intentions as if we were not being reactive. The context has been set; we step into the ring, knowing the boundaries and knowing that we don't have to hold back anything—we have permission to be outrageous.

Our task is to do this full-out; if we get self-conscious or only express ourselves partially, we can deliberately exaggerate our outrage, allowing ourselves to be melodramatic. In this, we're going for sheer vitality, not humor—though such rants can be hilarious once they're fully rolling.

The conscious rant practice described in chapter 2 was for emotion in general. The practice below is specifically for anger. If your partner or a close friend is there with you, do not proceed if your anger is at them, unless it is over a relatively mild concern. If you are loaded with anger toward the other, it's best that you do your conscious rant without them, either alone or in the company of a therapist who is comfortable with intense emotional expression.

Practice

CONSCIOUS ANGER RANT

Stand in the middle of a room private enough to allow loud sound. And if such a room is not available, stand in the middle of whatever room you have, with a firm pillow in one hand. Your partner or a close friend can be in the same room, having already cocreated with you an agreement for the parameters of the conscious rant you are about to have. (Those parameters include having a clear starting and ending point for the rant, doing it all out, causing no physical damage, and so on.) And if you have no one (or cannot have anyone there) to witness what is about to happen, that is fine.

Fully focus on what is angering you, closing your eyes if necessary. Breathe more deeply, bending your knees slightly. Now let your anger speak, and speak uninhibitedly; don't be polite, don't be careful, don't try to adhere to any model of clean anger. Bust loose! (If you have to keep the noise down, hold the pillow to your face so that it completely covers your mouth. Squeeze the pillow as hard as you can, and let fly!) If you feel self-conscious, be more outrageous. No rehearsing! Stomp your feet, make fists, speak with your whole body. If you have a gripe, blow it up to major proportions; if your tax bill is unexpectedly high, blow the roof off with your indignation; if you feel as if you were treated unfairly, lay into whoever dared treat you that way, and so on.

Keep your rant full-blooded, keep it dramatic, keep it spontaneous, and exaggerate it whenever you feel yourself energetically fading. Give your conscious rant at least two minutes of full-out expression. After that, you may continue for a bit, but stop when you truly start to run out of steam, and lie flat on your back spread-eagled and breathe slowly and deeply for a couple of minutes. Then let your breathing return to normal and slowly rise.

GENDER AND ANGER

In modern Western culture, we have far less flattering labels for women's anger than men's. An angry man is hotheaded, blowing off some steam, raising hell, kicking some ass, straightening out things, taking a stand, taking care of business, cutting loose, being assertive, taking charge, letting loose some firepower, showing who's the boss, and so on. And an angry woman? She's often called a nag, a hysteric, a bitch. He's just being a guy, she's being a bitch. There are, of course, exceptions to this, but not enough to make a real difference. And when a woman is complimented on her anger, her "achievement" may be described in masculine or tough-guy terms: "She's got balls" or "She sure ripped him a new one."

An angry woman often is considered less feminine than a nonangry woman, at least in most circles. If she's just a touch angry, she might be considered cute or sexy, but if she's really angry, then her sexiness quotient drops. Even if her anger is skillfully managed, she might be categorized as a "castrating bitch"—there's something about her anger, her fury, her outrage that more than a few men find emasculating and threatening. This fits in with the metaphors that imply men are the victims of womanly wiles (and hence under "her" control): "She put a spell on me" or "She brings out the beast in me." Is it any wonder that women are so often portrayed as objects of male aggression and disgust in much of pornography, when the primary viewers are men? This is not to say that enormous progress hasn't been made in the area of women's rights, but there's still a long way to go when it comes to women and men being true peers—and this bridging, this sorely needed mutuality, has as one of its key requirements that women's anger be given the same respect as men's, and not just intellectually or politically.

Anger-In practices have been more popular with women than with men; after all, good girls don't get angry. They are "sweet" (a complimentary adjective for a woman, but often a label of weakness for a man). It's OK, of course, that women get sad or depressed, so long as they don't make a fuss—so many women, despite cultural advances in women's rights, are still stuck in a let's-not-rock-the-boat paradigm, putting up with situations that would either end or radically transform if they fully stepped into the anger they feel.

A woman cut off from her anger invariably has weak or overly porous boundaries, drawing to her men who, out of their own unresolved wounds, prefer women who are relatively passive (except when it comes to their sexual openness to him). And more often than not, such men end up in the relationship-eroding position of expressing both their own anger and that of their partner.

When women cannot successfully depress—literally "press down"—their anger and are not in a position where their anger can be truly heard and respected, resentment and bitterness can easily take root, making relational intimacy little more than a fantasy. And successful anger repression has a cost, using up an abundance of life energy to keep the fire from taking flame, and therefore increasing the odds of illness. Is it any wonder that some women get a splitting headache or a stomachache every time they repress their anger toward their partner? Years of this simply runs us down, drains and erodes us, consuming the very energy needed to either leave the relationship or spur it into a more life-giving direction.

For anger to be a resource in relationship—a force that truly serves a relationship—it needs to be equally valued in both women and men and known well enough to be expressed skillfully. It moves me deeply when I see men and women together facing and working with their core wounds, honoring each other's journey through such pain, which inevitably includes opening to and fully embodying their anger, their vulnerable and wonderfully potent anger.

During couple's work Diane and I invariably see problems with anger, be it overexpressed, underexpressed, or turned into aggression or contempt. When men who are emotionally shut down get angry at their partner during such work, we often see that she likes seeing him come alive, regardless of his content, because he's energetically engaged with her, with his other emotions starting to surface. By contrast, when women who are emotionally shut down get angry at their partner, we often see that he dislikes this and to varying degrees freezes in the face of her anger. So her anger usually represents more of a threat to him than vice versa.

Why do so many men fear women's anger, even when it is nonaggressive? Is it because during their early history maternal anger signaled either a loss of love or approval, or some sort of danger? Perhaps. The loss, or threatened loss, of mother-love when they were very young doesn't necessarily disappear because they've gotten older. If their tremendous dependency upon their mother during their very early years was badly handled, men will almost inevitably have a problematic orientation to any kind of dependency on a woman, especially when their need/desire for her (emotionally, psychologically, or sexually) reaches a certain intensity.

So when the primal helplessness a man felt during his childhood resurfaces, his tendency is to do whatever helps him not feel helpless, such as having substantial control over his environment and his key relationships. If this is part of a man's operational core, he is very likely going to feel threatened when his partner gets angry, because when she's angry—whether her anger is skillful or not—she will *appear* not to be the loving mother/food source that is so, so important to him or, more precisely, to the little boy in him.

What men need to really get here is that a woman's anger does not necessarily mean that he's going to be left or neglected or unloved—which means that when she's angry he needs to look at her not just through the eyes of the infant or little boy he once was, but also through the eyes of the man he is. That is, he needs to really see her and feel her, being with her hurt and anger just the way that he'd like her to be with his.

The answer is not to tame women's anger so men will feel safer with them—or vice versa. What is called for is not the domestication of anger but a deep honoring of its wildness and capacity to serve our highest good. Sadly, the anger-wildness in men often gets crushed or channeled into savagery (however smartly dressed it may be), and the anger-wildness in women just as frequently gets smothered, channeled into sexual strategies, reduced to nagging, or trivialized as mere bitchiness.

Cutting through the tendency to view male anger as somehow more legitimate than female anger is essential if we are to have anything approaching healthy relationships. It's time to let anger out of its cage, in both men and women, so that it can be a resource for us all and a guardian of what really matters.

Imagine the individual, female or male, who is intimate enough with anger to deliver it responsibly as well as with full-blooded passion and heart. Imagine this individual can also receive anger without crumpling, pulling away, or getting defensive, receiving it not like an invader but like a guest. This is what we are called to embody. Our capacity for anger asks for nothing less, as does our capacity to be in truly fulfilling relationship.

EXPRESSING ANGER, RECEIVING ANGER

> I was angry with my friend;
> I told my wrath, my wrath did end.
> I was angry with my foe;
> I told it not, my wrath did grow.
>
> —WILLIAM BLAKE

Becoming skillful in expressing and receiving anger asks much of us, including a high degree of self-awareness, but with consistent practice it will feel more and more natural to handle anger in ways that serve rather than hinder our relationships.

To reach the point where we can *express* anger effectively, there are a number of things to consider:

1. We need to know the differences between unclean and clean anger, and know this more than just cognitively.
2. We need to recognize the degree of reactivity, if any, that is showing up in our anger, and not let that control us as we proceed.
3. We need to remain aware of the *energy* of our anger—as opposed to the *content* of our anger—and keep it from straying into aggression and hard-heartedness.
4. We need to resist the temptation to get into our anger's content before we have established at least some emotional resonance with the recipient of our anger. This means simply saying—angrily so—that we are angry, and at the same time giving ourselves and the other enough time to digest this and resonate with it. At this point there is nothing to argue about; your anger is a fact, not an opinion, and it needs to be heard as such.
5. We need to remain aware of the impact our anger is having on the other person and take that into account as we continue, being willing to shift course if necessary. For example, if the other is getting overwhelmed or is triggered, stop and address that. In so doing, you're making your relational intimacy more important than driving home your anger's message.
6. We need to remember that anger and compassion can coexist.
7. We need to take the time when we're overloaded with anger or are in a very reactive mood to have a conscious rant (as described earlier in this chapter), or to go to a place in our home where we can get totally physical with our anger: pounding pillows, punching and kicking a heavy bag, wringing a towel with all our strength, biting hard on a rolled-up towel—anything nondestructive that helps discharge the energy of our anger. And we can always go for a hard aerobic workout.
8. We need to remember that the expression of anger and the need to take action are not the same thing. Expressing our

anger is about exposure and sharing, but the need to take certain actions in a certain way has more to do with power.

9. We need to stop restricting the expression of anger to verbal combat only. There are times when it is far better to put the verbal sharing on hold and simply express our anger without words—just pure vocalization, however embarrassing that might be to our egoity.

10. We need to keep our anger as vulnerable as possible, without diluting its energy and passion.

11. We need to keep making intimate connection more important than being right.

In order to reach the point where we can *receive* anger effectively, there are also a number of things to consider:

1. Knowing the differences between clean and unclean anger, and knowing it more than just cognitively.

2. Having the capacity to hold our boundaries firm yet also to let them be permeable—so that when unclean anger is being expressed to us we can say a solid "no" to it, and when clean anger is being expressed to us we can open to it without abandoning our boundaries.

3. Being able to separate the energy of anger from its content.

4. Staying grounded and present as we receive anger, not like a cement wall but like a well-rooted tree bending with the wind.

5. Resisting the temptation to argue with the content of the anger we're receiving (unless it's abusive) and letting ourselves stay with the raw feeling of it.

6. Not tolerating any aggression or abuse, though for the first half-minute or so we might tolerate *some* sloppiness in the anger coming our way *if* we can sense that this is allowing the other to get his or her anger flowing.

7. Speaking up *immediately* (or having an agreed-upon signal, like holding up one hand) if we feel ourselves getting triggered or reactive.

8. Staying vulnerable without any internal collapsing or loss of dignity.

9. Making intimate connection more important than being right.

10. Listening both to what is being said and to what is not being said. Listening with our whole being.

11. Learning to let the energy of expressed anger pass through us as though we were a sieve or like the wind passes through the foliage of a tree.

If anger is to support and enhance relational intimacy, it needs to be expressed skillfully and be received nondefensively and empathetically. A deep listening is necessary, a listening in which agreement and disagreement with what's being said remain *secondary* to our caring for the one expressing anger to us.

When we close off to the other's anger, we diminish our intimacy with them, forgetting that anger and love can coexist. Rejected anger—anger that is denied compassion—is the very anger that shreds intimacy.

Sharing anger skillfully in an intimate relationship can be a fiery process, scary at times, exciting at others, as it cuts through emotional deadwood and life-dulling habits. If done wholeheartedly, it usually does not take very long to reach a mutually satisfying resolution.

Practice

SHARING ANGER NONVERBALLY

This is a practice for when you feel angry with your partner or a close friend, and only then if you clearly trust her or him with your openly expressed anger. Make sure there will be no interruption. Sit facing the other on the floor. Have a large, firm pillow between you. Hold eye contact—not staring but steadily gazing. Breathe more deeply. Remind him or her what you are angry about and that you are going to express it vocally but nonverbally, without any physical contact.

The other's task is to be aware of each breath he or she takes, no matter what happens, and to be like a sieve while you're expressing your anger—not fleeing from it but letting it pass into and through them.

You can squeeze, pound, or shake the pillow while you let the raw sound of your anger pour forth. Keep your throat open, breathing fully. After a minute or so, stop and sit silently for another few minutes simply gazing into your partner's eyes.

Practice

SHARING ANGER VERBALLY

Follow the instructions in the previous exercise, but this time add verbal content to your expression of anger. Be as succinct as possible, and don't let yourself slip into blaming or name-calling. Stay vulnerable. Some righteousness is inevitable, but if you find yourself getting overly righteous, back off some. After a couple of minutes, stop and silently gaze at the other, even if you still feel angry. Focus your attention on the energy of your anger. Slow your breathing.

If you are the recipient of the verbalized anger, stay with the other energetically, no matter how much you disagree with what he or she says. Make your connection with her or him more central than your desire to argue against their content.

Continue to sit facing and maintaining eye contact with each other for at least another five minutes without speaking. Silently count at the end of each exhale; when the count reaches five, start at one again. If you lose count, start at one again. Do this counting practice for about five minutes, then let it go.

Now discuss the anger-inducing situation, or set up a time to do it later on.

FROM REACTIVE RAGE TO WRATHFUL COMPASSION

Anger is a very powerful force. Whether it helps or harms is in our hands and in our hearts. In the crucible of anger that's handled with skill, passion and compassion coexist, as do heat and light. When we stop viewing anger as something primitive or beneath us, we can start harnessing it for worthy causes, both personally and collectively. Anger ought to be our ally, but this cannot happen so long as we are at war with it, treating it as though it is nothing more than aggression.

It is easy to view anger as dangerous and to thus feel justified in keeping our distance from it, but *not* getting close to anger, *not* being significantly intimate with it, is a dangerous choice that estranges us from the very power that might already be operating in the service of aggression and hatred. Not knowing our anger intimately greatly increases the odds that we will be violent instead of simply angry.

The fiery intensity at the heart of anger asks neither for smothering nor mere discharge, but for a mindful embrace that requires no dilution of passion, no lowering of the heat, no muting of the essential voice in the flames.

Bringing some heart into our anger is an act of caring for ourselves and for all of us, because then we're less likely to let our anger mutate into aggressiveness, hostility, or hatred. Anger doesn't vanish as we awaken—in fact, it may become even more fiery, burning more and more cleanly, serving the well-being of all involved.

Intimacy with our anger deepens our integrity, vitality, and capacity to be in truly deep relationship. Through such intimacy, we embody a passion as full-blooded as it is responsible. Anger ought to be our ally; let us treat it as such.

Honor the vulnerability in your anger. Keep its hurt and transparency within range of your heart, no matter how heated your anger may be. Doing so lowers the odds that you'll dehumanize those with whom you're angry, which makes it more likely that there will be at least some compassion in your anger. Even a trace of caring for the other can greatly alter the course our anger takes. Anger and compassion *can* coexist.

12

Sadness

Loss Taken to Heart

Crying is not something we need to outgrow.

My life sings and bleeds in colors bare and bright
Riding waves of shattered moon through the night
Nothing is moving yet everything's in motion
Only broken waves will ever know the ocean

SADNESS IS LOSS TAKEN TO heart. Loss of love, loss of stature, loss of sunnier times, loss of money, loss of health, loss of connection, loss of friends, loss of sight, loss of what we have taken for granted. Whether or not we allow our sadness to surface, we feel its presence and weight in our heart.

Sadness draws us downward, below our usual self-presentation. There we may stay, dipping into our tears, or we might try to insulate ourselves against them or seek some sort of lift to a less overtly sorrowful place. Yet if we remain with our sadness, allowing it its natural gravity, giving it room to breathe and flow and have a voice, we usually will find ourselves not drowning or withering in it but soberly restored and eased, with our heart opening in unexpected ways.

We may conceive of sadness as something to get over, but in fact it is something to get *into*, something to allow. In sadness we are registering loss; it doesn't matter how big or small that loss is, so long as we let ourselves fully feel it and give it fitting expression. This doesn't mean getting mired in sadness or excessively dramatizing it, but simply yielding to its natural flow, as if easing ourselves down into a stream, letting ourselves be carried toward deeper waters. As such, the open expression of sadness is a kind of surrender, a temporary loss of face and control, a release that can be as healing as it is cathartic. Sadness can be a trickle, and it can be a deep outpouring, especially when it shifts into grief.

A sad face is hard to disguise. Visualize the uplifting, however subtle, of the inner eyebrows and cheeks, the droop of the upper eyelids, the downturning of the outer corners of the lips, all together conveying sadness to whatever degree. Try arranging your face in this pattern. Breathe a little deeper and notice how you feel—chances are that you will feel at least some trace of sadness. Notice your reaction to such an emotional shift. How do you greet it? Those who find a sad face unpleasant are likely uncomfortable with their own sadness.

When we're comfortable with our sadness, we don't fight its heart-hurt but let the ache of it move unhindered through us. As much as this might pain us, it also cleanses us, giving our sense of loss enough room in which to be fully felt. Sadness has the capacity to bring us down without sinking us completely, neither bogging us down in sorrowful shallows nor stranding us at the bottom of the well with no lifelines in sight.

In well-handled sadness, we let our tears come even if their arrival leaves us shaking with sobs—we feel the pain without slipping into self-pity or other victim-centered translations of our hurt. When, however, our sadness is expressive of unresolved wounds from our past, we may allow our pain to morph into *suffering*—meaning that we lose ourselves in the dramatics of our pain, weighing ourselves down with old grievances as if we had tied heavy stones to our ankles.

Sadness doesn't have to tie us down; it can bring us down to where we're close enough to our pain's core to really let the floodgates open wide. For example, we might feel sadness welling up after we're reminded of a lost love. We could allow such sadness to simply be there, noticing it, feeling it, weeping, without getting lost in it. Or, in contrast, we could bring to mind our resentments about that love and start going over and over a particular theme that stood out at the time, like "I always lose love" or "I'll never have a great relationship." This creates enough mental looping and internal drama to maroon us from the simple reality of our sadness.

So often we hear well-meaning statements like "Don't be sad" or "Look on the bright side" or "Cheer up." These convey the message that we shouldn't be sad or that being sad is somehow negative or a "downer," with the implication that if we had it together we wouldn't be sad. But what sadness can bring us to is a heartfelt—and sometimes gut-wrenching—acknowledgment of loss. If we stop short of that depth, we'll remain stuck in unattended sorrow, no matter how "up" or stimulating our life seems to be.

The upside of "being down" is that we're in a position to see, if we wish, some of the originating factors of our core sorrows, such as the details of an early sense of abandonment that pervades our current relationships. Seeds grow in the dark. So do we. Our tears keep things fertile, readying the ground for new growth and easing our ability to let go of what no longer serves us.

When we feel sad, we don't always cry—sometimes because our sense of loss is small, sometimes because our sense of loss is big enough to temporarily numb us, and sometimes because we associate crying with weakness.

It's commonplace to neglect or reject our sadness as though it were a distraught child we want to distance ourselves from. We fear feeling what that child is feeling. Such unattended sadness leaves us out in the cold, though, estranged from healing tears. So many of us have shame about crying, especially in front of others, not because crying is inherently shameful but because we've learned to associate crying with unpleasant consequences. For instance, when we cried we might have been told we're a baby or a sissy; we might have been put down for it ("Will you *please* pull yourself together!"), or we might have been punished for it ("Stop crying, or I'll give you something to really cry about!").

SADNESS AND GENDER

There's less cultural approval for men to cry than there is for women, and I'm not talking about a few manly tears at a press conference or some other brief tearing up. To be able to cry hard, to really sob, to let a flood of tears pour forth, is not so easy for most men, even though men experience as much sadness as women do.

When men are sad and don't want to show it, they have to invest energy into keeping their sadness out of sight. And emotional repression is hard work! Many men learned at an early age to not express or even show a hint of certain emotions because of the unpleasant or even dangerous consequences, such as being rejected or shamed. Picture a little boy fighting back tears, learning that the angrier he gets, the less his sadness will show. Picture the same little boy being shamed or mocked for his tears, finding some solace in getting aggressive with younger children, beginning the process of hardening his heart and turning away from his capacity for empathy. As a man, he is then likely to do the very same things and dispassionately rationalize them— which in turn diminishes his opportunity for connection with others. He is being run by his buried sadness, however subtly, regardless of how developed he may think he is. The deeper the sadness and the deeper the desire to keep it from surfacing, the stronger the walls that "protect" such sadness from showing outwardly. These walls, usually constructed of numbness and anger, are so common in men that they almost seem a natural part of "being a man." In such cases, a man may be so removed from his underlying sadness that he doesn't know that he *is* sad.

We can find all kinds of things to be angry about when we feel sad and don't want to show it, such as shortcomings in whomever we're feeling sad in front of. We can easily get ourselves so riled up that we lose touch with the softness and raw hurt of sadness. This allows us not to lose face, hence reducing our shame level. Losing face in anger is usually preferable to the facial meltdown we might experience if we let our sadness flow through us. Such a use of anger is more common in men than in women, given that there's even more shame in losing face for men than women.

Sometimes the opposite happens: we feel angry and shift to sadness before it's obvious that we're angry. Even if our anger is totally justified, we may block or smother it with sadness. You could say that we're putting out the fire of our anger with the water of our sadness. The stronger our anger and our aversion to expressing it, the stronger and more engrossing our flow of tears will likely be. Not surprisingly, this is much more common in women than men. And why? Partly because the expression of anger is less culturally approved of for women than men (remember the derogatory labels for angry women) and partly because expressing anger is generally less safe for women than men (an angry woman is more likely to be met with a man's rage/violence than a weeping woman).

SHAME OVER SADNESS

Sometimes our hands fly to our face when we're crying, as if to block others from seeing us in such a state. Often this indicates shame over "breaking down," especially when we collapse or curl into ourselves. At such times, we're experiencing extreme vulnerability, along with at least some sense of lacking safety. It's as if we're a snail suddenly bereft of its shell, with our softness exposed and trembling, completely vulnerable to unfriendly forces in our vicinity.

We aren't born feeling ashamed of our sadness—we're initially free of the burden of self-consciousness—but at an early age we easily get the impression that it's wrong to cry. We may be seeded with the pressure to cut off our tears. In our early years, we don't have the ability to suppress our tears, but we can feel shame about our failure to do so. We then feel conflicted when our tears come: on the one hand there's relief in crying, and on the other hand there's the heavy hand of shame pushing our head toward the ground.

When I work with men who have not cried for a very long time, I find that their tears naturally come once their shame has been clearly addressed and worked with—especially their shame over showing vulnerability. Often their shame is enmeshed with their anger, so when their shame is seen for what it is, they may start to feel very angry. As this finds fitting expression, the psychoenergetic armoring around their heart begins to crack and fragment, opening the gates, so to speak, for an even deeper anger and a surfacing sadness. Even if there is no anger, the exposure and peeling back of shame makes room for the expression of sadness.

When a man who hasn't cried for a long, long time cuts through his shame about openly crying, his tears often emerge spasmodically, with his hands over his face and his guts in a knot. When his belly, diaphragm, and jaw are energetically loosened, his hands often move to his heart, especially as he connects his crying to the events that first made him feel bad about crying and then to times preceding that. I call this *connected catharsis* (see chapter 29). Usually he emerges from this looking quite different: refreshingly alive and open, grounded and effortlessly embodied, full of shining boy yet simultaneously present as a man, a man with both guts and heart. He hasn't just had a good cry, but a transformative cry.

SADNESS AND DEPRESSION

If sadness were a color, it would be blue. Watery, cool, no yellow or red, just blue—and not a sky-blue but a deep-water blue with indigo undercurrents. No wonder we talk of "having the blues" or "feeling blue." However dark its depths or its weight, sadness is not necessarily depression. Whereas sadness is the heart suffused with a sense of palpable loss, depression is the heart flattened so much that it cannot be felt.

Sadness is an emotion; depression (discussed in chapter 17) is not. Although depression packs in plenty of feeling, it's more of a suppressive pressing-down of emotion. There is, of course, some overlap between sadness and depression, but they differ significantly. If we're sad and showing it, some people might interpret our state as depression, not seeing that our down-ness is a descent into the raw feeling of the loss of something significant to us, rather than a squashing or pressing-down of us. In sadness there is movement—down and in, down and out—but in depression there is almost no movement.

Where depression flattens us, sadness loosens us. In depression, we are immobilized; in sadness, we are flowing, however unpleasant that might be. While depression makes it difficult to take action, sadness provides a setting out of which action can emerge. Depression keeps us under the covers; sadness uncovers us. There's numbness in depression, but not in sadness. In depression we are drained, but in sadness we are cleansed. Depression is passive, sadness active. Where depression is repression, sadness is release. Where sadness is blue, depression is mostly black, shutting out the very light for which it aches. When we lift the lid of depression, getting out from under its heaviness, one of the first things we're likely to feel is sadness, not a moping or merely reactive sadness, but a sadness that breaks open our heart.

WORKING WITH SADNESS

The first step in working with sadness is acknowledging its presence. Out loud, if possible.

The second step is observing what we're doing with our sadness. We might, for example, be trying to keep it quiet or putting ourselves down for being sad; we might be welcoming it; or we might be trying to cover it with a smile. Or we might be doing nothing in particular with it.

The third step is to make as much room for sadness as we can, assuming we're in a situation in which this isn't problematic. So we inhale more deeply, especially into our chest, moving our sternum forward and up. We're not trying to cry; we're simply making more room for our sadness to emerge.

The fourth step is to let our mouth open, jaw loosen, and throat soften, giving ourselves permission to release some sound—again assuming that we're in a place where this isn't problematic. Our deep tears flow best when the front of our body, from belly to face, is open, and our throat is part of this. So if the tears start, don't deny them vocalization; sometimes our sadness needs to be far from quiet!

Practice

OPENING TO YOUR SADNESS

Recall the last time you cried, other than at a movie. Close your eyes, raise your inner eyebrows and forehead, turn down the corners of your mouth, lift your cheeks, and tighten your lips slightly. Breathe a little deeper. Keep your hands in your lap. As you do all this, let your head come forward a bit. If you were to cry now, what would happen to your posture? Your chest? Your mouth? Stay with this for about a minute.

Now bring your hands to your face, covering your eyes, perhaps having the sense of cradling your face. Do you have the feeling that you could cry more fully in this position? Or less? How does it feel to "hide" your crying face? Stay with this for a minute or so, then bring your hands back to your lap, lifting your head. Imagine gazing into the eyes of someone you feel especially close to, letting them see your full sadness. Let their compassion hold and support you. Now hold your sadness the very same way, caring for rather than shaming the sad you.

CONNECTING THROUGH OUR TEARS

Sometimes we cry because we've lost connection; and sometimes we cry because we've reclaimed or found our way back to connection. The following example illustrates the close link between the two.

> We are being very critical of another—our partner or a close friend. Though we have a niggling sense that we're going too far, we're not about to stop. Their defensiveness only spurs us on.

They ask us to stop, saying that we're coming on too strong and are hurting them, but we don't listen. We are on a roll. A minute later, loudly stating that we don't feel heard, we leave the room. Hours pass. A nagging sense of needing to set things right stays with us, no matter what we're doing.

Then the other comes to where we are, sitting down across from us. We notice that our heart is closed, our face mostly frozen, our breath shallow. Silence. We know that we need to speak. Suddenly, we clearly see the other and immediately tear up, now feeling our loss of connection with him or her. As strong as our temptation is to explain away what happened earlier, our desire to come clean is stronger. With a voice trembling ever so slightly, we say that we crossed a line, that we were out of control, and that we are sorry. The tears really come. Suddenly we have a very deep sense of what it would be like to lose the other person, and our crying deepens. The other softens, his or her eyes shining with tears, and we reconnect, even though we know that what happened earlier will linger for a while before winding down.

THE IMPORTANCE OF CRYING

Crying ought not to be something we outgrow. Deeply felt tears can be profoundly healing—at any age.

When we weep, we open the heart, ease the belly, quiet the mind, soften the body. It is a loosening-up and deep cleansing, a washing-out not just of psychic debris but also—at least to some degree—of biochemical waste. The composition of emotional tears is different than that of tears that result from cutting onions or from an irritant in our eyes. Emotionally shed tears contain more toxins (much like sweat does)—thereby helping cleanse the body—but also contain leucine enkephalin, an opiate. So such tears both cleanse and ease us.

Crying keeps us from drying out. It is easy to slip into aridity, hardening ourselves against the painful or hurtful aspects of life. We may find a certain safety in such ossification, greening our deserts of abstraction with oases of distraction, but still sadness stirs in us. We can put a lid on it or keep it in our darkest recesses, but still it arises, calling for our attention, our care, our recognition. The more we suppress crying, the shallower our lives become.

The most painful part of crying is right before its onset. As soon as our tears are flowing and our throat is open, we hurt less, unless we're fighting and tightening up against our undammed tears. Even if waves of deeper hurt arrive once we've begun weeping—as when the details of a betrayal freshly seize us—the pain pulses through us with less obstruction than before our crying started. There is hurt, but it is the hurt of contracted tissues expanding and stretching from the pressure of what's seeking to flow through us; the more we resist it, the more it hurts. When we don't resist it, the sheer pain of it subsides fairly quickly.

Each deep loss crucifies our attachment
Our ribcage unable to hold all the ache
It is not our heart that cracks
But its ossified shield—its bulletproof glass
A guardian from a much younger time
Crumbling to less than dust
As all constructions must

Practice

ALLOWING OLD SADNESS TO SURFACE

Generate a sad face as you did in the beginning of the previous practice in this chapter. Breathe more deeply, close your eyes, and remember a time or times when you felt especially sad as a child. Let that memory fill you, examining it in as much detail as possible and feeling it with your whole body. If possible, place your body in the position it was in at that remembered time. Feel your body as if you were that age. Notice how your heart feels, your throat, your mouth, your tummy, your back. Is there anything you feel like saying? What might you say if it was entirely safe to do so? Keep your face in sad mode, eyes still closed, without any pressure to cry. If some tears come, fine, and if not, no problem!

Let your tears come, and not necessarily quietly. Let them flow, flood, storm, shake, and wake you. Let your whole body cry, weep, sob. Drop below any shame you might have about crying so openly, letting your heart break, knowing that what is breaking is not your heart but its energetic encasement. If you feel like a child or infant as you cry, let it be; keep your mind out of it. We have so much unattended hurt, so much muted sorrow, so much life force tied up in keeping our tears, new and old, from fully surfacing.

But surface they must, if we are to truly come alive.

13

Joy

The Unbound Feeling of Being

Joy is elated ease—it's as if our whole being is smiling,
saying nothing more than "yes, yes, yes!"

The joy that comes from learning how to keep our heart open
during dark times constitutes true happiness, a core-level "yes"
that cannot be extinguished by the challenges of living and dying.

EMOTIONS THAT EXPRESS HAPPINESS ARE more difficult
to describe than the rest of the emotions. There is much to be said, for
example, about anger and fear—an abundance of telling particulars
and developmental considerations and explorations of expression. But
how much can we say about actual happiness, beyond how good it feels
and how dependent it usually is on certain conditions?

Happiness is ease-centered emotional pleasure, characteristically
lighthearted and expansive, ranging from contentment to outright elation. In happiness we can be carefree or calm, mellow or excited, full
of equanimity or uplifting excitement—all rooted in a fluidly pleasing OK-ness of being, without any itch or desire to be elsewhere. The
happiness family includes joy, exhilaration, contentment, bliss, peace-
fulness, ecstasy, equanimity, exuberance, *joie de vivre,* exultation, and
delight. And these are quite contagious—just writing this list makes
me smile.

If the literature on "happy" emotions (as opposed to the literature on
how to attain them) could be stacked up against the literature on less-than-
happy emotions, what might be a fitting image for such a comparison?

Certainly not two piles of comparable height! A shoebox beside a sky-scraper might be the accurate comparison. Imagine a novel in which everyone is already happy and stays happy throughout the entire book; imagine a novel in which there is tragedy, betrayal, darkness, detours, breakthroughs, love won and love lost. Which would you rather read?

Not that happiness has to be limited to formulaic plots or to being saccharine or bubbly, but its dramatics (think fireworks and soulful reunions) signal more of an arrival than a journey, and so they hold less interest for us. Where's the adventure, the challenge, the falls and breakthroughs? The great journeys of mythology would not have been undertaken if there were no drive for a deeper life—and the absence of this drive (along with regular injections of contentment) is precisely where the shadow of happiness lurks.

Think of all the books about how to achieve happiness, the sheer volume of which speaks to the rarity of happiness, the loss of happiness, the effort to stay happy, the drive to find and keep whatever it is that will make us happy. Such a pervasive pursuit of happiness! But this very chasing after it, this desperate search for it, this grasping for it, only generates more unhappiness, as various spiritual authorities (like the Buddha) have told us for millennia, pointing us to what they perceived as the root of our unhappiness or suffering. So we may have followed such teachings religiously but still found happiness to be elusive and far too ephemeral.

If we've suffered a lot, we may equate happiness with relief from our suffering, but happiness is more than that, being an uplifting of the heart and spirit, an expansive "yes" that pervades us, whatever the context. To reach it is to fully recognize (1) that it is not outside us and (2) that to access it we simply have to turn toward our pain and cultivate as much intimacy as possible with that pain. To not develop such intimacy guarantees our ongoing unhappiness, regardless of our moments of elation. Happiness is our birthright, but we cannot embody it if we keep turning away from our pain, trying to access the treasure without having faced the dragon. Put another way, happiness is our natural state when we are no longer at war with ourselves, are no longer striving to keep our suffering in the shadows, and are actively cultivating intimacy with *all* that we are.

Less-than-happy emotions all feature something that troubles us, something that generates suffering, something that catalyzes an impetus to be in a state other than where we are. This inherent struggle, however vain or failure-bound, is in many ways the centerpiece of our lives, the core challenge that can call forth the very best from us: the stuff of great novels, plays, films, songs. Yet in the midst of happiness, there is no such struggle. What we have been trying to reach, however shallow or antithetical to our well-being, has been attained. Even if our happiness is short-lived, there is no real struggle during the experience of it—no effort to cut through it, no drive to go beyond it. Our very contentment in many cases may be a kind of soporific, an obstacle to doing what it takes to embody a deeper life. But who wants to investigate—and therefore possibly disrupt—that contentment, that plateau of equanimity, that respite from life's difficulties? Yet, as we shall see, there is always the possibility that there could be a deeper happiness.

Let's flesh this out by exploring the emotion perhaps most commonly associated with being happy: joy. Joy is happiness in the raw, an energetically expansive, strongly pleasurable feeling of unobstructed openness and connection, ranging from a mild sense of euphoria to outright bliss. In short, joy is elated ease. It's as if our entire being is smiling, with nothing more to say than "yes, yes, yes!"

There's not much cognitive complexity to joy, which makes it a refreshingly straightforward emotion—no ambiguity, no mental log-jams, no heavy-duty infusions of information-soaked considerations and contextual concerns. What a joy it is to be filled with joy! What a pleasing influx of ease!

Unlike ecstasy, joy is not supercharged with positive stimulation, but pervaded with an easiness that is more than just contentment. In joy, we are not amped up but *opened* up. With no goal to be elsewhere. And how are we opened up in joy? There's a sense of effortless expansion, as if our ribcage can no longer contain us. We radiate outward and usually upward, with not just our heart blooming wide, but also our belly, our throat, our face, our skull, our entire being.

Joy is much more than the mere absence of suffering, much more than the pleasing sensations that arise when an extremely tight pair of shoes is at last removed or when we're otherwise extricated from some sort of suffering. Its presence signals a palpable "yes" that pleasurably radiates all through us—a "yes" that celebrates the relaxation and spaciousness and primal sense of OK-ness that pervades us.

Joy lifts the sternum and brow, opens the arms and eyes, lifts the head and step, loosens the jaw and belly, and ultimately causes the entire body to soften and expand. It breathes us open, loose, easy. No wonder we so persistently seek it and so highly value it!

TYPES OF JOY

Million-dollar moments can certainly catalyze joy: winning the lottery, getting a yearned-for job, unexpectedly completing a marathon. Such moments lead to *situational joy*—joy that is dependent on certain events taking place—but joy can also arise when outer circumstances are unpleasant or uneasy. The deepest joy—*nonsituational joy*—does not depend on outer circumstances. It is found not in having, but in being.

Almost all of what we refer to as joy is situational joy, based on the occurrence of specific events; this inevitably casts a shadow on our joy (a shadow initially obscured by our joy's brightness), given that the event or conditions that generate and coexist with our joy may be gone or altered in a very short time; they're beyond our control. So in situational joy we're on unstable ground, our very celebration tainted by the impermanent, often fleeting and fluxing nature of its originating factors—along with the recognition that our usual patterns are still intact despite the reality of what's brought us joy.

Nonsituational joy, on the other hand, carries no such shadow, given that it does not rely on the arising of particular conditions. It is the joy of simply being, regardless of our circumstances or mood, achieved by ceasing to turn away from life and instead developing intimacy with all that constitutes us. It has nothing to do with what we have or are getting and everything to do with what we are.

There is another kind of joy that could be called *realizational joy*. By this, I mean the joy that arises when we have achieved something very significant and recognize it as such without any egoic inflation. For example, we've worked hard—very hard—to reach a certain capacity in our vocation and now have clearly done so. There is no mistaking that we have arrived at this place in our work and are now established there. The joy that arises from this depended—not depends, but *depended*—on certain conditions being met and now remains, usually as a kind of emotional background or backdrop, as we proceed, having already arrived at a deeper stage of our work.

Situational joy can be selfish or me-centered—and far from healthy, as when it arises at the expense of others' well-being. But it can also be we-centered, as in the elated/generous sharing of bounty or good fortune with others. And sometimes the contagiousness and openheartedness of such joy can stretch it into a bigger, far more expansive sense of we-centeredness, as exemplified by the Buddhist practice of *mudita*, a Pali and Sanskrit term meaning "sympathetic joy," a joy readily felt when others succeed or do well. Practicing mudita means, in part, meeting those aspects of ourselves that don't wish others well; it necessitates deepening our knowing of ourselves in more than just intellectual ways. As such, the practice of mudita helps pave the way toward recognizing our innate or nonsituational happiness.

And doing our inner and relational work, hard as it can be, has as one of its rewards the joy of knowing that all situations can be worked with, used to deepen and enrich us. This joy, the joy that comes from learning how to keep our heart open during dark times, constitutes true happiness, a core-level "yes" that cannot be extinguished by the challenges of living and dying.

SHADOW FORMS OF JOY

The most common shadow of joy is a self-centered pleasure in which we don't care about our impact on others, perhaps even exploiting them in the service of our own happiness. Bullying is one example; unscrupulous yet legally sanctioned financial profiteering is another.

In contrast to mudita (sympathetic joy), there is a low-grade, pinched mixture of disdain, vicarious aggression, and some degree of joy known as *schadenfreude* (there's no English term for this), meaning the pleasure we take in others' misfortunes. Schadenfreude—roughly translated from the German as "harm-joy"—is something we have all experienced, however discreetly or quietly. It is considered in detail in chapter 23.

Another shadow form of joy—or at least something resembling joy—is mania, which is happiness so intoxicated with excitation that personal boundaries are trashed and the ground underfoot is rendered dangerously unstable. (A somewhat more subtle relative of this is hypomania, a toned-down version of mania that is often taken to be a good or even admirable thing in much of our culture.)

WORKING WITH JOY

How to work with already-present joy? Make room for it without clinging to it. Stay present with it, keeping as grounded as possible, appreciating but not losing yourself in its pleasurableness. Don't let it blind you to others' difficulties. Don't chain its arising to having/owning/keeping something in particular. And how to work with the absence of joy? Acknowledge what is actually occurring emotionally, and do whatever it takes to compassionately shift your awareness to the heart of that, however unpleasant doing so may be. (Practices for this can be found throughout this book.)

If you want more joy, get as intimate as possible with *all* of your emotions, illuminating and honoring the basic energy of each one. There is a kind of joy that sooner or later emerges from such exploration, the joy of simply being present at the heart of whatever we are feeling. Such joy weeps as easily as it celebrates; its loss of face only deepens its presence. This is nonsituational joy at its best, the joy of being, the open-ended feeling of being. Not being this or that, but just being. An example of this is when we're feeling deep disappointment and are letting ourselves go to the core of our disappointment, dropping down into its painful landscape, and openly feeling its contractedness and hurt and perhaps some of its stark beauty. We cease resisting it; our desire to know it is stronger than our desire to distract ourselves from it. Then slowly but surely, a sobering joy starts to arise as we look at our disappointment through undreaming eyes—eyes for which disappointment is not disappointing.

Practice

JOY AND DEEPER JOY

Remember a time when you felt total, unadulterated joy. Close your eyes, letting the details of that time come into focus. Whatever position your body was in at that time, assume that now as best you can. Let your mouth open a little more, and breathe more deeply. Turn your hands palms up, letting your fingers spread wider. Notice how you feel: your face, your throat, your chest and belly, the back of your neck, your feet. Notice what your mind is doing. No pressure. Feel your entire body softening and expanding. Now let the memory go, and bring your attention to your life as it is now.

Start letting go of the notion that you can't be joyful if there isn't anything to be joyful about. No matter how hard or difficult your life is right now, speak out loud what you currently are grateful for—it could be as simple as gratitude for functioning eyes and ears, or for simply being here. A sobering joy is still joy. Again recall that time when you felt joy. Stay with it as you, at the same time, bring into your awareness your current circumstances, doing your best to let the two coexist. Don't measure the success of this by how much joy you feel, but by your capacity not to forget your inherent sense of well-being in the midst of difficult or otherwise challenging circumstances.

If you want more joy, don't wait for more auspicious circumstances. Simply get more intimate with your emotions, spelunking your depths, and practice being grateful, especially when you feel far from grateful. Practicing gratitude helps reset our emotional baseline, providing a nonconceptual perspective that helps awaken us to who and what we really are. It's very hard, if not almost impossible, to practice gratitude and remain ego-centered or selfish.

Practice

GRATITUDE MEDITATION

Find a comfortable place to sit or lie down, and settle in there, having ensured ahead of time that you won't be disturbed for at least twenty minutes. Close your eyes, and let your belly and jaw soften as much as possible. Become more aware of your entire body, starting with your feet. Do this for a few minutes.

Now focus on your feet, and silently say, "Gratitude for these feet." Feel into each foot with your full attention as you do this, letting yourself feel gratitude, to whatever degree, for being able to walk and to have functioning feet. (If your feet don't work, do the same practice for another, functioning part of your body.) Think of how readily you take for granted the presence of your feet, and imagine what it might be like not to have them. Focus on each toe for one full inhalation and exhalation, doing so without any hurry. A few more times silently say, "Gratitude for these feet."

Next, move your attention to another part of your body, scanning it closely so that you feel as if you were there, and then silently say, "Gratitude for [name this part of your body]." Again, recall how easily you take this part of yourself for granted, and repeat your gratitude for it. Keep your belly and breathing soft.

Bring this practice to another two or three parts of your body. Don't worry if your gratitude expression feels a bit shallow or flat or insincere; simply stay with it, and you will eventually start to feel some sense of gratitude emerging, perhaps along with a sense of increasing internal spaciousness. Give yourself about five minutes for this.

Now focus on your entirety, silently saying, "Gratitude for being." Feel as though you are breathing in your totality, sensing your core aliveness and presence, and breathe out gratitude for this, including gratitude for the very capacity to do such a practice.

Last, focus on what is most essential about you, most central to you, what is more you than your personality, what is simultaneously transcendent yet still uniquely you, and allow yourself to feel gratitude for this, not so as to get away from anything but rather to include all that you are in the circle of your care. Rest here as long as you like.

Variation: When you feel far, far from any sort of gratitude, such as when things have gotten very difficult, do the practice in the appendix, and then do the above practice, initially focusing on the parts of your body you most feel cut off from. After five or ten minutes of this, shift your attention to whatever emotional pain you're in, including numbness, and silently say, "Gratitude for the ability to see and approach this pain," touching it the way you'd touch a distraught child. As you bring more compassion to your places of hurt, practice being grateful to be able to generate—or even intend to generate—such compassion. There's no "should"-ing here, no pressure to be grateful in any conventional sense. All that matters is that you open to the possibility of being grateful for simply being here, able to function in whatever ways you can.

When we settle into the raw reality of who and what we really are, joy inevitably arises, as the unbound feeling of simply being. We may not necessarily feel good at such times, but we don't really mind because we know in our heart of hearts that we are on track and that each time we get sidelined and then recenter ourselves, we are deepening our capacity to skillfully navigate whatever arises, high or low, dark or light, pleasant or unpleasant. Having such a capacity on tap keeps us plugged into joy.

Learning to live in intimacy with all that we are roots us in a joy that is more foundation than goal, a joy that is not washed away with the inevitable tides of emotional and relational pain. Joy is utterly natural to us; let us stop trying to produce it and instead simply open to it, and not stop short in that opening.

14

Grief

The Heart Broken Wide Open

Where reactive sorrow contracts and isolates us, unimpeded grief
expands and connects us, grounding us in natural openness.

WE ALL HAVE GRIEF, HOWEVER much we may mute, delay,
or bypass its expression. There is grief over the death of a loved one,
grief over shattered promises, grief over missed opportunities, grief over
great pain endured by someone close to us, grief over the sheer suffering of so many of us, grief over planetary destruction. So much grief,
and so much of it denied full expression.

Grief is what we feel when our heart fully registers a loss that is of
deep significance to us. It is intensely personal, even when it stretches
us far beyond our usual sense of self, shaking us to our marrow. And it
breaks the heart, however concretized its "casing" may be. The broken
heart can go into endarkened contraction (a myopic "going to pieces")
or it can go in a very different direction. If allowed to, grief doesn't just
break the heart but breaks it *open,* ultimately opening us to unbroken
being and our innate wholeness.

Grief includes sadness but is much more than just sadness. Its tears
may burn and overwhelm, but sooner or later they also illuminate. In full-
out grief, we are stripped down to our feeling core, registering the bare
fact of suffering—and quite often not just ours—without any buffers.

We begin with "my" grief and may remain there, but sometimes
we shift to "our" grief as our rawness of heart starts to radiate out to
include the suffering of others close to us. And then we may shift even

further to "the" grief as we feel our collective suffering and allow that feeling to pervade us—which doesn't just bring on more sorrow, but also more love, love that remains itself even as it freely weeps. Here there is huge heartache, enormous hurt, and deep opening—together carrying us through the extremes of sorrow into a spaciousness as naturally compassionate as it is vast. In such heartfelt spaciousness and such exquisitely raw openness, there is eventually room for all.

When asked what could be done about the Middle East conflict, a rabbi once said, "Both sides have to grieve together." *Together.* The deepest grief is, however solitary its expression, a communal event. It touches all. Its hurt blows the cover off its sky, carrying us far beyond the dramatics of conventional sorrow.

Grief—unlike sadness and sorrow—is a passion. And like other passions—rage, lust, ecstasy—grief has the power to overwhelm us, for better or worse. Grief usually works best when it's uninhibited. Many people want to muzzle or mute it, perhaps to minimize potential embarrassment; such suppression is quite common at funerals. Anyone who really wails, really lets it out, is often looked upon as behaving poorly or inconsiderately. Not surprisingly, many of us end up in therapy years after the fact to deal with grief that wasn't fully expressed.

Unleashed grief is not mere venting or self-indulgence, but rather healing life energy on the loose, cutting new channels in the terrain of self, uprooting stands that no longer serve us. Such a wild storm grief can be; such a dark, yet luminous, outpouring; such a radical ripping of the heart; such a deep dying into life, birthing a truer "us" in its wake.

Practice

THE EXPERIENCE OF GRIEF

Make a list of what you have felt grief about. Is there anything on your list that you have not fully grieved? If so, recall what was happening at the time. Imagine now having the freedom to openly grieve the loss you suffered then.

Close your eyes, breathe more deeply into your heart, and keep your focus on the object of your grief. Stay with this for at least five minutes, without any pressure to cry, taking whatever body position feels most fitting. When you are done, lie down somewhere comfortable, with one hand on your heart and the other on your belly, and let your body soften. Finish with the practice in the appendix.

GRIEF UNDAMMED

More often than not, grief is as messy as it is healing; in it there are not only deeply felt tears, but also wild mood swings, times of disorientation, sudden spiritual openings, and intense flurries of anger. Grief has its own timetable, and it doesn't take well to being fit into a schedule. When unzipped, grief can also be quite noisy; it is more prone to wailing or broken sobs than to politely shed tears.

Ceasing to suppress the anger we might feel over a big loss can catalyze the undamming of a feeling of loss so immense and so deep that it resonates with other big losses—tragedies that belong to all of us (like the deaths of those we love)—thereby making deeply significant links with many, many others across space and through time. Thus we move from the interiorized community of voices that makes up our usual sense of self to the community at large (humankind), widening the circle of our reach, our love, our caring. Grief can blow us open that much.

Initially, grief bends and breaks us, shaking us to our core and washing away our footholds, leaving us with nowhere solid to stand. This can be frightening, but it's not as chaotic as it seems, any more than is a river plunging through a jagged canyon. The seeming lack of order simply reflects the unpredictable directions our grief takes through our internal structuring—directions that are largely dictated by the major choices we've made in life. For example, if we've kept a stiff belly whenever conflict has arisen, we may do the same when grief arrives, so that its energies have to either go around our tight gut or through it—in much the same way water behaves when it has to pass through a suddenly narrow passage. As such, grief can really loosen us up—if we will but lower our resistance to it and its currents.

However agonizing grief's intensity of heart-hurt might be for a while, it softens us—and the softer we are, the more readily we can allow the grieving process to work upon us. Eventually, there emerges some sense of a sobering ease, the ease of simply being—not being this, not being that, but simply being. This is not the bliss of immunity-seeking transcendence or of flight from painful feeling, but the natural joy of simply existing, equally at home with the high and the low, the dark and the light, the dying and the undying.

Such is the prevailing condition of the heart that, though bruised, is nonetheless sufficiently open to have room for all that we are, however dark or lowly or frightened. In grief, the heart is broken in much the same way that a stream rushing through a mountain forest is broken: seemingly in pieces but still unified in essence, its elemental dying only strengthening and affirming its fundamental aliveness, its rough-and-tumble course only furthering its dynamic yet vulnerable surrender.

Practice

ALLOWING GRIEF TO FLOW AND EXPAND

Close your eyes and remember a time when you grieved. Stay with this for a few minutes. Now imagine others who have suffered over the very thing that catalyzed your grief. Feel the circle of your grief expanding to include these others. Stay with this for a few minutes, imagining the energy of your heart extending in all directions with no dilution of its core feeling. Feel your feet solidly planted, and let your arms open out to the sides, palms up, moving in a very slowly lifting gesture of openness and prayer. Keep lifting your arms until they are parallel to the floor, keeping your shoulders and belly relaxed. Now slowly bring your hands in an arc back toward your chest, still keeping your arms parallel to the floor.

Once your hands have reached your chest, keep them there, and imagine that someone you lost (to death or through a relationship's demise) is sitting across from you. Remember the grief you felt regarding that loss, and recall the feeling of it as best you can. At the same time, let yourself feel this person sitting across from you, and bring them into the circle of your heart-hurt without any expectation that they respond in a certain way. Wish them well, either out loud or silently, letting your hands drop into your lap. Rest here for a few minutes.

Where reactive sorrow contracts and isolates us, unimpeded grief expands and connects us, grounding us in natural openness. Grief can be just as spacious as it is earthy, existing as a deeply personal yet also significantly transcendent sense of loss pervaded by a deeply visceral recognition of the inevitable passing of all that arises.

As such, grief provides a bridge not only between the personal and the transpersonal (with neither having a "higher" status than the other), but also between suffering and love. That bridge awaits our step, our crossing, our wholehearted contact.

15

Disgust

Oral/Moral Rejection

Anything that we believe could contaminate
or dirty us can elicit disgust.

Healthy disgust helps us separate from toxicity,
whereas unhealthy disgust contaminates us with
aberrant notions of cleanliness and purity.

DISGUST IS PROBABLY THE EMOTION that's most difficult
to disguise. Its characteristic crinkling of the nose and lifting of the
upper lip are hard to miss, even when subtly expressed. When we're
feeling disgust, it's as if we've just smelled or tasted something foul.
Whether that repugnant thing is experienced in the physical, psychological, or social realm, our disgust curbs any attraction we might have
toward it, usually quite emphatically.

The origins of disgust exist in the oral domain, beginning when we
were infants. Picture the face of a baby who, disliking the taste of a
particular food, unceremoniously ejects it. This kind of reaction stays
with us as we get older, and not just physically. The food rejection that
a disgusted child displays may show up in a disgusted adult as an other-
rejecting look (e.g., "looking down one's nose"), thought, or comment
denoting something repellent. The classic stiff upper lip is often just
frozen disgust (often in conjunction with frozen sadness). Haughtiness
is little more than dressed-up disgust, reinforced with a shot of pride.

Like anger, disgust says an unmistakable "no!"—but unlike anger,
disgust is not primarily out to right a perceived wrong (although it

might help catalyze an anger of sufficient strength to take the stand that's apparently needed). Disgust, however powerful, is not seeking justice, but space and distance from the offending other (by trying to generate a clean zone between us and that distasteful one). Disgust and anger share plenty of overlap; when the two emotions mix, contempt arises. (See chapter 18 on contempt.)

Like shame, disgust involves rejection, but unlike shame, disgust (with the exception of self-disgust) does not render us painfully self-conscious; we are too busy pushing away what disgusts us. Combine shame and disgust, and loathing arises.

Like fear, disgust is an expression of aversion, but unlike fear, disgust does not paralyze or shrink us. When fear and disgust get together, horror arises.

When we let ourselves openly feel our disgust—including in our mouth and on our tongue—we sometimes experience nausea or a sickening sensation in our solar plexus region, as if we have swallowed something that does not belong in us, something we cannot digest.

As a pure feeling, disgust is projectile rejection. If the tongue doesn't protrude, it usually carries the intention to do so, as if rejecting words are on its tip.

Practice

EXPERIENCING AND EXPRESSING DISGUST

Raise your upper lip and nose a bit, think of something revolting, and notice what happens to your tongue and the inside of your mouth. Exaggerate it. Come onto your hands and knees on the floor and push your tongue out as far as possible and downward toward your chest. Open your eyes wide, and keep your mouth wide open. If you can push your tongue out any farther, do so. While holding this, think of someone or something you recently felt disgusted by, and release some sounds that express this, all while your tongue is fully protruding. It's natural that your jaw will ache as you hold this position. Keep the sound coming for at least half a minute, then relax your jaw, letting your tongue return to its normal position. Come back to sitting or standing, noticing how you now feel.

In disgust, our gustatory and olfactory systems are on high alert (including psychological and moral contexts) and are ready to repel whatever offending object is before us—such as a reviled politician's assertion. We may not be pushing out our tongue, but we might as well be, given the distaste and probable revulsion we're feeling. Disgust mixes the oral and the moral with a unified voicing, however muted, of "yuck!" After our initial experiences with disgust in infancy, we learn, directly or indirectly, to have a disgust response to things we might not have otherwise found at all revolting—like certain foods or sights or certain behaviors. Our own bodily fluids might become distasteful to us. As parts of us become "other," we are more likely to find them disgusting.

Such "otherness" is especially experienced as "not us" when it clearly lies outside us. For example, we ordinarily don't mind swishing around our own saliva inside our mouth and swallowing it; but if we were to swish it around and then spit it into a glass, how would we feel if we were to then drink it? Probably not so comfortable, with at least some degree of distaste. It's still the same saliva—our own—but once in the glass, it is "other."

HEALTHY AND UNHEALTHY DISGUST

Where we once, through our disgust response, literally defended our mouth—and especially the inside of our mouth—from contamination (real or not), we now similarly defend ourself from contamination (real or imagined). In our move from orality to morality, we develop a kind of disgust evaluation code that we may stick to even when it violates others. This is an evolutionary survival mechanism designed to protect us, to keep potential poisons, real or imagined, out of our bodies, our selves, our familial and cultural grouping. In this we find the shadow side of disgust, first cousin to toxic shame and hostility, wherein we dehumanize others, objectifying them to the point where we can readily abuse them.

Disgust defends us against impurity, real or imagined. Such impurity doesn't necessarily have to be something physical—perceived impurity can show up in moral or ethical issues. Anything that we believe could contaminate or dirty us can elicit disgust in us, leading in the extreme to horrors like genocide.

When we, in our disgust, overdo the "other-ness" we assign to whomever we find distasteful or repulsive, we are already neck deep in the domain of dehumanizing them. And of course the more we dehumanize them, the more easily we can legitimize both our disgust for them and the way we are mistreating them. It's as if they are dirty—hence the term "ethnic cleansing."

Healthy disgust does not degrade others. It focuses on *behaviors* that we find repugnant, giving us the impetus to so strongly reject such behaviors that we unmistakably stand apart from them while simultaneously standing in our integrity, not letting ourselves dehumanize those engaged in behaviors that disgust us. We have not retreated (as in fear) and we have not pressed forward (as in anger); we are simply standing our ground. And however strong our disgust may be, we are not letting it obscure our compassion.

It is worth noting that the word "disgust" is sometimes used when we're not actually feeling any disgust. For example, we might say that someone or something is disgusting, without experiencing any disgust. Disgust minus any feeling of revulsion or distaste is not really disgust, but just an emphatic way of voicing our moral disapproval.

WORKING WITH DISGUST

First of all, familiarize yourself with disgust so you can recognize and name it as soon as it stirs in you. Notice its facial gestures in others, even though they may flicker across a face for less than a moment. Second, explore your history with it: What did you find disgusting at different ages? What wasn't disgusting to you at one age, but disgusting at another? What do you now find disgusting that you know you were conditioned to find disgusting at a certain point? What things do you find disgusting? Which people? Which behaviors?

If there were things in our past that we could neither stomach nor ward off (like an older sibling's taunting aggression), part of our healing is to fully access and express our anger, so as to empower ourselves and set healthy boundaries. Another part is to fully access and express our disgust, no longer swallowing what we had to in the past.

Practice

WORKING WITH YOUR DISGUST

Make a list of ten or more things you find particularly disgusting. Imagine being forced into very close proximity to one of these. Notice the details of your response: Where do you first feel disgust in your body? What is happening to your tongue? To the roof of your mouth? Your eyes? Your throat? Your belly? Your hands? What sound most accurately conveys what you are feeling? Make that sound now, a few times.

Now think of someone whom you feel—or have felt—strongly disgusted by, someone whose behavior was repellent to you. Focus on that person without holding back any of your disgust and without judging yourself for the strength of your disgust. Maintain your face of disgust. Now view the object of your disgust not as a person but as a reviled "it": go ahead and dehumanize that person without any countereffort to be caring. Keep your heart hardened, your gaze removed, your distaste and revulsion nearby. No mercy. Stay with this for a few minutes, never straying from your disgust.

Now continue thinking of that person and allow yourself to feel your full disgust over what they are doing or did, but start viewing that person as a human being. Don't let yourself dehumanize him or her, even if the behavior in question nauseates you. Your heart may not open, but do nothing to harden it. Stay with this for a minute or so, then let yourself see more in this person than what disgusts or disgusted you. Sense him or her in different activities; sense any similarities between you. As you do this, maintain awareness of your disgust. Don't let your fledgling compassion for this person block your disgust, and vice versa. After a few minutes of this, step outside for some fresh air, or go into another room and stretch out for a short rest.

However much it may be in the foreground, disgust can coexist with compassion. May we not allow our disgust to obscure our heart.

16

Guilt

A Stalemated Parent-Child Bind

Feeling guilty about doing something enables us to do it again.

ARE GUILT AND SHAME THE same thing? No, but they do share plenty of common ground. Guilt is something we *do* with shame—just as aggression is something we do with anger and contempt is something we do with disgust. Whereas shame interrupts what we're doing, guilt short-circuits such interruption, putting on the brakes *after* we've acted out the behavior in question.

Guilt is little more than frozen shame—shame that's been infused with some degree of fear. Most of the time, guilt manifests as the self-punishing sensation of having violated some sort of private contract or moral agreement. When we're busy beating ourselves up, we're in all likelihood mired in guilt.

Where shame exposes us, guilt *splits* us.

In guilt one part of us, fixatedly childish or adolescent, does the forbidden or "bad" deed—the act that trashes our values—while the other part, authoritarian or rigidly parental, does the punishing. The stalemated relationship between these two is the essence of guilt. And it is this relationship, this codependent bind, that must be illuminated and worked with if we are to cease being stuck in guilt.

In shame we say, "I won't," or something similar, but in guilt we say, "I won't do this again," so as to justify doing it *now.* Thus does delayed gratification yield to delayed (and anticipated) punishment; yes, we will beat ourselves up, but not until *after* we've done what apparently merits such punishment.

Guilt doesn't just divide us, but keeps us divided, splitting us into two factions whose ongoing struggle with each other is so draining and so self-defeating—"divided we fall"—that we have little energy left for facing or outgrowing our guilt's agenda.

Shame says "stop" with the whole body, but guilt says "stop" with the mind—accompanied by an in-the-shadows "don't stop" counter-intention to *continue* the behavior that brought on the guilt. This counter-intention usually overrides any opposition to it, in much the same way that an addict's resistance to having another drink or another hit is shoved aside by the desire to do so.

The very feeling of shame halts us in our tracks; we simply cannot function as we usually do, losing our focus and coordination. This, when healthy, gives us a needed time-out to reconsider what we are doing or are about to do, which triggers our conscience. Of course, we may bypass this opportunity by dissociating from our shame, but if we stay present with it, we're less likely to follow through with what we were about to do before our shame arrived.

And the feeling of guilt? Unpleasant as it may be, it doesn't halt us in our tracks to any significant degree; in fact, guilt may even spur us on in anticipation of the possible pleasure or relief that our "bad" deed might provide—a pleasure or relief that we may have come to crave. This deed we are about to engage in against our better judgment meets only token resistance from us because in our guilt we know that we are off *and* we know that we will definitely be punishing ourselves (or be punished by another) for our misdeed—but not until *after* we've done it.

So our "guilty pleasure" or guilt-centered action coexists with our disapproval of it, with us pinned between the two.

Guilt is interwoven shame and fear. We feel bad about doing something we know we shouldn't do, and we fear the consequences even as we intuit that doing it will distract us from our fear. Facing the consequences of our "bad" behavior scares us, but not enough to stop us. Shame contracts us and so does fear; tie them together and we're in quite a knot.

Our faces may turn red with shame, as if in unavoidable confession of our transgressions in front of a critical audience, be it internal or external. But we don't turn red with guilt—even if caught red-handed!—because we anticipate with some degree of fear the consequences of our misdeed, including the self-recrimination we'll have to endure. So while we may blush with shame (from sheer exposure), we may blanch with guilt (from fear-infused contraction). There's a sense in shame of having our slipped behavior publicly lit up as if under bright stage-lights, but in guilt things are conducted behind darkly veiled curtains. Where shame focuses on defectiveness, guilt focuses on wrongdoing.

Practice

GUILT'S PARENT-CHILD DYNAMIC

Sit in a chair facing an empty chair a few feet away. Bring to mind something you feel guilty about now or have felt guilty about in the past. Imagine yourself as the one who did the "bad" deed, and that sitting across from you is the part of yourself who's about to punish you for it. Close your eyes. Sense yourself doing the misdeed, and notice how old you feel, how small or contracted you feel.

After a minute or so of this, sit in the other chair, feeling yourself in a position where you'd never do "the deed" and where you are appalled at the you who just did it. Notice what you want to do to the other you, knowing that when you do this, you will meet no resistance. This is the dynamic that centers guilt, a stalemated back-and-forth parent-child interplay.

Now stand up, move away from both chairs, and hold both positions in your consciousness. Feel your connection to both positions without getting absorbed in either; instead of going back and forth between them, you are simply present with both simultaneously.

CUTTING THROUGH GUILT'S DRAMATICS

Guilt is a toxic, internal cycle: we act out, then punish ourselves for doing so, then act out again, and so on. Knowing that we're going to punish ourselves for acting out "legitimizes" us doing it again—thus do we impale ourselves on guilt's twisted morality. And if we punish ourselves enough, we might feel justified in acting out again to more of an extreme. It is literally a hell of a deal, keeping us stuck on repeat, leaving us enmeshed in a stalemated parent-child (or parent-adolescent) relationship.

Guilt keeps us small and irresponsible, removed from having to be accountable—other than submitting to our own mode of punishment, which has been set up to be ineffective for altering our behavior. We might also broadcast the abuse we're suffering at our own hand—our self-incrimination and self-flagellation—to such an extent that we lessen the likelihood of "outside" punishment. If we're doing such a good job beating ourselves up, then who would want to beat on us more? And if our self-punishing is severe enough, we might feel even more justified participating in whatever it is that we "shouldn't" be doing.

Here's an illustration: Carol disparages herself so nastily and relentlessly for eating candy on the sly that she (1) decreases the odds that others who know of this will speak in similar fashion to her (unless they're hard on her for being hard on herself); and (2) feels that she's absorbed enough self-denigration—that is, done enough heavy-duty confession—to "wipe the slate clean," so she's thus justified in treating/rewarding herself with more candy. The more harsh her self-punishment, the more she'll crave a break from it, which she achieves in part by consuming candy. And so the cycle continues—before which she continues to both cringe and feel some relief (perhaps at the same time)—even as she protests that she's "trying" to cut back on her candy intake.

When we're immersed in guilt, we don't take responsibility for what we're doing but instead indulge in blaming ourselves, giving our inner critic total permission to flay us. (We may parallel this habit by blaming others for our misdeeds, perhaps even acting out this way to get back at them.) Responsibility is a self-empowering dynamic that fuels fitting action; any stabs that we, in our guilt, make at taking responsibility fall short, sabotaged by our underlying investment in changing nothing. Guilt's mantra is "I'm *trying.*" In other words, "I'm not really going to do it."

Try to pick up the pen or paper or cup in front of you. If you actually do pick it up, put it back down, for I didn't say to pick it up, I said to *try* to pick it up. Trying is inherently impotent, featuring the intentionality of only a *part* of us, along with an unacknowledged oppositional intention. To say we're trying to do something—and to say we feel guilty about something—is a confession of being so divided about it that we're probably going to leave it as it is. (And we may also say that we're trying when we fear that we won't follow through.)

Guilt can easily masquerade as our conscience.

The *self*-accusations that characterize guilt carry the same mean-spiritedness as the *other*-accusations of resentment. In resentment, we are busy dragging others down; in guilt, we are busy dragging ourselves down, nailing ourselves with enough condemnation to keep ourselves down. Resentment is just as heartless as guilt. Whereas guilt is an amalgam of shame and fear, resentment is an amalgam of shame and aggression—along with a sizeable dose of entitlement. Turn resentment inside out, and you'll get something like guilt. And vice versa.

Guilt is a kind of emotional incarceration. In it, we are repeat offenders, always found guilty, always about to be punished, lost in a courtroom drama in which we play both accused and prosecutor, repeatedly finding relief from our entrapment through redoing whatever justified our imprisonment in the first place. There's no compassion, no love, no real release.

Guilt means we don't have to grow up.

WORKING WITH GUILT

To effectively deal with guilt, we need to step back far enough to witness not only its operational dynamics, but also the shame and fear that constitute it. Also, it's crucial when working with our guilt to approach it with an open heart, setting aside any kind of moral righteousness. Feeling guilty about having guilt won't help!

Let's begin by considering the difference between guilt and healthy shame. When shame is experienced in its healthy state, it initially contracts us, obstructing our forward momentum. Then, once we've stopped our shame-producing behavior and registered what our conscience says, the contractedness within loosens, especially when our intention to take fitting action takes over. So if we've hurt someone, our remorse finds no obstacle to being openly expressed. There is healing movement. Our entire being becomes aligned with a consciously felt responsibility for our slippage. We have not let our shame morph into aggression or withdrawal, but have stayed with it, and now we're coming clean, healing, resolving, taking action.

By contrast, in guilt we're not truly interested in healing. Most of our energy is committed to the internalized child-parent (or adolescent-parent) conflict that allows us to indulge in doing "it"—whatever we "shouldn't" be doing—and to justify continuing to do "it," we have to keep the threat of parental punishment (from ourselves or from others) hanging over our heads, so that we can, in a sense, "wipe the slate clean" after our misdeed.

To work with your guilt, bring as much attention as possible to the shame that has become locked into guilt's framework. Stay with that shame, exploring it and your history with it, approaching the shamed you with as much compassion as you can. Don't let your inner critic trespass here. As you do this work, you will feel the childish side of guilt fleshing out more. Embrace that side and protect it, just as you would a shamed, frightened child.

Practice

WORKING WITH THE SHAME IN GUILT

Think of something you feel guilty about. Close your eyes and breathe in the feeling of your guilt, focusing as closely as possible on the details of whatever it is you feel guilty about. Instead of putting yourself down for your "misdeed," simply feel the raw shame of it, letting your body assume whatever position best fits or expresses this feeling. Stay with this for a few minutes.

Now pick up a small pillow and hold it against your heart and solar plexus with both hands. Keep your eyes closed. Imagine that the pillow is the shamed you when you were a child. Embrace that little one with a compassion at once tender and protective. You are not excusing the "misdeed," but are simply giving what is shamed in you room to breathe, open, and be present—and keeping it from "freezing" into guilt. Stay with this for a few minutes, then do the practice in the appendix.

FEAR IS PART OF GUILT

As was mentioned, fear is an ingredient of guilt, manifesting as the contractedness and anticipated self-punishment of guilt. Such fear may not appear very strong, as it often shows up flattened or deintensified by the shame in guilt, but it does nonetheless have quite a grip. Once we've isolated the shame in guilt, we can bring its fear into clearer focus and then work directly with that fear.

Here's an example: Bill quit smoking a year ago much to his partner's delight, but he has now resumed smoking in secret. Thus far his partner has not detected this. He feels very guilty about his smoking and about his secrecy regarding it. Right before he smokes he feels shame, but as soon as he's smoking he feels some relief from that shame—and also from the fear of being caught, the fear of what his partner might do upon discovering that he is smoking. Bill's fear of being found out is both unpleasant and exciting; it actually increases his desire to smoke. In this, he plays "bad" child, turning his partner into a potentially punishing parent.

Practice

WORKING WITH THE FEAR IN GUILT

Do the preceding practice, "Working with the Shame in Guilt" on page 192, isolating the shame within guilt and compassionately connecting with the shamed you. Give this as much time as you need.

Now recall the anticipated feeling of what was coming your way while you were immersed in your "misdeed." Let yourself feel the fear of that soon-to-arrive punishment: the harsh words, the condemnation, the lovelessness. It's as if you are in a dream that is shifting into a nightmare. Keep your eyes closed. Now imagine that the pillow you're holding against your heart and solar plexus is a frightened child, a child already hyperalert to the arrival of something unpleasant. Embrace that child, that frightened locus of helplessness, with a compassion simultaneously tender and protective. Breathe fully and slowly, expanding yourself, giving your fear the room to expand beyond itself, releasing it bit by bit from guilt's employ.

Once you've isolated the components of guilt—having identified the shame and fear therein—you've reached the heart of guilt. To cease automatically going back and forth between the parental and childish/ adolescent sides of guilt, you need to first recognize that neither side is you, that both take turns masquerading as you. They are but rigidly polarized personifications of guilt's script. Instead of identifying with either side, stand where you can see both at the same time, as detailed in the next practice.

Practice

WORKING WITH BOTH SIDES OF GUILT

Put three pillows on the floor in a triangle, each equidistant from the other two. Place them about a yard apart from each other. Sit on one pillow, imagining that it is the child side of guilt, and face another pillow, imagining that it is the parental/ punishing side of guilt. Speak as the child to the parent. As much as possible, talk spontaneously and animatedly, doing your best to hold nothing back. Do this for a half-minute or so, then switch to the parental/punishing pillow and face the child pillow. Immediately respond back to the child pillow, spontaneously and with obvious animation, doing your best to hold nothing back. Do this for about a half-minute, then switch back to the other pillow.

For a few minutes, move back and forth between these pillows, switching when it feels right to do so. Keep the dialogue vital; if you want to get noisy, do so. If the energy starts to slip, get more dramatic. What you're doing is making the relationship between the two sides of guilt more explicit.

Now sit on the third pillow, facing the other two. Breathe more deeply. Gaze at the child pillow, feeling what it represents as fully as you can without, however, identifying with it. Do this for a minute or so. Now do the same with the parental/punishing pillow. Be aware of each breath you take. Do this for a minute or so.

Now pull the two pillows close enough toward you so that you can put a hand on each. Find a way to do this that is physically comfortable. Imagine/feel their energies coming through your hands and up your arms into your heart. It's as if you are breathing in both at the same time, while feeling their separate energies. Stay conscious of your breathing as you do so.

Stay with this for at least three or four minutes, feeling both sides of guilt with equal compassion, deepening your intimacy with each, not losing yourself in either one. Envision them not going back and forth against each other, but resting more and more in you. It's as if they are clouds, and you are their sky.

One gift that guilt can bring us is the opportunity to see the workings and interplay of our childish and parental sides with remarkable clarity. Another gift is the opportunity to embrace a truly healthy shame, a shame that does not shy away from remorse and healing action. Working with our guilt helps us grow up, making us all but incapable of betraying ourselves or giving away our power, helping root us in our natural integrity and wholeness of being.

To not be split internally begins with seeing where we are thus split, and there is perhaps no better indicator of such internal divisiveness than guilt. Becoming intimate with our guilt liberates us from its programs, leaving us more whole, more able to make wise use of our shame, more able to take good care of all that we are and all of our relationships.

17

Depression

A Pain That's a Solution to a Deeper Pain

Depression keeps us under the covers but gives us no real rest.

THOUGH DEPRESSION IS NOT AN emotion per se, it is so common and so commonly associated with sadness, distress, and emotional collapse that it's important to be well acquainted with it. Depression is not so much a feeling as it is a suppression of feeling, a literal pressing-down of feeling—but it is not a *full* suppression, regardless of its degree of numbness. As much as we may feel weighed down or burdened or crushed by depression, we nonetheless feel such pressing-down, unmistakably registering its discomfort and how it leaves us feeling drained, sapped, enervated.

One could say that depression is the felt sense of not-quite-successful emotional repression. As much as our shutting-down flattens us emotionally, it still leaves us feeling wretched enough to darken even the brightest day. Depression, except at its mildest, is a kind of hell and at the same time is a "solution" to a deeper hell, keeping us significantly removed from having to openly feel and be with what is really hurting us.

If the pressing-down is massive enough—and such weightedness may be far from volitional—we will feel immobilized, sometimes debilitatingly so, pinned to the spot like a moth in a museum display. Depression can be that deadening, our wings but petrified dust.

Depression is often explained away as "a chemical imbalance." There is, however, no conclusive evidence of this, though it may be that antidepressant medications themselves cause neurochemical disturbances in the brain, which ease short-term symptoms but create a health-worsening addiction to such pharmaceuticals in the long term. Unfortunately, most depression is looked at in the context of such biological reductionism, with far too little attention given to its possible originating factors. It is, of course, much easier to give those suffering from apparent depression some pharmaceutical aid than to actually help them explore—and not only cognitively—the roots of their depression.

We all get depressed from time to time; circumstances sometimes knock us hard, flattening us for a bit. We feel down, blue, unmotivated— but we are still able to function. We may skip a few workouts, complain more than usual, or feel unhappy, but we know our mood will shift before too long. This is everyday depression, a dark and rainy day when we'd like to crawl back into bed and stay there for a long while, but still manage to get the basics done.

Once we've developed some intimacy with depression, we may find that we even can, in a certain sense, enjoy our time in it, looking through its relatively unhappy, sobering eyes at the world and ourselves in a way that deepens us. At such times I like to write, go for a workout, or meditate. Sitting with depression can be fascinating: sensing the layers of it, the sadness and departure from positivity; feeling through it into our existential condition with an awareness of our mortality close at hand.

And there is a darker, more insidious depression, one that doesn't just knock us hard but flattens us with such force that we stay down, finding it so difficult to get up that we all but lose the will to do so. Such heavy-duty depressiveness may be situational—as when someone very close to us has unexpectedly died and our shock is so great that we cannot cry. And it may be already in our system, "wired" there from long-ago circumstances. This kind of depression requires strong intervention; unfortunately, this is often limited to medication, frequently accompanied by the assertion that we'll have to be on it for life. Medication is sometimes required, ideally serving as a kind of crutch while we develop other resources through psychotherapeutic, meditative, physical, and dietary means. Once there has been some healing and reassertion of will, to the point where we can stand with some strength, then we can start weaning ourselves from our crutches, being grateful that they were there when we needed them.

When we fall into a deeper-than-usual depression, but not one that's truly debilitating, it's helpful to ask investigative questions such as: What had to be depressed in our early years so that we could survive or cope? Why? What did we have to shut down then? What was happening that necessitated this? How was such a pressing-down or shutting-down activated?

Investigating the dynamics and originating factors of our depression doesn't require years of psychoanalysis or other cognicentric therapies; a few sessions with a psychotherapist who knows how to work deeply with emotions will in almost all cases illuminate the roots of what happened—and how that connects with what is happening *now*—pointing the way to dealing with the roots of our depression in a manner uniquely suited to us: ongoing psychotherapy, exercise programs, meditative practices, dietary balance, and so on. This takes a lot more time and investment of attention and energy than filling out a depression inventory for a psychiatrist, but it's actually far more cost-effective in the long run.

For example, when Kevin was young, he was shamed by his mother, who repeatedly told him he was stupid and worthless. She often told him she wished he'd never been born. Kevin's father did nothing, setting an example for his son that he should simply take whatever his mother said. No matter what Kevin did, his mother continued to shame him, making no effort to disguise her disgust for him. Kevin, of course, assumed all this was his own fault. He survived her belittlement by shutting down, literally depressing himself. This wasn't something Kevin did consciously; nevertheless it became his default whenever he felt shamed by others or by himself (in the form of an inner-critic onslaught)—until he began working with a psychotherapist well-versed in connecting past and present in more than just intellectual ways.

There can also be biological—but not genetic—reasons for depression. During Carrie's birth, she suffered serious oxygen deprivation, registering this as a life-or-death situation: pure physiological panic. To survive, Carrie's whole system had to slam on the brakes; her vital functions had to be depressed to conserve her energy for the emergency. This literally wired her to shift into a depressed state—so as to contain her agitation—whenever she was in a sufficiently stressful situation, especially ones that "took her breath away."

As such, depression is a pain that walls off—or keeps under wraps—a deeper pain. Such repression may initially work (it *does* actually distance us from our core pain), but it consumes so much life energy that before long we're depleted,' run down, discouraged, further depressed. At best, depression helps us to lay low—and sometimes this is exactly what we need to do—but mostly it just exhausts us, as if we were back in the original circumstances that first necessitated it.

Depression is inherently draining. It keeps us under the bedcovers but gives us no real rest. A telling job description for it might be the "wretchedly insomniac gatekeeper of incarcerated pain or trauma." Depression's dreams are ones of hopelessness and meaninglessness. Our mindset during depression can easily reinforce our energetic flattening—we're in enough of a weakened state to sit passively before our inner critic's accusations, letting despair and thoughts of giving up occupy us.

Ordinary depression—which stops short of malignant despair or debilitating exhaustion—can provide us with a certain sense of security, a predictable and reliable weighting-down that generates an admittedly miserable yet also reassuring sensation of being anchored or settled, at least at some level. We may not be on truly solid ground, but at least we're not adrift in uncharted waters. Not surprisingly, we tend to prefer the burdened beasts of depression to the monsters of the deep.

But if we descend through the caves of our depression, entering what is walled off or buried, we find ourselves in the territory of our core or primal wounds. As scary as this is—and as important as it is to explore what's here consciously, caringly, and at the right pace—it is not depressing! The Minotaur (the mythic personification of our bottom-line fear) awaits us, its face none other than ours, our upcoming encounter with it readying us for a deeper wholeness. What our depression is "protecting" us from is precisely what we will need to face sooner or later; it is *not* something to be drugged, smothered, ignored, abstracted, or thrown into a dungeon, but something to unguardedly feel, something to cultivate intimacy with—and this begins with knowing our depression so well that we can reach *through* it.

Despite its flatness and capacity to dull our vitality, depression is an agitated state. If we are weakened enough, such agitation (usually presenting itself as a muffled, tightly corseted anxiety) may surface—easily running through us because we don't have the energy to push it back down—occupying our mind with dark thoughts and intentions, which only further depress us. Hence the importance of staying alert to the state of our mind when we're depressed, as we can through grounded meditative practices (see the appendix).

Depression is miserable in part because we're aware that it's a repression-centered state. It's very easy to indulge in. In a way, depression legitimizes our passivity; we can get away with grumbling about our discomfort and alienation from ourselves—without having to do anything about such states.

Depression is also a kind of numbness, lethargically and reluctantly facing its reflection in its stagnant waters. But when we look below the surface, we start to see and feel our core pain and unresolved wounds looking back at us. Then we begin to realize that in our depressiveness we've been treating such pain as an alien, a pathogen, something we are *allergic* to.

Depression, whether personal or collective, can easily slip into a toxic sulk, excessive passivity, or apathy. Depression says, "What can I do? It's no use," and its underlying agitation/hurt says, "I have to get out of here!" Quiet desperation and frenzied desperation, together reinforcing the trap. Or, depression can be used as a springboard into our depths, carrying us into the heartland of what really matters. It can be a doorway into what has generated it.

WORKING WITH DEPRESSION

The first step is to name it. Simply say "depression" to yourself a couple of times. Do your best not to say it in a depressing tone. Second, turn toward it. Face it. This is a movement through awareness, not through space—a shift from here to a deeper here.

Third, closely examine depression's various qualities: its texture, its density, its sense of color and shape, its directionality. Take your time with each of these, letting yourself be as curious as possible. Consider, for example, its directionality. This—its felt sense of movement—is very likely inward, a curling-into, a gravity-laden internal sinking, a withdrawal. You may think of yourself as down and out, but it is more accurate to say that you are "down and in." Keep your attention on this movement, noticing how it changes. Follow it without losing yourself in it.

Fourth, identify the sadness, hurt, and fear (and perhaps also shame and anger) in/under your depressiveness, taking time to feel and breathe into each. Finally, bring more attention to what underlies your depression—psychotherapeutic help is especially valuable here. As you do so, you will likely experience some very deep feelings, perhaps sensing yourself at a much earlier age. Approaching this can be a very vulnerable undertaking, so proceed only at a pace that allows you to remain present and relatively grounded.

Practice

WORKING WITH DEPRESSION

Next time you feel depressed, sit down with it and bring your attention to your breathing, doing nothing to alter it or your posture. Instead of trying to get away from your depression, sense yourself moving a little closer to it, even as you remain aware of the arrival and departure of each breath. Do this for a few minutes, then shift most of your attention to your mind, noticing what is happening there, both with regard to content and energy. What are you telling yourself? What are you deciding about yourself? How seriously are you taking this? What is the general feeling of such thoughts? What is the felt quality of your mind?

Ask these questions at least two or three times, keeping some attention on your breathing as you make room for answers. Do none of this to get rid of or evade your depression. Have the sense that you are sitting in your living room with an unpleasant guest whom you need to get to know better, regardless of your discomfort. Stay with this for a few minutes, then slowly raise your sternum and deepen your breathing, as if to give your depression more room in which to stretch and move.

Stand up, plant your feet firmly, bend your knees slightly, and start letting your body shake, gently at first. Keep your feet in place, allowing yourself to move like a tree in a strong but not too-strong wind. Shake out your hands and wrists harder, and now your shoulders, and now your knees and hips, still keeping your feet in place. Let your mouth open, allowing your face to shake. And your head and neck. Let your entire body shake, without any effort to do so smoothly or rhythmically. Shake as though no one is watching. Do this for two or three minutes, breathing deeply and letting your whole body loosen up. Then stop and stand still for at least a minute or two.

Open your eyes and prepare yourself for whatever aerobic exercise best suits you: jogging, walking, cycling, swimming, elliptical trainer, treadmill, and so on. Begin exercising as soon as possible. Finish with the practice in the appendix.

Depression is an energetic bog, a murky pit, a dark and despairing valley that invites our conscious entry, however indirectly. Descend into it, not resisting its gravity, feeling your way along its muddy footing through its undergrowth and dour mindset, wearing your awareness like a miner's headlamp, until you arrive at its heartland. Here there is an abundance of pure feeling, and also a sense of encountering who you were before you were gripped by depression. Do your best to embrace and protect this you, this locus of pure vulnerability and unthinking openness, and learn to stand where depression is no longer depressing.

18

Contempt

Disdainful Dehumanizing

I can be revolted or angered by what you've done
and still feel some genuine caring for you, but if I'm
contemptuous, I don't give a damn about you and don't
give a damn that I don't give a damn about you.

THE LOOK OF CONTEMPT IS unmistakable: the nose and
upper lip contracted up, as if smelling something revolting, and one
corner of the mouth also pulled up. Picture Clint Eastwood in one of
his spaghetti Westerns: his eyes narrowed to slits and his face displaying
pure contempt, as if he could spit on whoever has just displeased him.
Or picture a group of teens ruthlessly bullying a kid, trying to outdo
each other in their sneering disdain for their target.

When we're in the grip of contempt, our targets are always below
us, even if they occupy a higher rung on the social or workplace ladder.
Our nose may be up, but we are looking down it, like it's a gunbarrel with a sighting scope that helps keep the offending person in the
line of fire. Infuse disgust with a sense of moral superiority plus some
degree of anger—especially anger in the form of hostility—and the
result is contempt.

Contempt is a harsh judge, devoid of compassion, no matter how
soft its face might look. It's not as aggressive as hate, nor as bitter as
resentment, but it is just as dehumanizing. When we're caught up in
contempt, we hold ourselves morally above the object of our contempt;
after all, they're unworthy of standing on the same ground as us, are

they not? Those for whom we feel contempt are those for whom we have no respect. And so we, in our contempt for them, treat them not only as lesser than us, but as less than human.

Practice

THE EXPERIENCE OF CONTEMPT

Imagine that you're angry. Make the face of anger, and then add to it the face of disgust, letting both expressions mingle. Now let your face soften a bit while still retaining some of the amalgamated expression of anger and disgust, and imagine that you consider yourself to be morally superior to whoever has angered and disgusted you. Add to this face a slight turning up of one corner of your mouth. Hold this expression for a half minute or so, noticing how you feel.

CONTEMPT AS MORAL CONDESCENSION

In contempt, we are stranded from our heart. Our operational mode is that of having to bring our attention to trash or something similarly distasteful. However smilingly delivered our contempt may be, it simultaneously conveys revulsion and moral condemnation. Ours is then a kangaroo court, with our target not deserving, of course, to have any significant say.

So of what value is contempt? Its presence, if recognized for what it is, can alert us to our dehumanizing tendencies, reminding us that we are estranged from our compassion. Contempt also can alert us to the fact that we're out of healthy relationship with whomever we're feeling contempt toward. If that person is our partner, our contempt signals that our relationship is dangerously close to being over—and may in fact be finished if the contempt between us has gone on for a while.

Research shows that contempt is the greatest single emotional indicator that a relationship is over or on the rocks. And why? Because once we've lost respect for our partner, intimacy with her or him is all but impossible, except in the most superficial ways.

Disgust can coexist with compassion, and so can anger, but contempt cannot. I can be revolted or angered by what you've done and still feel some genuine caring for you, but if I'm contemptuous of you, I don't give a damn about you. In contempt it's easy to say things that can irreparably damage a relationship—both in terms of content and delivery—so when you feel yourself slipping into contemptuous territory with another, name your contempt, and notice your lack of respect for that person, as opposed to your lack of respect for what he or she has done. Notice how tempted you are to express outright disdain for that person; then, without delay, step back just enough to notice your breathing and posture, doing your very best to curb your tongue.

Disgust and anger can be directed at an action, but contempt is directed at a person, always. In contempt there is no significant connection to anything redeeming or healing. We might as well have mercilessly cast our offending person into a pit with no lifeline to anything that might help heal or remedy the situation. Contempt is a cold fuck-you, as calculating as it is cruel—a mix of icy disgust and toxic criticalness.

Where anger shows up as moral fire and shame as moral disturbance, contempt shows up as moral condescension. It is not out for justice (like anger) or remorse (like shame), but for condemnation. If we're on the receiving end of contempt, we're not on trial (as we might be in anger) or on the hot seat (as we might be in shame), but we're already sentenced as if from on high, with no parole. Contempt is resentment in snobbery's garb, finding enough satisfaction in its heartless dismissal of its target to offset any envy it might have toward that person.

WORKING WITH CONTEMPT

The first step in working with contempt is to learn to recognize its signs so that you can catch it before you begin acting it out. When you feel angry at someone, disgusted to whatever degree by something they have done, and feel your judgment or condemnation of them amplifying, you're well on your way toward being contemptuous. All it takes is a firmer closing of your heart and a more ruthless disrespect in your delivery. If you can keep your anger from mutating into aggression, you will not go into contempt. And the same is true if despite your disgust you can avoid dehumanizing the other. It is crucial that we distinguish, and keep distinguishing, between not respecting another's actions and not respecting that person. So in order not to get caught in contempt, it's imperative that we know our anger and disgust—and that we keep our compassionate heart open.

Practice

WORKING WITH CONTEMPT

Put your face in the "posture" of contempt: Wrinkle your nose and lift your upper lip as if you're smelling something disgusting. Let your whole face shift into the look of disgust— then lift up one corner of your mouth like you're smiling only with that part of your face. This is the sneer of disdain. Hold this, positioning your body so that it supports, or is aligned with, your facial expression, then bring to mind someone for whom you have lost or once lost respect. Sense the place in yourself from where you could spit on them. Let your head move in any way that resonates with your contempt; it may turn to one side, tilt, or fall back slightly, or it may hold still.

Imagine looking at this person—the object of your contempt— and finish this incomplete sentence without any hesitation: "My respect for you is _____." And then finish another sentence, again without any hesitation: "You are a_____." Repeat this with more aggression and revulsion, exaggerating the contraction in the upturning of the corner of your mouth, as if you are displaying a certain satisfaction in how you are treating this person.

Stay with this feeling for another minute or two, breathing in your anger and disgust, and breathing out your contempt. Now, doing nothing to alter your posture of contempt, focus more closely on the target of your contempt. Sense this person prior to whatever she or he did that incurred your disrespect; sense how he or she may have moved then, spoke then, felt then. Let yourself get more absorbed in their world. Now imagine that you are that person, still holding your mask of contempt in place. Imagine looking through their eyes at you. What do you see?

Breathe into your heart, breathe in that person, breathe in what they have done that disturbed you—not to excuse what they did, but to humanize them. Feel your display of contempt thinning. Sense its constituent anger and disgust. Divest it of its moral hauteur. Drop any arrogance that remains. Hold the other person accountable for what they did, but do not deny them your compassion. Sense their inner pain and fear, their woundedness, while continuing to hold them accountable. As best you can, stand in their shoes, actively humanizing them. Stay with this for a few minutes, then lie down somewhere comfortable and rest for a while.

Your contempt is a reminder to more fully humanize others—all others. If this does not feel possible (and it may not for a time), do the preceding practice daily for a while. In contempt we not only dehumanize the other, but ourselves as well, marooning ourselves from our heart in the process. So when contempt arises, name it as such and remember that you owe it to yourself not to act it out, nor to let it occupy you.

19

Self-Doubt

Fearfully Myopic Inner Questioning

As simple as this may sound, it works: doubt your doubt.

PERHAPS THE MOST COMMON MEMBER of the fear family is self-doubt. We all worry at times and usually are aware at the time that we are worrying, but we're less likely to know that we're caught up in self-doubt while we're in it. And why? Because self-doubt is so commonplace—and often so low-key—that we frequently don't register its presence. Among the many thoughts occupying our mind, the doubt-oriented ones don't feel all that different than those that are not, at least in their initial arising.

Furthermore, if we don't maintain some awareness of our mind—which doesn't mean *thinking* about it!—we won't have much of a sense of our mental activity, including that which is doubt centered. So self-doubt may not register with us until it has occupied our mind long enough to start showing up in our body as an agitated gut, contracted solar plexus, shut-down heart, shallow breathing, and so on.

Self-doubt is a myopic inner questioning injected with enough agitation and uncertainty to make it a mildly unpleasant state. There's a darkly compelling—and draining—ambiguity to it, which we ordinarily try to think our way out of, thereby only reinforcing it.

Typical self-doubt is only mildly fearful, nibbling rather than gnawing on us. But if we let it run untended for long enough, it can consume us. And it can slip into anxiety or dread if sufficiently fed. Self-doubt is also quite infectious, seeping into whatever mental content is nearby and framing it in a questionable light.

Self-doubt, if explored, offers us the opportunity to know our mind well, to cut through our identification with our thinking processes, to not allow fearfulness to infiltrate and recruit our mind. All we have to do is turn toward it without buying its messages, allowing whatever's left of its questioning to mutate into a clear-seeing skepticism.

Practice

EXPLORING SELF-DOUBT

Close your eyes. Think of something you're considering doing but have doubts about. Focus on these doubts without any outside perspective until it seems that you don't have them but that they have you. So each step you consider taking coexists with your doubt about taking it. With compelling conviction, your self-doubt keeps you from making any decisive move, other than to stay immersed in your going-nowhere inner questioning.

Stay with this as fully as you can for a few minutes, then shift your attention to your body, especially your chest and belly. What do you sense there? Can you feel any fear? What happens to your self-doubt as you keep your attention focused on your body? How strongly pulled are you to "return" to the cognitive side of your self-doubt? Focus more on the feeling of your self-doubt than on its contents, letting your belly and chest soften as you do so, deepening your awareness of your breathing. Stay with this for a few minutes, then do the practice in the appendix.

WORKING WITH SELF-DOUBT

Do we get caught up in self-doubt's sinking vortex? Do we try to operate from within its cognitive framework? Our challenge is to withdraw our attention from the messages of our self-doubt, not letting ourselves get so absorbed in it that we make decisions based on its input. Instead of adapting to its endarkened headquarters, we can step back enough to illuminate it and bring it out into the open.

The first step to working with self-doubt is to realize that a merely mental approach won't really work. We can think positively, affirming all kinds of wonderful things about ourselves, but in so doing we are doing little more than distracting ourselves from the less-than-positive aspects of our thinking processes. As soon as we let down our positive-thinking guard, our self-doubt reasserts itself, making it clear that it never really went anywhere—if our self-doubt could speak, it would probably say something like: "Wherever you go, there I am."

The clue here is to cease trying to get away from our self-doubt and to journey into it without losing ourselves. This means that we must deeply attune ourselves to the actual feeling of it while not letting its contents distract us. Within self-doubt is an abundance of cognitive entanglement, an easily entrapping complexity strewn with the debris of stalemated internal debating—so it's best to proceed without giving much attention to the mental details of our self-doubt. As we do so, we'll be able to deepen our focus on the actual feeling of our self-doubt, both as a fearfulness in our torso and as a sense of cranial congestion.

Practice

WORKING WITH SELF-DOUBT

Do this exercise when self-doubt is present. Close your eyes. For a minute or so, allow yourself to be wrapped up in your self-doubt, letting all its details and concerns and back-and-forths have your full attention. Now pull back a little, and notice the feeling tone of your self-doubt. If you were to draw it, what might you draw? If it had color, what might that be? How does it sound? What is its texture? What is happening to the topic of concern as you pay more attention to the energetic characteristics of your self-doubt?

Notice your breathing. Deepen it slightly. Still feeling into the presence of self-doubt "upstairs" (behind your forehead), bring your attention to your chest, feeling both the surface and depths of it, registering the sensations there. Is there any discomfort, any tingling, any electricity, any edginess? And also register whatever emotional presence is there. When you zero in on the fear there, stay with it, breathing just deep enough to give that fear a slightly larger "container."

Keeping some awareness in your chest, drop your attention to your solar plexus and belly, paying attention to them just as you did with your chest. What happens to your mind as you do so? What do you notice about your self-doubt? For a moment, focus on your topic of concern, and notice if any intuition about it arises. Make no effort now to think your way through your self-doubt—simply remain attentive to your bodily sensations, making room for the emergence of a truer response than that of more self-doubt.

DOUBTING YOUR DOUBT

One of the key components of working with self-doubt is to engage in the practice of doubting your doubt. This may sound odd at first, but when the doubting mind is turned back on itself, the machinations of doubt tend to come to a grinding halt. The very act of remembering to doubt our doubt gives us some distance from doubt, along with the impetus to question whatever our doubt may be telling us. Doing so usually brings a sudden spaciousness to the mind and opens us energetically. So instead of just doubting ourselves, we're making more room for ourselves in which to function.

When self-doubt does infiltrate and occupy you—when you feel driven to stay in self-doubt's domain—read its headlines the same way you would the headlines of a supermarket tabloid that has grabbed your curiosity as you wait in a long line. Don't get into the stories and their details; simply stay with the headlines. Enlarge them in your imagination, exaggerating their importance. Do this for no more than a minute, then shift your attention to the *feeling* of your self-doubt, and keep it there as much as you can. Imagine that you are now out of the supermarket; you could go back and read the tabloid some more, but you're already on your way somewhere else.

When you take your thinking mind out of self-doubt, you'll find that all that's left is fear—a mild fear that can be worked with like any other fear. The key is to actively and decisively *not identify* with our self-doubt.

Practice

CUTTING THROUGH SELF-DOUBT'S CONTENT

Do this exercise when you're caught up in doubt and your partner or a close friend can be with you. Sit facing that person. Breathe a bit more deeply, and act as if you *are* your doubt, speaking spontaneously and freely, exaggerating your delivery. Don't worry about your content; be dramatic! Do this for a couple of minutes. If you run out of steam, repeat yourself, improvise, trying to be as convincing as possible.

Now keep letting your doubt express itself, but in no known language—speak in nonstop gibberish, amplifying the volume a bit, doing your best to express your doubt this way. Let yourself be outrageous in this! Speak thus for a few minutes, then be silent. Soften your belly and eyes, keeping some awareness on your breathing. Let a minute or so pass, then speak *to* your doubt as if it's an actual entity, allowing yourself to feel as much compassion as possible for it. Give this several minutes, then settle back, resting in your contact with your partner or friend.

When you cut through your self-doubt, whatever remains won't be worrisome inner questioning, but gems of insight, intuition, a sense of direction unpolluted by the obsessive pro-and-con arguments of self-doubt.

20

Paranoia

Fear-Driven Delusion

> The contracted electricity of bare fear holding
> us hostage with the highlighted certainty of dire
> possibility—this is unattended paranoia.

SOME FEARS ARE SOCIALLY ACCEPTABLE—like worry—and some are not socially acceptable. Like paranoia. Most of us can readily admit when we're worried, but few of us can readily admit that we're being paranoid. (Sometimes, of course, we don't realize we're being paranoid.) Usually, those who worry are not ashamed of doing so—they may even consider it a virtue—but many who feel paranoia are embarrassed about it, as if it indicates a failure on their part, a certain defectiveness. When we're worried, we generally let our worry show, but when we're paranoid, we usually attempt to hide it, masking it as best we can.

Like self-doubt and worry, paranoia is fear that has gone to the mind. Where self-doubt and worry peer at the precipice from quite a distance, paranoia teeters right at the edge, flirting not with uncertainty—like self-doubt or anxiety—but with *certainty*, however bizarre the reasoning might be.

Paranoia is the fear-infested mind doing time in windowless cells of hellish possibility that threaten to shift from possibility to probability to literal reality at any moment. No wonder we feel so edgy when our paranoia shows up!

And let us not forget that paranoia can arise in all of us, however much we might think it is something that happens only to the mentally unstable or to those taking certain drugs. The dark certainty of para-noia may last only a few seconds, or it may insinuate its way into a fuller occupancy of us when we are destabilized—as when we start to suspect that our partner is cheating on us but have no tangible proof whatsoever, yet we let our suspicion fester and multiply.

If we're thinking paranoid thoughts yet are aware that we're doing so, and realize that they're but thoughts, we're still sane—however infused with unpleasant feeling those paranoid thoughts may be. We're possibly disturbed, fearful for sure, but not insane.

However, if we're thinking paranoid thoughts and cannot step back from them enough to know that we're in fact merely *thinking* them, our capacity for clear self-reflection has become absent or crippled. That's when we have entered insanity's territory, regardless of our periods of sanity. Insanity doesn't necessarily mean the absence of sanity, but rather too little anchoring time spent in basic sanity.

If you know that you're paranoid and can openly admit it, the odds are that you'll be able to work with it effectively in psychotherapeutic and spiritual contexts. But if you're paranoid and don't know that you're paranoid—or refuse to admit it—then the odds are that you cannot be worked with very successfully, any more than a religious fundamentalist can be persuaded that his or her certainties may not be so certain.

Practice

BRINGING COMPASSION TO PARANOIA

This following practice addresses the everyday paranoia that all of us have felt at some point. Note: Don't do this practice if you're suffering from serious paranoia and are not under the care of a qualified professional. (Serious paranoia is something that overwhelms you or that you take as conveying literal truth.)

Sit with your eyes closed, and recall a time when you felt paranoia. Perhaps it was when a relationship started to derail or when you got overly absorbed in a conspiracy theory or when you smoked pot, or perhaps it arose with no apparent cause. If you cannot remember having felt paranoia, imagine feeling it now, thinking of something you dread that seems unlikely to occur suddenly seeming extremely likely to occur, despite the absence of any outward signs supporting this. Go over and over the details of this for a few minutes and then open your eyes, letting your gaze slowly go from side to side, as if trying to see something at the extreme corners of your vision.

After a minute or so of this, relax your eyes and jaw, and bring your full awareness to your belly. Breathe more deeply. Keep withdrawing your attention from the content of your thoughts. Breathe more into your chest, putting your hands there, imagining bringing the paranoid you into your heart. Notice how old he or she feels. Have a sense of both cradling and protecting this one, letting your compassion soften and stabilize you. Stay with this as long as you want. Finish with the practice in the appendix.

SELF, SANITY, AND PARANOIA

The ability to hold two or more perspectives in mind while remaining embodied and relatively intimate with each of them is a hallmark of sanity. In paranoia we lose this ability, locking ourselves up in a mono-focused, disembodied fearfulness. If we do sense another perspective, we don't really open to it; we just view it through the lens of our paranoia. (This is also true of worry and self-doubt, but in paranoia we are much more fanatic about what we believe.)

As much as we might like to think of ourselves as a sentient single-ness or an intact "me," each of us is more of a community—or even mob!—of "me's," an internalized collective of personified habits, every one of which, when given center stage, tends to refer to itself as "I." Each of these pretenders to the throne of self—some of which are birthed from deep wounding—possesses *and* is possessed by its own unique perspective, which needs to be recognized and known well but not allowed to assume the role of overseer or master.

In becoming intimate with each of these apparent selves that consti-tute us—and with their perspective—we become increasingly capable of not identifying with any one of them. So paranoia may still arise for us, but we don't let it get behind the wheel. Instead we let it rest in the backseat, keep a compassionate eye on it, and stay attuned to its ener-getic presence rather than to its patter.

Real sanity is about recognizing and taking good care of *all* that we are, without letting any one aspect of us take over the others; this means maintaining a functionally fitting position for each aspect of ourselves, in the spirit of a parent who dearly loves his or her child. Keeping our habits where we can clearly see them is an essential practice in our maturation. To journey into our paranoia without getting significantly paranoid is basic sanity in the courageous crunch.

CULTIVATING INTIMACY WITH OUR PARANOIA

Journeying—at the right time and at an optimal pace—into something as challenging as paranoia without having to know what's going to happen once we're "there" is real freedom in the making. The way toward a deeper sanity is not that of rising above, marginalizing, or otherwise avoiding our scary states—and paranoia can be *very* scary—but rather that of entering and passing *through* them, step by conscious step, cultivating intimacy with them and letting whatever arises, however frightening, awaken us to who and what we really are.

Let us touch our paranoia with tenderness and presence, entering it until it is but the contracted electricity of bare fear trying to hold us hostage with the certainty of dire possibility—and then not even that, but only primal aliveness, now energetically available for something other than the hallucinogenic certitude of paranoia.

When we thus relate to our paranoia rather than from it, we feel our way past its contents and dark edginess into its core of heightened sensitivity until it is nothing more than exquisitely responsive attunement to whatever is arising.

Paranoia can be an entry point into what lies prior to and beyond all fear. All we have to do is move toward it when it arises, however counterintuitive that might seem at the time, while opening ourselves to whatever assistance we might need in order to do so. Each step thus taken, however small or halting, reinforces and deepens our basic sanity, giving us much of the ground we need for living a deeper life—a life unburdened by paranoia's programs.

21

Jealousy

Heart-Stabbing Rejection

Jealousy can be an extremely uncomfortable visitor, darkly aflame and massively disrupting our lives, but it is worth sitting down with and getting to know very well.

OF ALL THE EMOTIONS THAT we find painful, jealousy is probably the one that stabs most sharply. Though it can be subtle, a faintly stabbing flicker—as when first picking up the scent of possible betrayal—jealousy usually is painfully obvious and impactful to a sometimes overwhelming degree. It easily cuts us to the core, especially when there's been a completely unexpected, major betrayal. We may feel as if we've been stabbed in the back as well as the heart. If we could speak at such times, we'd probably say we'd been violated. This can, of course, be done extremely dramatically—featuring us as a larger-than-life victim—but it also can be just industrial strength heart-hurt devoid of drama. Pure agony.

Jealousy is a painfully consuming reaction to—and also a compelling dramatization of—being rejected or replaced, whether this is real or imagined. There's nothing furtive about jealousy; at its peak, its heart-shredding anguish surges through us with riptide intensity, impaling us on its moral outrage. It can be devastatingly intense—it's as if we have been slammed in our chest with a sharply spiked wrecking ball. If the jealousy-catalyzing blow is powerful enough, we may go to pieces initially, carried by our pain and disbelief—and shock—in multiple directions, with no one at the helm. In the midst of such upset, we may find ourselves considering doing things we never thought we were capable of, ricocheting between numbness and excruciating hurt.

When jealousy possesses us, we may behave badly: getting destructive, making incredibly rash decisions, losing ourselves in massive melodrama. Jealousy can be like that. Crazily consuming. Plates flying, loved objects destroyed, accusations barbed with poisonous intent, physical violence, damage done that cannot be repaired. A mean-spirited mix of twisted anger and exaggerated hurt up on a righteous soapbox. It's not hard for jealousy to stray into such toxic territory. No wonder so many view jealousy as a negative emotion.

So what's it like when we handle our jealousy well? We stay vulnerable in it, we don't take its thoughts and intentions as living truth, and we don't dehumanize the other, no matter how furious we are at them. When working with our jealousy in a healthy manner, we do no damage, holding it as we would a child who is overwhelmed with both pain and the certainty that she or he has been treated unfairly. We may rage, we may sob, we may feel ravaged, but we don't lose touch with our core of being for any significant length of time. We do not, in short, let our jealousy possess us.

Given how exceedingly painful jealousy can be—as anyone who has writhed in its grip knows all too well—most of us strive not to provide fertile conditions for it. Nevertheless, jealousy may still manage to sprout up—green, not from a sun-embracing reach, but from a dark and sometimes venomous force.

However, jealousy is not an inherently unwholesome, negative, or inappropriate feeling. If we discover that our partner has been cheating on us, jealousy is natural—we'll feel a mixture of hurt, anger, resentment, grief, and possibly shock, all of it intensified when we think of our partner with his or her new lover. And we'll probably feel like taking various actions, some of which would only make things worse (like getting violent), and some of which would improve matters (like establishing and maintaining clear boundaries).

However much jealousy hurts and destabilizes us, it can be used to deepen our lives, if we become intimate with it. The slightest threat, groundless or not, of being rejected, replaced, or bumped to less-than-central status by a significant other can trigger jealousy, especially if we're already insecure in our relationship with that person. It may even seem that our very survival is at stake.

One flicker of not trusting an esteemed other in his or her inter-actions with another—especially if we sense we're in danger of being replaced—can set us on the road to jealousy. Of course, sometimes we *are* intuiting something that needs to be addressed—something high-lighted by the arising of our jealousy—but at other times we are just acting out some of our unresolved woundedness (such as being replaced by a younger sibling when we were young), the very presence of which may be obscured by our absorption in our jealousy. This is why we need to learn to step back a little from our jealousy so as to bring it into clearer focus, to make sure that it is not simply a playing-out of our condition-ing, our unresolved fears.

HOW JEALOUSY CAN MANIFEST

Jealousy can manifest in many ways, ranging from a subtly gnawing sense of being rejected or replaced (even if the other keeps reassuring us that they love us and would never leave us), to a burning certainty that we are being betrayed, to an over-the-top fury and vengefulness that runs through us with acid ease.

We may talk of jealousy as though it were a single emotion like anger or fear, but it is in fact a compound emotion, mixing together anger (moral upset), grief (*very* impactful loss), and anguish (deep-cutting aching), along with usually at least some degree of resentment and shame. Sometimes the anger is in the foreground, sometimes grief, sometimes anguish—but they are all present in jealousy's cauldron, stirred to overflowing by an achingly real sense of being unwanted or cast aside, replaced, or rejected.

More often than not, jealousy features a compulsive drive to blame our offending other—or our apparently offending other—for what *we* are doing in our jealous state. After all, we might think, if he or she hadn't done what they did, we wouldn't be feeling this way! That may be true, but this attitude relieves us of any accountability for how we're framing and handling our jealousy. That said, it's important that we not downplay or marginalize what is catalyzing our jealousy just because we are not dealing with it very well—because a true betrayal or bound-ary violation may have taken place.

The core message of jealousy cuts to the quick, along the lines of "You don't love me" or "You don't want me" or whatever else implies deep-cutting rejection or betrayal-centered loss. Closely aligned with this message is one that is torture for the jealous: "If you really loved (or wanted) me, you wouldn't be doing this." So the fact that the other *is doing this* eats away at us, claiming most of our attention. And if the other's jealousy-generating doings are indeed unloving, the pain at the heart of our jealousy will only be reinforced and intensified.

As painful as it is to feel unloved or unwanted—or to be loved or wanted in a lukewarm fashion—it is even more painful to know that a significant other is giving to another what we have been yearning to receive. This is the bleeding wound of jealousy, the gut-slam, the heart-piercing agony of in-your-face rejection.

Being rejected or replaced is not easy to deal with, but its degree of difficulty diminishes as we approach our jealousy more skillfully. Unless we avoid all attachment, we still become jealous as we mature, but we will learn to take care of it in ways that serve us. We will still get angry, still get indignant, still get wounded, still shake in disbelief that another could do this to us—but we won't lose touch for long with our core of being. We won't indulge in blaming even as we go for full accountability; we won't slip into aggression or violence; we will stay vulnerable without losing our spine or dignity; we will allow our grief to fully flow. In all this, we're committed to exploring jealousy's realm, going right to its heartland rather than setting up camp somewhere on the outskirts from where we can righteously snipe and gripe.

And we start learning to love when we are not being loved, instead of waiting for the other to come around and love us. So there's no more being held hostage by the hope that the other, the one whose behavior got us jealous, is going to give us what we want. (This does not mean we've forgotten that they have betrayed or rejected us, but that we do our very best not to lose touch with our heart, regardless of our anger and hurt.)

JEALOUSY AND ENVY

Jealousy and envy often get confused. They may feel similar, especially in their contractedness and sense of getting a raw deal, but jealousy is far more of a *moral* emotion than envy. In jealousy, we assume that we have a right to whatever it is that has been or is being taken from us, but in envy we don't make such an assumption. The jealous employee sees his boss giving another employee the very energy and attention that he not only wants but assumes should be his and his alone. On the other hand, the envious employee sees the very same dynamic at play, but does not make the same assumption of entitlement.

In envy we look to those who seem to have what we want but don't have, and we feel impotent or passive about it. In jealousy we look to those who have what we want but don't have (or are apparently losing), and we feel outraged about it. In envy we're not concerned about deserving "it"—whereas in jealousy we are.

Practice

EXPLORING THE ELEMENTS OF JEALOUSY

Think of a time when you felt especially jealous. Close your eyes and recollect as much of that time as possible. Breathe more fully, visualizing yourself then. What do you see? At the peak of your jealousy, what did you tell yourself? What did you do? Imagine yourself there, facing whoever catalyzed your jealousy. Describe to that one what they did to you and the impact that this had on you, speaking with as much feeling as you can. Stay with this for a few minutes.

Now focus solely on the hurt of it, noticing what happens to your chest and your face, especially your brows, cheeks, and lips. How penetrating was that hurt? How deep? How hard did you cry? What were you losing or seeming to lose? Give this a few minutes.

Next, focus solely on the anger of your jealousy memory, noticing what happens to your belly, hands, and face, especially your lower eyelids, jaw, and nostrils. How angry were you? If you had held none of your anger back, what might you have done? What outraged you the most? Give this a few minutes.

Last, focus on the hurt and anger at the same time, letting the sense of being rejected or replaced pervade you. Notice the degree of caring, if any, that you have for yourself as you do this. Stay with this for a minute or so, then imagine you're seeing the jealous you from a slight distance, while at the same time holding that you with compassion. Let your jealousy memory fade until you are simply present with whatever you're feeling.

Given jealousy's power to erode and undermine—and, at the extreme, to destroy—it is extremely important to be able to deal with it skillfully, which begins with knowing it from the inside.

WORKING WITH JEALOUSY

Working with jealousy is not so easy. This is partially because we may be so absorbed in its energies and viewpoint that we have little or no desire to examine it, but mostly it's because jealousy can be so excruciatingly painful. If it already wounds us deeply, getting closer to it—which is essential to effectively working with it—might hurt even more. But if we keep distant from our jealousy, leaving it uninvestigated and therefore free to slip into toxicity, we risk more than if we were to explore it.

A good place to begin, once we have acknowledged that we are indeed feeling jealous, is to ask—and answer—some exploratory questions, about both our current jealousy and how we've handled our jealousy in general. Such questions are presented in the following practice.

Practice

GETTING BETTER ACQUAINTED
WITH OUR JEALOUSY

Read each of the following questions, taking whatever time you need to answer each one (via pen or keyboard). Don't limit yourself to short answers; feel free to expand on what you are saying, considering yourself both currently and historically. Take a couple of conscious breaths before moving on to each new question.

How lost have you gotten in the dramatics of your jealousy?

What have you told yourself that has bound you even more tightly to your jealousy?

Did you ever hate the other for betraying you or casting you
aside, and if so, what did you do with that hate?

Did you feel sorry for yourself?

Did you stay with the slash and burn of your jealousy, or
did you go up in righteous flames, busying yourself with
fantasies of revenge?

Did you throw caution to the proverbial winds and give your
jealousy a megaphone, or did you stew in private bitters?

Do you tend to dissociate from your jealousy, claiming to have
transcended it, or do you tend to sink so far into it that you
are completely possessed by it?

Do you deny that it's happening, plastering nonpossessive
smiles over your pain, or do you submerge yourself in its
reality, forgetting to come up for air?

Do you shame yourself for being jealous?

Do you think that only the immature get jealous?

When you have suspected the other of betraying you, what have
you usually done?

When you have felt jealous because another is getting more
attention than you, what have you done with *your* attention?

What have you done when you've felt jealous and have known
that the other has done nothing whatsoever to warrant
your jealousy?

Don't try to eradicate your jealousy. Don't trash it. Don't shame yourself or let yourself be shamed for having it. Listen to it closely, noticing
what it is conveying beneath all the dramatics. Is your jealousy just

a possessive reactivity rooted in your early history, or is it something more, something that is arranged around an intuition you have—or have been having—about the other?

Turn to face your jealousy, separating the raw feeling of it from its message. Pay closer attention to that feeling, identifying the anger, grief, and anguish in it, noticing the degree of intensity of each. Deepen your breathing as you do so, making more compassionate room for each emotional state. As you do so, keep the message of your jealousy in a peripheral position.

Don't let the message of your jealousy take over your mind. As agonizing and shocking as that message might be, it's best to consider it when you are *with* the feeling of your jealousy rather than reacting to it.

At the same time, don't reject your jealousy. Don't abandon it. Hold the hurt of it the way you'd hold a distraught child. Let the grief of it freely pour through you. And don't let the anger of it turn into overt aggression or violence, even as you make room for its full-out expression.

Practice

HOLDING YOUR JEALOUSY

Close your eyes and do the meditative practice described in the appendix for at least ten or fifteen minutes. Now imagine watching yourself at your most jealous. Remain aware of your breathing. Witness the churning mix of anguish, grief, and anger that is surfacing in the jealous you. Witness the stabbing sense of rejection/replacement, the despair, the sheer hurt of it all. Stay with this for a few minutes, then imagine moving closer to this jealousy-ridden you, breathing in his or her state without getting caught up in its content, bringing as much compassion as possible to your witnessing. Do this for a few minutes. Now move even closer, until you have a palpable sense of holding and making room for this you with great care. Remain with this for as long as you like.

JEALOUSY AND ATTACHMENT

Jealousy is made possible through attachment. What I mean by attachment is a felt sense of connection that bonds us to another or to a particular condition or state. This bond secures us, at best giving us stable ground from which to venture forth: think of young children finding a life-enhancing stability through feeling that they're truly wanted by their parents. Of course, attachment can be mishandled so that its connecting power becomes more bind than bond, but without attachment, we are cut adrift, marooned from intimacy.

Not surprisingly, some of us strive for nonattachment in relationships, perhaps as a way of seeking an end to jealousy—or at least to relational hurt. Without attachment, there would be no jealousy—and there would also be no compassion.

Do not allow yourself to make a problem out of attachment, and beware of teachings that present attachment as a problem, something to be shed or transcended, with the exception, of course, of our attachment to such teachings themselves. It's very easy to get attached to not being attached. Yes, attachment does have pathological possibilities such as addiction, but attachment itself is not necessarily a sign of neurosis or immaturity. We are born with an innate drive to form attachments, beginning with deeply bonding with our mother. Attachment comes with relational intimacy and in fact may deepen as we become truly closer and more vulnerable, even as it simultaneously becomes more transparent. Jealousy doesn't necessarily go away as we mature; we simply handle it more and more skillfully, mining it for whatever nuggets of intuition it might contain.

JEALOUSY AND LOVE

If we are habituated to give love only when we're already being loved and feeling loved, we will be hit especially hard by jealousy. When we *depend* on the ready supply of another's love, the withdrawal or loss or redirection of that love is devastating. Even the imagined threat of such loss can trigger jealousy, injecting us with chronic suspicion, reducing us to part-time sleuths sniffing around for signs of rejection or outright betrayal.

Many relationships are polluted by some degree of this. Perhaps one partner periodically feels a nagging sense of jealousy, assuming that the other is either betraying her or him or is going to, and so keeps a suspicious eye open. The other partner gets busy reassuring the first one, claiming that she or he has nothing to worry about. The mistrust breeds more craving for reassurance, which in turn breeds more mistrust. This can happen whether the jealousy is warranted or not.

It takes great courage to not shut down our heart—or not to keep it shut down—when we're being rejected or replaced. To give the love that we ache to receive in the midst of feeling the pain of dwindling or withdrawn love asks that we leave our comfort zone. This doesn't mean that we ought to be openhearted with those who have betrayed or abandoned us, but that we need not let our jealousy toward them take us down.

When we're gripped by jealousy and torn by the rejection it signals, it's crucial that we not reject ourselves—as can happen when we blame ourselves for the other's turning away from us. We don't have to love our jealousy, but sooner or later we do need to start loving the place in us—vulnerable, dependent, and so, so soft—that is chained and screaming in the black pit of our jealousy.

Finding our heart while we are jealous does not necessarily mean that we won't be angry. If our significant other deliberately incites our jealousy, perhaps to feel a desired sense of control, we might feel for them in their neurotic ritual, but we can also let our anger flame forth by clearly saying "no" to what is being done. And if there has been a major betrayal? Rage is an entirely natural response, and we may have to cut loose with it—skillfully—for a while before we can bring in our heart. We may not reach the domain of wrathful compassion for a bit, but we will reach it if we let our rage flow fully in a noninjurious way while working not to dehumanize our offending other.

When we're jealous it's important to openly admit that we are feeling rejected or unwanted—and it's just as important not to let this feeling balloon out of proportion. There's plenty of hurt in rejection, but when we overfocus on being rejected, we lose touch with its underlying hurt and arguably even reject *that.* And so we might end up doing to ourselves what our jealous-inducing other is apparently doing to us. When we're being truly loving, we do not reject the other, but we may reject—and need to reject—something that the other is *doing.*

Practice

TURNING TOWARD WHAT WE REJECT IN OURSELVES

Think of something that you tend to reject or turn away from in yourself. Closing your eyes, imagine turning toward it. Do you feel resistance to doing this, and if so, how does such resistance manifest? How do you feel as you turn toward whatever it is that you ordinarily reject or turn away from? Stay with this feeling as much as you can for the next minute or two.

Now imagine that what you have turned toward is your jealousy. Sense it as an energy field, noting its shape, texture, color, density, movement. Make your curiosity more central than your aversion. The closer you move toward it, the more clearly you can see it. Keep paying attention to it, watching it the way you'd watch a full-flaming fire in a fireplace in a dark room. Both observe and feel it. Stay with this for three or four minutes, then lie back and let gravity have your body, resting for as long as you like.

Once jealousy is held with compassion—without repression of its essential energies—it eases its defenses, becoming a nonviolent expression of relational hurt and wounding, a heart-opening confession of attachment that has been intensified by rejection. This leaves us no longer bound by the possibility of potential rejection, no longer fearful of getting jealous, which allows us to adopt a nonproblematic orientation toward jealousy.

When jealousy arrives, treat it neither as an enemy nor as an excuse for getting reactive. Separate what is neurotic in it from what is not. Stay present with it until its righteousness ebbs and its vulnerability and hurt are clearly in the open. Jealousy can be a very uncomfortable visitor, darkly aflame and perhaps massively interruptive of our lives, but it is worth sitting down with and getting to know, and know very well.

22

Exultation

Fiery, Elated Affirmation

There's a fieriness to exultation that often carries at least some
signs of anger, especially when it signals a moral triumph.

JUST AS UNPLEASANT OR DISTURBING emotions are not
all the same, pleasant emotions are not all the same. We ordinarily
clearly distinguish between fear, anger, and shame, but we may view joy,
exultation, and ecstasy as just different forms of happiness.

Consider exultation. Is it simply a kind of heightened happiness? Not
necessarily. There's a fieriness to it that often carries at least some signs of
anger, especially when it signals a moral triumph. We commonly see exultation in athletes who have just achieved something extraordinary—the
most recognizable image of this perhaps being a fist-pumping, full-bodied
explosiveness that's simultaneously uplifting and strongly grounded.

Exultation overflows with pleasure, but it's far from mellow. It's not
at all modest or burdened by self-consciousness. In it there's a sense of
deep uncoiling, a surging forth, a full-blooded "yes!" Exultation is an
amalgam of joy, immense relief/release, and often some degree of anger,
featuring a pumped-up intensity and a hugely expansive openness. Its
smile is not the smile that masks anger (as in boxers who act as if the
blow they just received didn't hurt), but a smile of unabashed triumph.

Whatever anger exists within exultation is not out to attack but to
emphatically *affirm*. Its voice, however explosive and impassioned, blends
with that of pure joy in a shout from our entire being that says YES!!

We could call exultation fierce joy, fiery joy, joy that dynamically celebrates our having arrived somewhere highly significant. Our feet may stomp, our body may pulse with pleasure, our fisted arm may powerfully pump. I think of tennis legend Jimmy Connors at the US Open at the end of his career, passionately pacing around the court after each improbable winning rally against a much younger opponent, the crowd a thrilled extension of his obvious exultation.

Exultation affirms what we have achieved, with great force and openness. It cannot be kept in, and we don't care about keeping it in—we are not at all embarrassed by our display. In exultation, heart and belly function as one.

Practice

THE EXPERIENCE OF EXULTATION

Think of something you achieved that asked much of you and that took quite a while to reach. A real milestone, a big breakthrough. Perhaps you were quiet or subdued at that time, but imagine now that you don't have to hold back at all.

Stand up, plant your feet firmly with your knees slightly bent, and pump your fists vigorously while letting out a sound that conveys a resoundingly emphatic YES!! to what you achieved. If you feel any self-consciousness, make your movements and sounds even more emphatic. Notice what happens to your jaw, your gaze, your chest as you do so. In all this, what is the message you are conveying?

Exultation is strongly body-centered; there is nothing spacy or ethereal about it, despite its sense of elevation. If we are standing, our stance is powerful, rooted, and vibrantly expansive; if we are lying down, our stance is equally powerful, perhaps spread-eagled on the ground with arms and face spread wide.

We are not so much "beside" ourselves with joy as we are explosively emanating from ourselves. Our whole body is hugely smiling. Exult in your capacity to exult. The "yes" it expresses is good medicine for us, an expansive upsurge of affirmation that serves our entire being.

23

Schadenfreude

Finding Joy in the Misfortune of Others

THERE'S A VERY COMMON EMOTION for which there's no word in English (other than perhaps the extremely obscure *epicaricacy*), an emotion that is all about deriving pleasure from others' misfortune or suffering, especially when we think that they deserve it. This may not be the kind of emotion that we readily admit to having, but who among us hasn't felt it to at least some degree?

When people who have done us harm or committed a crime are obviously suffering—having been "brought to justice"—we may feel justified in taking pleasure at their downfall and might even do so publicly. At other times, however, we may feel the same kind of pleasure over the suffering of others who have done absolutely nothing to disturb or harm us, nor committed any sort of crime. In this case, we're not inclined to show our pleasure publicly or privately—or even to admit it to ourselves.

German has a word for this emotion: *schadenfreude*. This translates as "harm-joy." Many other languages have a word for it, but not English. We have phrases that hover around or hint at it, phrases that convey some of the feeling of it but usually without the overt pleasure— as if we're embarrassed to admit that we actually feel it and that it can feel good.

For example, we may say, "He had it coming" or "I hope she suffers" or "It was just a matter of time before he fell." These phrases hint at a certain moral satisfaction we might feel upon seeing someone take a spill or go downhill. However, these statements usually do not come very close to indicating any real pleasure. But schadenfreude with a stiff upper lip or impassive countenance is still schadenfreude.

If we think someone deserves to take a fall, we'll not only approve when it happens, but we're likely to take some pleasure in it. This could be called *justified* schadenfreude. There's no malice in it, no sadism, no overt cruelty—just a kind of righteously moral pleasure. We are not shouting for blood, but when it appears, we look on with undeniable satisfaction. As such, schadenfreude is passive; we are in no way trying to bring misfortune to those we deem to be deserving of it. And we might even say that our pleasure is not so much based on the suffering incurred by the "deserving" other as it is on justice being served.

Unjustified schadenfreude may be our most ubiquitous guilty pleasure, often springing—unlike justified schadenfreude—from envy. Such envy pleasantly dissipates when we witness or hear of the demise of the envied other, leaving only a dark stain in the back corners of our psyche. Put another way, schadenfreude takes the suffering out of envy, leaving us in a place of undeniable satisfaction.

Practice

EXPERIENCING SCHADENFREUDE

Think of a situation that has aroused schadenfreude in you. Close your eyes and remember the feeling of it. Imagine that you are not holding back such feeling at all; if you could speak, what would you say? What was your judgment of those involved in that situation? When you are sure that someone has wronged you and later you hear that misfortune has befallen them, what do you usually feel? Is this different than what you think you should feel? Write down your answers to these questions, noticing what the process of answering them stirs in you.

SCHADENFREUDE AS A VICARIOUS SHAME-FEST

The more we consider schadenfreude, the more we realize how common it is, both personally and collectively. The tabloids on sale at most checkout counters provide an instant schadenfreude high: celebrities without any makeup, celebrities messing up royally, celebrities down in the dumps. Their travails invite us to look upon these celebrities in a state where they're not only just like us, they're worse. Their fall is our rise, leavening us with tiny bursts of satisfaction, like a sweet milk-chocolate bar downed in the midafternoon while watching a soap opera. It's a vicarious shame-fest—we're close to their shame but not that close, so we can see it and feel it without having it contract or shrink or expose us. The enormous coverage given to celebrity failings—including major news networks—is largely fed by a powerfully pervasive cultural schadenfreude.

How quietly yet pointedly delicious it can feel to be on the other side of the glass. Someone else's fall amplifies the fact that we have not yet fallen; thus does schadenfreude give us a little hit of immunity, which in itself provides a small but noticeable shot of pleasure. And this is often accompanied by the relief we can feel when we hear of problems we don't have.

SCHADENFREUDE AS ARMCHAIR JUDGE

Much of schadenfreude's ancestry lies in the triumph we felt—and this goes back a *long* way—when the overcoming or downfall of others improved our lives in some way. The better this felt, the more fully we'd participate in it. This can also be seen developmentally, when young children display pleasure over getting something that another child clearly wants. Being higher up on the food chain can be a thrill, despite the cost.

As we get older and more cognitively sophisticated, our capacity for schadenfreude deepens. Although we may still be driven by competitiveness and a corresponding envy—along with our own sense of justice—now we can bring in finer and finer distinctions as to what constitutes a fall in others. We also may drag into the mix such potent ingredients as the ability to shame others. And if we ourselves can be shamed relatively easily, we may seek to offset this not only through being aggressive with others, but also through honing our capacity for schadenfreude.

Our sense of justice and our schadenfreude leanings are directly related. If we feel that others have behaved unjustly, we're more likely to feel some schadenfreude toward them than if we knew they had not thus behaved. In schadenfreude, we play armchair judge; the others' misfortune is their sentence, which pleases us because our value system is being upheld by the powers that be. Sometimes we might ask another, "Would you rather be right or happy?"—perhaps forgetting that there are times when being right (or apparently being right) is quite pleasurable.

SCHADENFREUDE'S LACK OF COMPASSION

There are many shades of schadenfreude, ranging from the malicious to the primly righteous, but all involve an absence of compassion, coupled with an us-versus-them mentality. As such, schadenfreude works against mercy and forgiveness, and how could it not, given how it dehumanizes the offending or fallen other?

Just think of the ancient Romans packed into the amphitheater for a day of rousingly entertaining bloodshed—schadenfreude as a spectator sport in the voyeuristic extreme. Whatever its scale, schadenfreude keeps us emotionally separate from the downfall or misfortune that's providing us with pleasure. Thus does it disconnect us, even as it connects us to others who are also enjoying observing the same downfall or misfortune.

Schadenfreude can be brought into clearer focus by examining its opposite, *mudita* (a Pali and Sanskrit Buddhist term), which basically means sympathetic/appreciative joy—the pleasure we take in others' successes and achievements. Many of us know this emotion in its purest form through the joy we feel over our children's breakthroughs and triumphs. Mudita has an open heart; schadenfreude does not. Mudita does not lose touch with the humanity of others; schadenfreude does.

So what can we do about our schadenfreude? First, become sufficiently aware of it so that you can name it as soon as it arises in you. Then bring your full attention into the actual feeling of your schadenfreude, without making it wrong. What catalyzes schadenfreude in us says much about where we stand morally—which may contradict where we claim to be morally. So to explore our schadenfreude is to explore our morality, clarifying what constitutes justice to us.

Practice

WORKING WITH SCHADENFREUDE

Recall a time when you clearly felt schadenfreude, and do your best to recollect the details and actual feeling of it. Feel into the pleasure of your schadenfreude. Notice the limit of its expansiveness. What feels contracted in you in the midst of it? And where do you sense this contractedness in your body?

Now imagine feeling an extra strong sense of schadenfreude—as if just finding out that someone who has hurt many people (without any legal consequences) is now down and out—and notice what happens to your mouth, lips, and chin. Exaggerate it. Stay with this for a minute, then imagine facing this person who has fallen, shorn of his or her adornments. Feel your judgment of this one, and hold it steady for a minute or so. Then look more deeply, relaxing your face and torso. Breathe into your heart. What do you now see? What do you now feel? Stay with this for a few minutes, keeping your attention on your heart and the other's eyes. Make no effort to shed your schadenfreude; let it coexist with your deliberate humanizing of the other. Finish with the practice in the appendix.

Instead of merely judging or dissociating from your schadenfreude, have compassion for the you who tends to indulge in it. Everyone has some schadenfreude; all we need to do is see it for what it is, and not allow it to sit in the driver's seat. Don't worry about getting rid of it; rather, let it sit in the backseat, and give it some quality playtime with mudita.

24

Envy

Sideline Craving

Envy doesn't really care about morality, being all but bereft of
any serious sense of entitlement. In envy there's an absence
of feeling that we actually deserve the object of our envy.

ENVY'S TERRAIN IS LONELY AND painful, with the only
neighbors being greed, resentment, jealousy, and shame. Its credo of
coveting but not having what some others have renders it an unpopular
emotion, one we tend to keep from showing fully. And to top this off,
envy is listed as one of the Seven Deadly Sins. To better understand envy,
it's important to compare and contrast it with its neighboring emotions.

ENVY'S RELATIONSHIP TO GREED,
RESENTMENT, JEALOUSY, SHAME

Greed is the demand for more and more, often insatiably so. Envy
is not so overtly desperate as greed, but nonetheless it's still centered
around a sense of not having enough. Whereas greed grabs, envy craves;
in both cases, we're convinced that we need more. Our greed for the
roses weds us to the thorns, and yet our appetite for more continues
unabated. Envy is not as painful or driven, but it still hurts, like a splin-
ter wedged far enough under our skin to generate a mild infection, a
locus of encapsulated pus. How we deal with that infection determines
whether or not our envy erodes or serves us.

Envy and resentment are also close; resentment could be described
as a mix of hostility, entitlement, and envy. But as dark as envy can

get, it's no match for resentment. Ill will is often present in envy, but it's present at a much higher concentration in resentment—often to the point of toxicity—emphatically dehumanizing the person who has what we think we *should* have or who has what we think they *shouldn't* have. Envy, on the other hand, simply *wishes* that it had what another has. Resentment is more of a moral state, filled with the conviction that the other doesn't deserve to have what they have—or what we think *we* deserve to have.

Envy—like greed—doesn't really care about morality, being all but bereft of resentment's sense of entitlement. In fact, in envy there is an absence of feeling that we actually deserve the object of our envy.

And jealousy? Both it and envy are emotions in which we experience ourselves as being left on the sidelines. In jealousy we're excruciatingly aware of having what we want slip away from us, whereas in envy we're in a much less sharp sort of pain and don't even have our desired something in a position where it *can* slip away from us. As such, envy is far more passive than jealousy. We don't flare up with envy, but we do a slow burn, keeping our distance from what we crave—usually without taking responsibility for keeping that distance. Jealousy is constellated around rejection, envy around lack.

And shame? When our envy is largely automatic, we don't question its presence, being almost totally focused on what lies outside us and far enough out of reach to leave us impotently resigned or embittered. But when we start to see our envy more clearly, sensing its slinking desperation and self-induced suffering, we may slip into shame about having it, judging ourselves as pathetic or otherwise lesser, which only reinforces the neediness and impotence at the core of our envy.

ENVY AS INSPIRATION IN PASSIVE DRAG

What is most potentially insidious about envy isn't its felt sense of lack, but its "comparing mind" component: there is in envy a contracted flood of repetitive thoughts about those who have what we want. When we let such a state of comparison—which features us outside looking in—run unchecked through us, we're left embittered, tightly knotting ourselves up when we think of whomever we envy. When we don't let such comparisons so firmly grip and occupy us, we're left more in a state of longing than bitterness, recognizing to some degree what we'd need to do to have what we don't—assuming, of course, that it's within our reach.

So envy can spur us toward a deeper life, or it can eat away at the one we have. As such, envy can veer between admiration—however begrudging—and resentment. When we feel envy rise in us—when we're eaten up thinking about what we don't have and wish we did—we have a chance to make wise use of this emotion, ceasing to be so focused on the differences between us and our envied others.

When I was twenty-one, stuck in a doctoral program in biochemistry, I found myself taking increasingly frequent breaks from my scientific studies to read authors whose protagonists were filled with wanderlust. Jack Kerouac's madcap hero (patterned after the real-life exploits of Beat-generation icon Neal Cassady) especially pulled at me. I envied his wild spirit and on-the-road exuberance, not caring about his excesses. I didn't resent him, but I started resenting my doctoral program, regardless of how well I was doing in it. My envy for Cassady stayed strong, catalyzing my own wanderlust. Within a year I could take no more and left my program, heading for the open road. Now I no longer envied Cassady, but simply appreciated him for inspiring me to travel a truer road. The traveler in me came fully alive, and I was on my way, ripe for adventure.

Envy brings us down and can keep us down; there, we tend to do nothing to alter our situation and simply settle for being embittered about what another has that we wish we had. In thus submitting to our envy, we miss an enormous opportunity to make a better life for ourselves. Even the effort to cut through our envy's mindset can shift us internally for the better, so that even if nothing changes externally, we are still furthered.

Practice

WORKING WITH ENVY

Think of someone you envy (or someone you have envied, if there is no one at the present). Close your eyes, and imagine they're sitting across from you. Tell them what it is they have/ had that you wish you did. Notice how you're speaking. Envision this person as just someone who has something that you wish you had. Feel your lack of that particular something, taking your attention into this feeling as much as you can. If other times when you felt envy show up during this process, let the presence of that amplify what you are feeling. Stay with this for a few minutes.

Now ask yourself this question: Am I willing to do what is needed to have what this person has (assuming, of course, that it is possible)? And another question: Do I deserve it, and if so, why? Notice how your answers register with you. Did you feel any resistance to answering them? Take a few minutes to be with these questions and your responses to them. Now look more closely at the person you envy (or envied). Imagine they are suddenly without whatever it is that you wish you had. What do you see? What do you feel? Breathe into your heart, allowing yourself to feel some compassion both for the envious you and the envied other. As you do so, notice what is happening to your envy.

Envy can serve us if it is allowed to coexist with mindfulness and compassion—compassion for both ourselves and for the one who has what we don't have but want. Let us hold "I envy you" and "Thank you for inspiring me" not as two far-apart, seemingly unrelated statements, but as two deeply intertwined statements.

Envy can be a gift, if we don't just spin our wheels when it arises, miring ourselves in passivity. If we can envision envy as chained inspiration, inspiration in endarkened drag, we have a chance to ride it into a deeper life, a life in which the differences between us and others move us to take life-giving action.

25

Surprise

Wide Open in One Inhalation

BEING THE SHORTEST-LIVED EMOTION, surprise gets the shortest chapter in this book. Despite its brevity, lasting just a second or two, surprise is one of our primary emotions: it is not a combination of other emotions; it is not something we are doing with another emotion; and it is not negative. It manifests as a sudden openness that pervades our entire system. As quickly as it may give way to other emotions—anger, sadness, joy, fear—surprise itself is neutral, having no shadow side. While what follows it may be healthy or unhealthy, surprise is simply psychophysiological openness: a kind of emotional reset button that readies us with extreme rapidity to respond to an unexpected event.

Why is surprise so short lived? Its purpose is to, as quickly as possible, both shift our perspective and open us up to what's now happening. Once this is achieved, surprise does not need to be reactivated. When we're surprised, it's as if we've been energetically and contextually stretched and reset, opened very wide to allow the intake of as much information as possible in a very brief slice of time, which readies us to respond as freshly as we can to an unexpected event.

Though surprise is so quickly gone—typically lasting no more than one very sudden inhalation—our facial expression when experiencing it is unmistakable: wide-open eyes and mouth, without the brow, eye, and jaw tension that comes with fear and anger. It is as if the whole face pulls back from top to bottom, from side to side, into one big "O" (a perfect aperture for a full-bodied gasp). The expression of surprise is more dynamically open than of wonder; there's much more of a stretching as the eyes and mouth widen. Wonder is in part an extension of surprise, having a much longer lifetime than surprise.

Surprise is often likened to being startled. But a startle is merely a physiological reflex. When we are startled—which lasts just a fraction of a second—our eyes usually snap shut (one super-quick blink) then open wide, whereas in surprise our eyes don't close (though they may do so as other emotions arrive). Also, being startled usually involves some lower-face tension such as instant grimacing (a horizontal lip-stretching), displaying the extreme readiness of fear, or the teeth-gritting anticipation that can precede an impending crash. (Being startled looks much like fear before it feels like fear.) Furthermore, we don't really enjoy being startled even if we *know* the explosion or shout is about to happen, but we often do enjoy being surprised.

The sound of surprise is also unique among the emotions, employing inhalation—usually just one!—as the key source. That one gasp, that sudden and clearly audible intake, is just as much a core indicator of surprise as its dramatic facial display.

Surprise creates an on-the-spot sense of radical reevaluation, as if a completely unexpected internal shift has just occurred right behind our eyes, dramatically altering our sense of reality. We may even jump into the air. But whatever our response may be, our attention is totally focused—riveted—on what has surprised us. What was concerning us right before we were surprised falls into the background, so that we can bring as much of ourselves as possible to what is now happening.

Surprise is often quickly followed by other emotions. For example, if we have just been surprised by disturbing news, the openness of surprise may rapidly mutate into deep sorrow or perhaps flaming rage. If we are surprised with good news, we may very quickly shift into joy or exultation. Such emotional intensity can easily obscure the fact that we began with surprise.

It's worth noting that being surprised and saying that we're surprised are often far from related. For example, I may tell you that I am surprised that it's raining today or that no mail arrived today. But in fact I am not *feeling* any surprise at all. Surprise is very difficult to feign, for if we already know what we're about to be surprised by, we won't naturally *feel* any surprise.

Other emotions—especially fear and shame—can halt us in our tracks, but none so quickly as surprise. This is its gift to us, to almost instantaneously shift our perspective and state of being, thereby making room in us for whatever emotions and actions to emerge that fit the moment.

26

Awe

The Full-Blooded Intuition of Innate Mystery

We cannot get used to awe, for it is ever fresh, ever new, taking us not from here to there, but from here to a deeper here.

AMAZEMENT IS WONDER INFUSED WITH a touch of surprise. Add a stronger dose of surprise, and the result is astonishment. Rev this up a bit, and we shift from astonishing to astounding—jaw-dropping to deeper jaw-dropping.

And beyond this is awe. Less surprise, more depth and transformational impact. Awe is the feeling of nonconceptually recognizing and connecting with the essential and unspeakably significant nature of reality. Awe plugs us into bare mystery, leaving us not trying to figure it out but simply bearing witness to it with our entire being—at least, that is, until we filter it through our interpretive or sense-making lenses.

The unusual can amaze or astonish us—a spectacular sports moment or a much-better-than-expected report card—but in awe we directly encounter the transcendent, the numinous, the heartland of what really matters, in even the most mundane of circumstances.

For example, we might be having an ordinary discussion with our partner or a good friend, and suddenly our usual sense of familiarity vanishes, leaving us watching the other as if we're seeing them for the first time, not only marveling that the interchange between us seems to be happening all by itself, but that it's happening at all. Our heart is ever-expanding openness, our appreciation knowing no bounds. It's as if we are gratitude in the flesh. And while this is happening, we continue our conversation as if nothing extraordinary is occurring, which makes it all the more extraordinary. Pure awe.

Likewise, there are moments in sports that we don't just enjoy watching—we're amazed or astonished by them: a thundering slam-dunk, a one-handed end-zone reception, a dazzlingly impeccable gymnastics routine, a blazing-fast final lap in a ten-thousand-meter race, a lunging forehand winner. And there are other moments, much rarer, that touch us to our core, moments that *emphatically* transcend the sport. When Bob Beamon broke the world record for the long jump by almost two feet in the 1968 Olympics, many who were watching—including me—felt awe. Both stunned and blown open. For a while, nothing else existed. When Beamon realized what he had done, he fell to his knees, his forehead on the ground, obviously overcome; he wasn't demonstrating elation, but awe. The enormity of his feat seemed to humble him to the core.

Amazement and astonishment momentarily shake us but don't alter our self-sense. We are still the usual us, experiencing amazement or astonishment. In awe, however, our self-sense does not remain intact but is momentarily supplanted by a self-transcending center of being. Awe has the power to transform us if we stay in touch with what it has stirred in us.

Awe includes not only the rapt attention and radical openness that characterize deep wonder, but also a sense of veneration. Amazement and astonishment may not bring us to our knees, but more often than not awe does. It is *that* humbling, decisively stripping us of our self-importance so that we're centered not by ego but by being.

In full-blown awe, the realizations that arise can be liberating and joyful, and even sometimes frightening—especially if we're strongly attached to our usual frame of reference. Arms may be raised in weeping gratitude, and a few breaths later our entire frame of being might be stormily shaking, lit with a fearful reverence. It's enough to simultaneously exalt and deeply humble us. We then bow not because we choose to do so, but because we simply have to. What we're facing is that profoundly compelling and vast.

Awe is a direct acknowledgment of and response to sublimity; it reconnects us with visceral immediacy to the heartland of life, literally plugging us back into a deeply felt sense of primordial significance, depositing us in a domain where revelation outshines explanation.

THE SHADOW OF AWE

Awe may not necessarily be as wonderful as it sounds, however, because it can arise at any stage of development and can be used in less than life-giving ways. For example, if religious fundamentalists experience awe, they will very likely interpret it through the lens of their belief structure, using it to reinforce and further legitimize the very fundamentalism in which they are embedded, while leaving its harmful features intact. When those who have outgrown fundamentalism experience awe, they will interpret it very differently. Same awe, different filters.

AWE AS SELF-TRANSCENDING
INTIMACY WITH MYSTERY

Strip awe of whatever conditioning colors or clothes it, and all that's left is a speechless uprising of uncommon recognition, a deeply emotional yet self-transcending intimacy with irreducible mystery. In the same sense that life could be said to be the poetry of being, awe could be said to be the poetry of revelation, too real for translation.

The gift of awe is full-bodied revelation. However briefly it lasts, it provides us with enough of a break from our usual ways to glimpse something deeper, something that if taken to heart and not allowed to be swept aside by our usual certainties can be a catalyst for changing our lives for the better.

How wonderful it is that we can feel awe! We are hardwired for it. We cannot get used to awe, for it is ever fresh, ever new, taking us not from here to there, but from here to a deeper here. My words fall down speechless as awe pervades me, leaving sentient openness in the raw, personalized just enough to keep things thing-ing, without any intrusion of everyday familiarity.

Awe is all the proof we need for the really big questions. Silence may be the answer, but awe is the answer in full bloom.

Part 3

Deepening Emotional Intimacy

27

Directions Feeling Can Take

Feeling Into, Feeling For, Feeling With

WE USE THE VERB "FEEL" in many ways, ranging from outright emotional expression to indicating actions that are not expressions of feeling per se (such as thinking and perceiving). A common use of "feel" is in combination with certain prepositions—like "into," "for," "with"— to indicate what we're doing or intending to do on a feeling level. So we may "feel into" a particular situation; we may "feel for" another's dilemma; we may "feel with" the concerns that a close friend is expressing. All three of these usages are explored in what follows.

FEELING INTO

Feeling into others is all about sensing and *nonconceptually* reading them—especially emotionally and energetically—bringing an embodied, finely tuned attentiveness to them. We cannot do this very effectively if we remain stationed or isolated in our *head*quarters; we need to be solidly and spaciously present in an intuitive, body-centered sense. This allows us to operate from a relatively clear and grounded focus while we establish a significant resonance with those whom we are feeling into.

When we feel into others, we remain alert to subtle shifts in their facial expression, body language, emotional presence, and vocal tone. Our scanning of them is usually more than skin deep; we zero in on details while keeping an eye on the overall picture.

Feeling into others is a largely intuitive undertaking, wherein we're more sensitive than usual to their emotional signals and emanations. What we're reading is an ever-shifting three-dimensional phenomenon—the marvelously intricate processes that constitute a person—that churns out data very rapidly. To the degree that we're emotionally and somatically literate, we'll be able to use such data to better understand those we're feeling into.

But as helpful and necessary as feeling into others can be, more is needed when it comes to deepening relationship and emotional intimacy. To only be feeling into others can keep us somewhat distanced, "safely" removed from entering into truly vulnerable connection with them. In our practice of feeling into others, we may not yet have gone very far into feeling *for* or *with* others, even as we "hold space"—or attempt to hold space—for them to be in the condition they are. One can be adept at feeling into others and use this ability for less than life-giving purposes, such as sexual seduction. So it's crucial not to limit our feeling toward others to just feeling *into* them.

FEELING FOR

Feeling for others brings in more empathy, more obviously heartfelt connection, more caring and reciprocity. Those we're feeling for will likely feel safer with us than if we were only feeling into them. Now we are able to attune to them, and also to be more empathetically present with them—which asks of us a nonstrategic, or agenda-free, vulnerability. When others sense in us this quality of vulnerability—an undefended, emotionally open transparency—coupled with our steadiness of presence, they will probably relax even more, connecting with us without losing themselves in such connection.

The biggest challenge to the realm of "feeling for" is being *too* open or *too* absorbent—as when we get overwhelmed or flooded by another's emotional state. This is the dark side of empathy: losing ourselves in another's feeling state.

It's easy to empathize so strongly with another's plight that we abandon our boundaries in order to be close to them, to hold them with nothing between us. Yet in doing so, we have abandoned the little bit of distance needed to maintain a clear focus; instead of relating deeply to them, we have in a sense *become* them. Fusion. This is a oneness that does not serve us or them, for we, being without boundaries, are in a position where we cannot see what needs to be done.

The solution is not to hold our boundaries tight, but to *expand* them—at the right pace and at the right time—to include the other, to bring that person into the circle of our heart's reach. Doing this allows us to maintain our autonomy while simultaneously bringing us very close to the other. In this process, our empathy can flower and spread without pulling us too far into the other's state. Then we truly feel *for* them—and, to a certain degree, even *as* them, giving ourselves without giving ourselves away. And what does this do for the other person? It provides both connection and safety because our closeness to them does not blind us to what may or may not need to happen between them and us.

FEELING WITH

Feeling with others makes things even more mutual. Now it's not just us sensing, reading, and empathizing with others, but also us being with them in a clearly resonant mutuality. Instead of sitting *across* from us, now others sit *beside* us—assuming of course that they're also emotionally connecting with us. Here there is both emotional resonance and the presence to stabilize it, a shared attunement that both deepens and holds relational mutuality.

The shadow side of "feeling with" is cultism, or a tightly encapsulated "we space" that's overly bound to its core beliefs and that doesn't significantly allow for inside dissension or outside feedback. If we're operating from within such a structure, we will very likely not recognize its cultic nature, keeping our distance from (or even discrediting) those who might point this out to us.

If we are thus entrapped, our emotional communion with each other only strengthens the web, increasing the odds that we'll stay put in our cultic bubble. "Feeling with" in this context can easily arise in conjunction with "feeling against" those who are not part of our setup, so that our sense of "us" is like an island in an us-versus-them paradigm—whether we're in a codependent relationship (arguably a cult of two) or a this-is-*the*-way religious, spiritual, or political movement (arguably a cult of many).

Feeling with others works best when we emotionally connect with them while also retaining our capacity to question and challenge our relationship with them. If there is no space to rock the boat, then our connection loses its vitality, flattening into a mutual pact not to make waves. Many people slip easily into this, marginalizing what isn't working in their relationship because facing it might necessitate some big shifts in their relationship, or even make it clear that they need to part.

When our feeling with others is healthy—honoring both our autonomy and our togetherness in contexts unpolluted by cultism—we are side by side with them in mutually empowering communion, enjoying both their individuality and their interrelatedness with us.

Put together the best of feeling into, feeling for, and feeling with, and what do we have? Intimacy.

28

De-Numbing

Thaw until Raw

Our emotional numbness must be approached with great
care, given the extreme vulnerability that it so often blankets
or encases—but approach it we must if we are to truly live.

NUMBNESS IS A COMPLETE OR near-complete absence of
sensation or feeling. It denotes more than disconnection: when we disconnect emotionally, we pull away or "vacate the premises," but when
we go numb emotionally, "the premises" themselves have become
devoid of feeling and significance, which we may or may not view as
our own doing. In disconnection we flee; in numbness we freeze.

When we register our numbness, we only "feel" it in the sense
of noting its presence and whatever sensations—or echoes of sensation—might characterize it. There's *physical numbness*—the absence of
sensation due to shock or nerve damage; there's *cognitive numbness*—
the absence of registered significance regarding difficult or unusually
challenging circumstances; there's *spiritual numbness*—the absence of
palpable connection with anything beyond the personal; and there's
emotional numbness—the absence or blunting of feeling in situations
that normally would elicit strong emotional responses from us. And
these various forms of numbness can share considerable overlap.

Emotional numbness is a survival strategy and needs to be responded
to as such, rather than as an occasion for self-deprecation or shaming,
especially given how automatically emotional numbness usually arises

and the likelihood that it has prerational origins (for example, as a coping strategy in the face of sustained family violence). It's not as if we rationally decide to numb ourselves.

If we have just badly cut ourselves while slicing vegetables, the numbness that initially forms around our wound makes our pain more manageable, increasing the odds that we will properly tend to it; this clearly serves us. If we suffered trauma as a child, the probable emotional numbness that arose then—dissociation and a tucked-away encapsulation of the trauma—served us at a survival level, allowing us to keep on functioning to some degree. However, that very same numbness does not serve us as adults, other than to remind us that there is much encased in and below it, namely the very wounding that first generated our numbness, and this hurt calls to us through all that we do, no matter how long we ignore or try to ignore it.

Numbness is not a feeling per se—although we could arguably call it a kind of "frozen feelingness" —but rather is simultaneously a suppression *and* a container of feeling. It is a coping strategy, a kind of disembodiment, an endogenous flight from and flattening of pain. Numbness must be approached with great care, given the extreme vulnerability that it blankets or encases—but approach it we must, if we are to truly live.

WORKING WITH NUMBNESS

The first step toward working with numbness is to recognize and name it. This might not be as easy as it sounds, for if we have any shame about being emotionally numb—especially if we're in an intimate relationship—we may be loath to acknowledge its presence. What if our intimate other takes it personally, accusing us of emotionally abandoning them—even though it's more accurate to say we've abandoned ourselves? What would happen if we met their show of affection with our undisguised numbness? It all depends on how we present our numbness.

When we admit our numbness without any defensiveness, we start to feel some degree of vulnerability and perhaps some sadness that we are so out of touch with our feeling core. I have seen many clients begin to access their tears as soon as they cease hiding or denying their numbness; it's as if they were young children again, but in a far safer environment than the one in which they grew up. It's crucial to approach another's numbness or tendency to freeze in nonshaming ways; if we slip into shaming another for being numb, we increase the likelihood of them becoming even more numb (while perhaps denying that this is happening, so as to take the edge off their shame). A caring, nonaccusatory approach to illuminating another's numbness can soften the edges of their numbness enough so that what underlies it can be more and more clearly seen and felt.

It is crucial to become aware of how we numb ourselves to our numbness. This means doing our very best not to reject, disown, look down upon, or otherwise bypass our numbness. Face it. Move closer to it. Contact it. Listen as attentively as you can to it, attuning more than your ear to what is within and below it. Listen for the echoes of your past in your numbness, not letting your inner critic intrude.

Acknowledge the presence of your numbness without shaming yourself for having it. Take your attention *into* it with undivided focus and great care, noting its details. How thick does it seem to be? How dense? Is there any movement in it, and if so, what kind of movement? Get as intimate with your numbness as you can. Look inside it deeply enough and eventually you will meet your own gaze, however young that might be.

Feel into your numbness, feel for it, feel as it, feel through it. Give it a voice, however inarticulate. Let what is within and under it have a voice, even if you have to begin with the quietest of whispers. Sense what has been muted in you, pressed down, straitjacketed, and let yourself speak *as* that, breath by breath. No rush. Be aware of the cushioning, the protectiveness of your numbness, being grateful for how it has served you even as you explore what's within and below it.

Keep making your way through it, however slowly, until you reach its heartland, which is far from numb. There you will encounter, among other things, the originating factors of your numbness. Do this fully, thoroughly, openly, and caringly. Before long you will find yourself more alive, more loving, more whole, more here, more your full self. And don't expect to never be numb again! When it returns, to whatever degree, treat it not as a problem but as a chance to reenter your feeling dimensions ever more fully.

29

Collective Overwhelm

If we don't pay close attention to collective overwhelm, we become a host for it, a means through which it can seed and expand itself in a kind of cellular and organismic imperialism.

WHO HASN'T FELT OVERWHELMED at times? We become stressed, pressured, slammed with too much stimulation and demand, and a certain emotional threshold is crossed, leaving us flailing in a chaotic flood of feeling, gasping and grasping for a lifeline to a more settled, grounded place. Mostly this lasts only a short while, but other times it lasts a lot longer, at worst sweeping us out to sea and stranding us from our basic sanity long enough to seriously disrupt our life.

In considering such personal overwhelm—which none of us is immune to—it's important to understand and take into account the fact that contemporary culture is itself deeply entrenched in chronic overwhelm, unattended overwhelm, overwhelm without any significant relief in sight, overwhelm that continues to pick up steam, overwhelm that is so hugely and deeply pervasive that its signature pressurizing and distress-making gets only token challenges. Such is the presence of collective overwhelm.

Collective overwhelm is a global destabilizing condition that combines excessive stimulation, massive information overload, unrelenting pressure, and a dread-infused numbing. Collective overwhelm keeps us in energetic debt, borrowing from our reserve tanks until we're all but running on empty. We're behind on the payments, and we're paying far too high a price to keep up the pace to which we've committed ourselves.

Because collective overwhelm has largely become the norm, adaptation to it remains only superficially questioned in most places. Nonetheless, collective overwhelm is fully here, insidiously ubiquitous and voraciously viral, occupying—*colonizing*—so many people and places that it often is only partially recognized for what it is. Collective overwhelm is more common than the common cold and more infectious than any plague.

Collective overwhelm blocks emotional intimacy by scattering and disorienting us and—most of all—by keeping many of us in so much chronic fear that we tend to view others as threats: more competition for resources and stability. In collective overwhelm we're often just too drained and scattered to expend the energy and attention needed to take better care of ourselves, including doing what it takes to develop emotional intimacy.

If "future shock"—the result of too much change in too short a time—is collective overwhelm's past, systemic depression is its present. This flattens and presses all too many of us down (hence "de-pression"), driving us into compensatory flight, obsession with stimulation, and other distractions from our suffering until we crash. This kind of future—assuming it remains unchecked—is not something to look forward to, one possibility being a technologically hyperadvanced, yet densely regressive singularity—a superficially diverse but nonetheless homogenized and largely dehumanized world culture, for which amnesia's infectious anesthesia would be the drug of choice. Prolonged depression can only be kept down for so long.

Fear (anxiety, angst, dread) and anger (irritation, frustration, hostility, rage) are collective overwhelm's predominant emotional correlates, operating on so much adrenaline that the only respite from them for far too many of us is eventual exhaustion and a tagalong apathy that features us being numb to our numbness.

Is collective overwhelm the emotional supernova of humankind's social and ecological myopia, an avalanching force choking on its own exhaust? Or is collective overwhelm a preparatory catalyst, an at-the-brink precursor to an unprecedented psychospiritual and ecologically literate awakening? Whatever it is, it's here in the metastasizing raw, generating more and more momentum, feeding itself on itself. And its tipping point? Probably already passed.

It's extremely overwhelming. No wonder the reported incidence of depression has shot up by more than 1,000 percent in the last five decades. No wonder there's widespread anxiety; no wonder there's so much addiction and such a massive intake of pharmaceutical medication; no wonder there's so much hell on earth, regardless of our advances. The time for denial is over. What we as a species have feared is already here, looming ever larger, and it isn't just "slouching toward Bethlehem"—it's eating its way into just about all of us, its appetite as voracious as it is blind, and it apparently has no more interest in its own survival than does cancer.

Yet all is not lost. In fact, there is much to be gained here, but only if we get off the overwhelm express and cease to let ourselves be fed or seduced or engulfed by it. Yes, it will continue to affect us, sometimes intensely so, but we do not have to let it occupy us. And this begins with seeing it for what it is and becoming as intimate as possible with the fearfulness at its core.

If we don't pay close attention to collective overwhelm, we become a host for it, a mere means through which it can seed and expand itself, in a kind of cellular and organismic imperialism. The good news is that if we play close attention to collective overwhelm and name it for what it is, we can start to cease being a host for it. We may not have stopped the vehicle, but we are no longer riding in it. Its noise and smell and presence still impact us, but not to the same extent as before.

For instance, we're at a major airport in a very long line that's moving slowly enough to generate anxiety in us. Even though we arrived early, we're starting to fear we'll miss our flight. We hear regular announcements that the alert level is at its highest for reasons we're not privy to, so there's more fear than usual in the airport crowd. But instead of letting our own fear possess us, we deepen our awareness of the general fear occurring, the pervasive sense of low-grade collective overwhelm. No one is making a big fuss, but there's an unpleasant tension running through the entire check-in line. As we attune ourselves more deeply to all this, separating it from our own fear, we become more present, more embodied, letting ourselves settle into the moment-by-moment flow of the line, accessing some compassion for ourselves and everyone around us.

Another example: We like to think we're keeping up with things as we watch and read the news daily. Our own life is not going so well, and we look forward to taking breaks from it by absorbing ourselves in the news, usually for at least one or two hours each day. As we skim the various headlines, we feel a certain pleasure, as if we're in control, in relative safety, keeping up with things. But today is different. What's not working so well in our life has taken a big turn for the worse. The news stories of violence, horror, and shocking loss just make us feel even sadder. There are truly horrible things happening in many places, and we, due to our life crisis, are no longer numb to them. We can now feel the presence of collective overwhelm and can name it as such, readying ourselves to stop being so passive in the face of it.

WORKING WITH COLLECTIVE OVERWHELM

To effectively deal with collective overwhelm, we need to make sure we're not under its spell, not caught up in any sort of cultural trance that keeps us distracted. So first of all, as described above, we need to be sufficiently familiar with collective overwhelm so as to be able to recognize and name it. This means not just having a conceptual grasp of it, but also having the capacity to sense its signs moment by moment.

Second, we need to do in-depth work with our fear (see chapters 8 and 9 on fear and collective fear) and our tendency for numbness (see chapter 27 on numbness), given how central they are to collective overwhelm.

Third, we need to do whatever helps to cut through depressiveness (see chapter 17 on depression), and do it full out. No more pressing down of our pain, no more wasting our vitality, no more energetic or emotional flattening. What's helpful here is a mix of the following: aerobic, heavy-sweat workouts at least every other day (ideally alternating with some weight training and mindful stretching); a grounded meditative practice as described in the appendix; well-supported self-exploration that connects the dots—intellectually and emotionally—between our past and present; and an in-depth, emotionally open sharing of this with others, until such work is not just personal, but *interpersonal*, liberatingly relational and collective.

And last but not least, we need to develop the endurance and patience to stay the course. What's required is not just a weekend of good work, or a month of it, or even a year of it. It's a life's work, and it needs to be treated as such. Yes, there will be plateaus, but these should not be occasions to quit but rather chances to rest and rejuvenate so that we can keep extending our edge, continuing to make haste slowly, letting all the damage awaken rather than merely embitter or fragment us.

Spiritual stamina is essential; don't postpone developing it. Go to the heart of collective overwhelm, beyond the fear and anger and numbness and shock, and there you'll find an enormous grief. Get into it, opening channels for it to flow, to cut loose, to break open your heart, until its cry is your cry. Then what's below and beyond all the pain starts to shine forth, inviting us into what we never really left but only dreamt we did.

This is the healing through which we embody a deeper life; this is the healing that calls to us through all that we are and all that we do. Yes, it may overwhelm us at times, but it's the kind of overwhelm that cleanses, purifies, heals, awakens. It is time to move toward it, for the sake of one and all.

30

Connected Catharsis

Sloppy or naïvely managed cathartic work—along
with the emotional "dumping" featured in many a
relational conflict—can make it all the more tempting
to assign a negative connotation to catharsis.

IN ANY IN-DEPTH CONSIDERATION OF emotional expression, the topic of catharsis almost inevitably surfaces, often accompanied by debates about its value. Catharsis—derived from the Greek word *katharsis,* meaning "to cleanse or purge"—is an emotional release that makes us feel as if we have emptied or drained ourselves of the emotion (or emotions) in question. Its discharging—or undammed venting—of emotional energy is frequently associated with literally getting something "out of our system." Whether we "blow our lid" or "erupt" or "cry a river"—we are engaged in full-blown emotional release, however healthy or unhealthy that might be.

Heated arguments about the pros and cons of catharsis are commonly found in Anger-In versus Anger-Out concerns (as discussed in chapter 11). The deeper concern, however, is not about whether it's best to keep anger in or let it out, but about *how* we keep it in or let it out. So the question before us is not whether we have a "yes" or a "no" for catharsis, but rather what kind of catharsis doesn't serve us, and what kind does.

Catharsis has a long history as a cleansing or purging process. In many ancient cultures, there were periodic rituals in which intense emotions were stirred up and then emphatically expressed, discharged, and released. As wild as these rituals could be, they usually were contained within preset structures, so as to minimize damage. Forty years ago in a tiny village on the Indonesian island of Flores, I watched two costumed men rhythmically trying to whip each other; both were intoxicated on palm wine, their moves part of a fiercely flowing ritual dance. Surrounding them was a circle of villagers, clearly affected by the aggression they were seeing. Once the blood began to flow—the blows were hard—the whip dance was stopped. Everyone present had experienced aggression stirred in them and then discharged, at least to some degree, through what they were witnessing.

A year before this I witnessed an even more cathartic ceremony in Bali. It was late at night, and the only light came from lanterns and a full moon. During a trance-dance that lasted several hours, masked dancers enacted an archetypal encounter between forces of good and evil. Live music, mostly percussion and gongs, accompanied this, helping maintain the trance state of the dancers, who were deeply *possessed* by the good and evil forces. I was mesmerized. Near the climax of the ceremony, obviously entranced men—under the influence of the Balinese epitome of evil—began stabbing themselves with daggers and screaming. The emotional intensity was electrifying. I sat just a few feet away and saw no bleeding, no injury—even when some of the men lunged down upon their knives. Later this was explained as the result of the countering power of the Balinese epitome of good, in whom the dagger-wielding men had complete faith. What a huge arousing and release of fear and aggression for all the dancers and audience! I left feeling stunned, deeply moved, and emptied of all tension. I had just been in a mass exorcism of extraordinary beauty and power.

Exorcism is dramatically cathartic, with the explicit aim of "driving out" or otherwise expelling whatever dark forces—"demons" or "evil spirits" or wrongful "inhabitants"—are supposedly possessing those who are afflicted, even if that means overpowering them. Such possession has been—and often still is—taken literally by those engaged in exorcism-like rituals. In contemporary psychotherapy—of which exorcism is the ancestral prototype—possession is of course very common (in the sense that we can be possessed by our reactivity and habits), but it's usually not taken to be a matter of a literal entity occupying us.

Confession is another long-established cathartic process. Though it's less dramatic than exorcism or possession rituals, it can be even more effective, given how it connects personal content with at least some degree of emotional release. We are not just blowing off steam or vicariously discharging some pent-up emotion, but are *specifically* connecting with what precipitated our current emotional distress. Whether done in a Native American sweat lodge, a Catholic confessional booth, or in psychological chambers that honor personal history, confession is cathartic, even when it remains quiet.

In talking or writing out what we have kept muted or secret, we open up energetic channels in ourselves, so that the forces we had employed in keeping things quiet can now flow into more life-giving purposes. In so doing, we are akin to young children talking to themselves out loud, letting the unspoken be clearly voiced, acting out roles obviously representative of their inner workings. Theirs is an organic confession unburdened by self-consciousness—as is ours, when we let ourselves go fully into it. Artistic expression—creative writing, painting, singing, dancing—can also be cathartic. When we're "possessed" by the creative urge, there's often an abundance of emotional expression and release.

CONSIDERING THE VALUE OF
EMOTIONAL DISCHARGE

Central to catharsis is emotional discharge, but such an "emptying" is not in itself necessarily valuable. What's the point of such discharge if we are not going to shift, change, or cease repeating the behaviors that seemingly necessitate such release? Part of the difficulty with catharsis (including such work in therapeutic contexts) is the often unquestioned value attributed to it. Yes, emotional unloading and purging can be helpful, even healing, but usually only when it's knowingly and non-injuriously connected to the *roots* of what is disturbing us. Otherwise, what we are doing may be little more than emotional masturbation—a blowing off or dissipation of energy that briefly relieves us of tension.

What about when it's more valuable to contain and metabolize our emotional energy? We need to stop viewing catharsis as an unquestioned good, despite how undeniably valuable it can be at times. For example, you're in a group devoted to personal growth. You haven't yet "opened up," but you feel pressure to do so from both the group and its leader. No one notices your shame. Reminders of the dangers of keeping your emotions "bottled up" are directed your way, along with encouragement to "go for it." Others have done so already, and they look happy—or at least they're relieved their turn is over. Not surprisingly, they're trying to reassure you that you'll feel a lot better once you stop holding back. So you go ahead, following the leader's directions; you're uncomfortable but know you'd probably be even more uncomfortable if you didn't "go for it." You rage some, cry some, and soon feel better. You feel part of the group now.

Not long after the group, you feel strange, destabilized, and in touch with some old pain, but you're in no position to truly face it. Your "opening" has closed you more than you were prior to the group. And you feel enough shame around your rising pain and sense of failure to not want to share it—which is a replay of your earlier years. Did the group leader work with your shame? No. Did he or she help you become more intimate with your resistance to "opening up"? No. Did your catharsis help you? No. Was there a more skillful way to work with you? Yes.

Sloppy or naïvely facilitated cathartic work—along with the emotional "dumping" featured in many a relational conflict—can make it all the more tempting to assign a negative connotation to catharsis. Overvaluing and overrelying on emotional discharge is as common as it is unfortunate. Resorting to such cathartic "unloading" when we're emotionally frustrated or reactive does little more than make a habit of it, the expression of which we may confuse with being emotionally "open" or "honest."

Nevertheless, catharsis can be an immensely valuable process. Those therapies that view catharsis negatively often claim that it just amplifies (and leads to more of) what it is supposed to "reduce"—anger being the primary example. But these therapies don't recognize that an *increase* in what's supposed to be reduced may actually be beneficial. For example, if we associate danger with showing anger, then learning how to openly express our anger cleanly *and* with whatever intensity is needed is an important developmental step.

Also, a so-called reduction in an emotion is not necessarily an accurate term, given that the supposed evidence for that (a self-reported lessening of symptoms) might signal nothing more than just a successful suppression of that emotion. What's needed is not "reduction" but a *deepening* of the capacity for healthy expression—and this might well mean an *increase* in expression, intensity, volume, and depth. Is crying that brings on deeper crying a sign of failure? Is anger that brings on the rage that we had to suppress long ago a proof that catharsis doesn't work? All of this brings us to the consideration of what I call *connected catharsis.*

THE NATURE OF CONNECTED CATHARSIS

With connected catharsis, we allow for a full-out expression of emotion *in context*—so instead of emotionally unburdening ourselves without knowing the roots of what is catalyzing our emotional discharge, we do so while recognizing the *origins* of such expression. In such plugged-in catharsis, what we do emotionally fits with both our core pain and our current circumstance.

For example, Sharon says something mildly critical to her friend Anne, who feels a surge of rage. Anne realizes that this reaction is far too big for what Sharon just said to her. Even so, she starts to get really angry at Sharon, feeling some satisfaction when she sees the shock on Sharon's face. Anne has energetic momentum, her mind is abuzz with other things Sharon has done that she didn't like but kept silent about. Suddenly, Anne remembers her older sister mercilessly taunting her and how her parents did nothing more than tell her to try harder to get along with her sister. All Anne's anger in those days turned to tears and shame. She couldn't stop her sister, and fighting back would have made her sister treat her even worse.

Realizing this as she's about to erupt at Sharon, Anne sobers enough to say something about her sister—whom she hasn't mentioned for years—and to let her rage go in her sister's direction. She still wants to hold Sharon accountable for how she just spoke, but Anne's old—and still present—woundedness around her sister is now in the foreground, and she is very angry. Soon she also begins sobbing deeply, noticing that her crying sounds like it did when she was four or five years old. Anne knows what she's raging and weeping about as she curls over in pain. Looking up, she sees Sharon gazing at her with tears in her eyes, and she lets herself settle into Sharon's presence, feeling grateful to be with her.

Such a contextually fitting, openly felt expression of our core pain sharply contrasts with disconnected catharsis—in which the discharging of the felt energy of pain is stranded from its originating factors. Getting outraged because our partner doesn't like how we cooked the asparagus, or because someone in a movie is being humiliated, is very different than getting outraged because we're emotionally remembering our mother or father humiliating us when we were young.

In connected catharsis, there's a sense of containing whatever is being released, not so as to reincorporate it, but to keep a conscious eye on it. So instead of dumping our emotional charge (or energetic buildup) into a garbage pit, we're treating it with ecological care, so that it isn't just shit, but compost-to-be. Call it psychoemotional recycling: taking care of our own mess.

Being intimate with our personal history makes connected catharsis possible. We need to know the specifics of what we're emotionally disturbed by, so that when catharsis occurs we are aware of more than just the surface presentation of our pain. And if we're in therapy, we need to make sure that our therapist both understands this and knows how to guide cathartic processes, ensuring that our emotional releasing occurs in a way that allows for proper digestion and integration of what's been opened up in us.

Connected catharsis can be overwhelming, but is not pursued in a way that generates (or legitimizes) overwhelm. There is no agenda to blow things open, to somehow try to purge our way to emotional freedom. We know that our emotions are not things we can "get out of our system" but rather are processes that involve body, mind, and social factors. So we don't get rid of, say, our anger, no matter how emptied of it we may feel—instead, we deepen our intimacy with it, knowing it both in its full-throttle peak and in its quiet undercurrents.

In connected catharsis, there's no overriding of our deeper pain, no ambition to breathe ourselves away from such hurt (in contrast to therapies that have us overbreathe or even hyperventilate), no settling for superficial release or blissed-out altered states. Time is made for proper digestion and integration. Staying grounded remains of paramount importance. All of this deepens our capacity for emotional intimacy.

Connected catharsis is not formulaic: no preestablished breathing patterns to follow, no one-size-fits-all directions. And no investment in having some sort of emotional breakthrough. When connected catharsis is underway, there's as much awareness of boundaries as there is of whatever emotions are present, along with a far-from-naïve openness.

Such openness—which is not a submission but a dynamic and self-illuminating surrender—is the operational preference of an explorer of those depths that "store" more than just our old wounds. When the waves, the sometimes overwhelming waves, of rising feeling come, they are neither fought nor fled, but instead are allowed, at the right time, to "take over"—in digestible doses—without focusing on their destination. In trusting this process, we not only ride the waves, but become them even as we simultaneously remain aware of them. Their power then becomes ours, not to have but to be. Here, catharsis is not just release, not just a break from our suffering, but an inherently liberating undertaking.

31

Phantom Limbic Pain

Emotional Healing and Breakthrough

> Our issues are not just in our tissues. Our unresolved emotional
> wounds don't merely hang out in our cells but exist as
> personalized energetic fields that not only pervade and alter
> our cells (including biochemically) but can easily outlive them.

IMAGINE THE FOLLOWING SCENARIO: You lost your left
arm from the elbow down two years ago, and you often feel as if that
missing section of limb is actually still here, especially when "it" hurts—
and sometimes "it" *really* hurts, no matter how much you tell yourself
that it's just phantom limb pain.

So you don't have a left hand, but you nonetheless frequently feel
the fingers of that hand curling in with painful intensity. No matter
how often you tell yourself your left arm is gone from the elbow down,
something in you is convinced otherwise, something that's impervious
to even the most compelling arguments.

Now imagine that you didn't lose your left arm (or any other part
of your anatomy), but two years ago your longtime partner, to whom
you were very close, was killed in a car accident. You grieved heavily,
slammed again and again by maddening shock, understandably having
an extremely hard time dealing with daily concerns for the first year or
so after your partner's death.

So now you function reasonably well but still are far from "over" what
happened, despite the well-meaning advice of friends who keep telling
you that it's time to move on, to let go of the past, that what happened

was long ago, et cetera after well-meaning et cetera. All kinds of things remind you of your partner, and when you are thus reminded—or haunted—you often feel yourself sinking into a crushingly dark sorrow, a despair that closes in on you with brutal ease. Medication helps some, but you're sick of (and from) the side effects, and the psychotherapy you've done hasn't helped much. But you know that you have to do something different, because this phantom *limbic* pain—the limbic system of the brain deals with emotion—is slowly killing you.

Telling others that the pain of their unresolved wounds is all in the past, or just something they're creating, is akin to telling those with phantom limb pain that such pain is not really there or is just something they're creating. But they *do* feel pain "there" now, sometimes to the point of suicide. Their lost limb is a phantom, but not its neurological correlates. Their brain is still mapping, or "re-presenting," that gone-limb area, still treating it as though it were very much present, thereby generating a corresponding pain. This happens in much the same way that in our sleep-dreams, our foot usually hurts when we kick a stone wall—a dream foot and a dream stone wall, yes, but not necessarily a dream pain.

If we feel pain in our nonexistent arm, we may intellectually grasp that such pain is being created by our brain and not by our departed arm, but our felt sense of it is that our phantom limb is producing the pain—after all, that's where we're feeling it, right? And in the same vein, if we feel emotional pain over what happened long ago (as in the example given earlier), we may understand that such pain is not actually being created by that long-gone event, but we nonetheless still strongly associate our pain with that particular time, including when we're not resurrecting it through our thinking processes.

We might say that we have been "storing" the feelings and imagery of this long-past event in our memory—or that it is wired into us—but *where* exactly is this thing (or activity, for it may be more verb than noun) that we call memory? And is its storage like that of literal containment, or is it more like that of a largely nonmaterial field of presence?

The here-and-now presence of certain aspects of our past is not necessarily just a ghostly hangover from our history. The presence of our past may in fact be running our life far more than we want to admit.

In fact, our issues are not just in our tissues. Our unresolved emotional wounds don't merely hang out in our cells, but exist as uniquely personalized energetic fields that not only pervade and alter our cells (including biochemically), but that can easily outlive them.

Such neuropsychological occupying forces broadcast and establish themselves through generation after generation of cells, keeping our past very much present, until we do the necessary work to resolve such wounding.

It is well known that unhealed emotional wounds and traumas are not just embedded in our minds, but also in our bodies. How great it would be if all we had to do was think differently or take on a new set of beliefs to heal our old hurts, but it just isn't that easy, despite various assertions to the contrary.

We don't so much need "better" beliefs as we need to change how we relate to our beliefs, along with doing deep somatic, emotional, and psychological work. If we truly want the treasure, we're going to have to face the dragon, realizing that our very encounter with it—that is, journeying to the heart of our pain—prepares us to make use of the treasure as wisely as possible.

Just as we can get trapped in negative thoughts, we can also get trapped in positive thoughts, blinding ourselves—and likely also emotionally numbing ourselves—to the more painful or troubling dimensions of life, confusing dissociation from them with actual transcendence of them.

Dramatizing and otherwise indulging in our pain—turning it into suffering—is obviously an unhelpful strategy, but so too is disconnecting from, fleeing, and otherwise avoiding our pain. How ironic it is that when we treat our pain as though it is but a phantom, we ourselves become more phantomlike when we try to get away from it. "Up, up, and away" is the mantra of unhealthy transcendence. The mantra for healthy transcendence? "Going beyond all, excluding none."

We need to develop the capacity to both stand apart from and relate to our thinking process, whatever its contents may be, not letting ourselves get absorbed in it to the point of forgetting that it is simply thinking. The nonconceptual holding of our capacity to conceptualize can be very liberating; thinking still arises, of course, but we don't get lost in it—including thinking about thinking.

If we don't maintain such clarity at least to some degree, we will find ourselves feeling *phantom thought pain:* the thought is gone, but its psychoemotional tagalong energies (the emotional charges that often accompany certain thoughts) may have taken partial root in us, which in most cases simply revives the original thought or something akin to or supportive of it. And how interesting it is that though thoughts are basically just electronic apparitions, they so often are, with our unwitting cooperation, resistant to giving up the ghost.

Our thoughts and beliefs can be very seductive—and so too can our emotions, especially when we automatically take them as living truth, not bothering to distinguish reactive emotionality from its nonreactive counterparts. It's so easy—and commonplace—to grant legitimacy to doing something by saying that we feel it, as if its having some emotional heft or backing automatically makes it more real.

The visceral quality of emotions makes them seem unphantomlike, but sometimes they're not much more than melodramatic ghosts with resoundingly impactful footsteps—as when they arise in reaction to something that is perceived as a threat but that in fact is not at all. So just as there is phantom limb pain, there is phantom *limbic* pain (again, emotions are primarily processed via the limbic system of the brain).

WORKING WITH PHANTOM LIMBIC PAIN

Those with phantom limb pain have in recent years often found significant relief through innovative work with mirrors—viewing and moving their functioning limb (their right arm, for example) as though it were their missing limb (their left arm, for example)—so that their brain maps the movements of their real arm as if it were the missing one. This means that immobilizations in the missing limb—which were there *before* the loss of the limb (from being in a cast, for example)—can be unjammed, loosened up, deparalyzed, rewired. So by literally seeing (through an ingenious placing of mirrors) the missing limb as the nonmissing one, the pain-inducing contractedness or frozenness in the missing limb—or, more precisely, in the part of the brain that's still mapping it—starts to loosen and expand, thereby significantly lessening phantom limb pain.

Similarly, we can bring our current capacity to function into our areas of dysfunction—areas haunted by unresolved trauma and pain—and generate needed movement there, using a combination of viewpoints ("mirrors") and psychotherapeutic savvy (intuitive bodywork, emotional release, fitting breathing patterns, and so on, in conjunction with therapeutic direction and insight) to generate a way of being that allows us to shift and give liberating voice to what has previously been stuck or frozen in us.

For example, we may have desperately wanted to run away from an abusive parent when we were little, but we didn't dare do so for fear of getting even more hurt. So we kept our running—and perhaps also fighting—urges intact, under wraps, and immobilized, and we don't yet connect our later and current times of actual fleeing and/or fighting with our original sense of entrapment.

Imagine being in an environment in which we feel sufficiently safe to reenter that "old" pain, and are able to mobilize our legs—and our entire body—in the very way we once needed to but couldn't, while at the same time recalling, emotionally and otherwise, the original events of our pain. Then we are no longer in a paralytic nightmare or numb trance, but are clearly awakening, kicking free the covers, kicking through the abuse, kick-starting our whole being into full-out expression, the very expression that arose in us long ago but had to be suppressed.

This is much, much more than a temper tantrum or mere emotional discharge! It is a literal reentry into—even a gatecrashing of—our preserved (or encapsulated) personal history, with enough awareness and mobilizing capacity to defossilize and deconstrict that time, bringing it into a present that unknots and unravels it, freeing its energies for something far more life giving. Thus is phantom limbic pain allowed to give up the ghost. Echoes may remain of such pain, but it is no longer in a position to run the show or masquerade as us.

Just as phantom limb pain does not need amputation but freeing movement, so too does phantom limbic pain need the same sort of movement, movement *through* the emotionally knotted context of then, movement that unshackles us, transporting us into the healing we need.

Our original woundedness, however phantomlike or hidden, remains present until we decisively bring our wakefully embodied presence into it, enlivening and liberating and giving full voice to what was previously frozen and mute. Through such psychoemotional ghostbusting, the knots and immobilizations of yesterday become fluidly alive now, serving rather than obstructing us, leaving us anchored in our heartland.

The Feeling of Being

THE ENGLISH WORD "EMOTION" IS far from universal; there's no corresponding term in many other languages. Among the concepts common to all languages, "feeling" is included, but not "emotion." So the *concept* of "emotion" is culture-bound.

Does the absence of a term for an emotion prove that the emotion it refers to is actually absent? No. English speakers, for example, certainly experience *schadenfreude* (taking pleasure in another's misfortune), despite the fact that there's no word for it in English. The considerable difficulty—or near impossibility—of mapping emotion words from one culture onto those of another with any meaningful accuracy does not necessarily mean that the actual phenomena to which such words refer exist only as cultural or social constructions.

These phenomena—nonlinguistic feeling-centered realities—exist whether or not they possess a name in a particular culture, as when English speakers experience, but do not label as such, the emotion of sweetly passive dependence known as *amae* in Japanese culture.

Since emotional experience is conceived of differently in different cultures, we might assume that it must therefore also vary from culture to culture. But how do we know? Perhaps all that varies is simply what is *done* with such experience, including alignment with the emotional display "rules" of each culture, as signaled by the vast variety of words and metaphors—whatever the language—that are applied to the experiencing of emotion.

When we relate to emotion not as a *thing*, but as an ever-in-flux process that both includes and transcends its parts, then its definitional boundaries become more open and permeable, allowing it to outgrow and spread beyond its original cultural confines. When the raw *feeling* of each emotion is sensed as being present in all of us—regardless of our cultural and familial filters—and that feeling is held with lucid compassion, we are all brought a little closer. And even closer when we cultivate intimacy with our emotions.

Emotions are the lifeblood of relationship, providing largely non-verbal, yet finely nuanced communicative channels that keep us in more-than-intellectual touch, helping us to illuminate and navigate whatever relational terrain we find ourselves in. Some of this is auto-matic—biologically preset—and some of it is far from automatic, depending on how well we know our emotions, including those for which we have aversion.

Becoming more conscious of our emotions does not mean that we have to keep away from them—like scientists maintaining an antiseptic distance from the subjects of their studies—but that we develop the abil-ity to stand back just far enough from them so as to keep them in focus.

This small but highly significant distance, coupled with an up-close compassionate investigation of our emotions, allows us to develop intimacy with them and their originating factors. As chal-lenging as this may be, it's an immensely rewarding undertaking, greatly enhancing our capacity for relational intimacy and for living a deeper life. This is especially true of those emotions that we tend to avoid or marginalize.

Implicit in developing more intimacy with our emotions is the act of turning *toward* our pain, however small or halting our steps in that direction might be. This is not about losing or overabsorbing ourselves in our pain and its possible dramatics, but about bringing it out onto the dance floor, engaging it wholeheartedly and as con-sciously as possible.

Through such deliberate connection-centered movement—such res-olute willingness to face all that we are—everything we've disowned or rejected in ourselves starts to shift from an unwanted "it" to a reclaimed aspect of "me." Even our most distressing or darkest emotions, once reclaimed and known from the deep inside, serve our healing and awakening and capacity for relational intimacy.

When we start making our longing to be truly free more central than our longing to distract ourselves from our suffering, we are on track for a deeper life—a life in which passion, love, integrity, and awareness function as one. And what better place to practice this than in the domain of our emotional life, where every day we are presented with opportunity after opportunity to turn toward what we'd rather turn away from?

Emotion connects body and mind, surface and depth, past and present, intention and action, impulse and reflection, containment and expression, biochemistry and biography, the personal and the interpersonal in an organic flow that invites our awakened participation.

Given that there is no getting away from emotion, we might as well do whatever it takes to make wise use of our emotions, and this begins with developing intimacy with them. Such an undertaking asks much of us and gives back much, much more—bringing us into an ever-deepening wholeness, a life as richly alive and embodied as it is compassionately awakened.

THE FEELING OF BEING

Each emotion has its own terrain, its own hallmark sensations, its own somatic signals and peculiarities, regardless of the unavoidably fuzzy boundaries between it and other emotions. Even so, at the heart of every emotion is a singular *meta-emotion,* a primordial feeling as palpable as it is subtle, manifesting as the "sensation" of self-transcending sentient presence.

This feeling—the feeling of Being—never leaves us. But we leave it, drift from it, forget it. Away from this feeling wanders our attention, fastening itself to an enormous array of objects, both inner and outer. Fasten-ation. Attention that's Velcro-ed to objects and that's overly absorbed in details and storylines is attention that's inattentive to *us.*

And still the feeling of Being persists. It doesn't begin here and end there. It's neither in time nor in space, having no temporal or spatial coordinates. It is, however, still a feeling—not a feeling of anything in particular, but nonetheless a feeling.

The feeling of Being is all but inseparable from Being. To directly *feel* Being is to—however slightly—start to recognize oneself *as* Being. Such recognition, such primal intuition, comes into clearer focus as we develop intimacy with our emotions—simply because the more at home we are with feeling, the more easily we can relate to Being from a feeling level.

However lightly or fleetingly it may register with us, the feeling of Being continues to pervade us, registering as our felt sense of bare existence. When we settle into the feeling of Being, remaining attuned to it as we engage in our daily activities, we may feel as though we are both right here—taking care of business—and nowhere in particular. And we might sometimes also feel as though we are both here for but a moment and also for forever.

None of this constitutes a paradox to Being. Paradox is just the mind's reaction to—and translation of—the inherent Mystery of Being. Cultivating intimacy with the Mystery of Being sooner or later leaves us in the position of knowing nothing (in the sense of knowing we don't know what anything actually *is*) and recognizing everything.

Silence probably speaks most eloquently through the feeling of Being. Everything's said without anything needing to be said. Silence is the answer that dissolves every query, the answer that literally makes light of even the deepest questions. Universes come and go. Silence remains.

And so too does the feeling of Being.

Listen. What do you hear? What is the sound of sound? When there is no sound, what do you hear? And when you stop trying to make sense out of it, what remains? Listen even more closely, including to the space between your thoughts and the space between the end of your exhale and the beginning of your next inhalation. Is there not some sense of a reality-unlocking realization close by that's about to dissolve our would-be translations, leaving nothing in its wake but us, lit up in our little boat of consciousness and feeling, at once shipwrecked and safely moored?

Even now, no matter what our condition, emotional and otherwise, the feeling of Being runs through it and all of its permutations, like the string of a necklace through its beads. Sacred connection in the raw.

Get friendly with whatever emotional state you are now in, divesting it of its egoic agendas and riding it into the feeling of Being—that is, letting the feeling of Being become foreground—and soon something more real than answers will seize your attention by the heart, rendering you all but incapable of distraction.

When we invite our suffering onto the dance floor, we're taking the hand, however clammy or shy, of our feeling self. If we won't dance with that one, if we won't touch and care for that one, we'll simply reduce the feeling of Being to a concept, a goal, a mere abstraction on which to hook our spiritual ambition.

Dance with anger, and you might have to go a few rounds with rage, but eventually that rage might, if worked with skillfully, mutate into joy—the joy of being nakedly alive.

Dance with grief, and you may have to curl up in an agony of deep sorrow for a while, but sooner or later your very rawness of heart will both ground you and give you a sky vaster than you can imagine, emotionally connecting you to all that is.

Dance with fear, and you may have to spend some time with dread and maddening expectation, but keeping that fearfulness close to your heart will eventually bring about a miraculous transformation: the monster will fade, leaving a quality of deeply embodied acceptance that is but the human face of a peace that surpasses all understanding.

Dance with shame, and you might well have to take a spin in guilt's sleazier hangouts, but staying there, befriending both the parental and childish sides of guilt, will divest it of its fear, until it is but shame unplugged, and then not even shame, but only forgiveness in its merciful purity.

Dancing with it all, holding every emotion, we make our way Home.

Before thought, feeling
Before feeling, sensation
Before sensation, presence
Before presence, this

Before persona, individuality
Before individuality, spirit
Before spirit, this
Birthing us out of the blue
Not yet separating journey and goal
Not yet broken enough
To be truly whole

Before now, a deeper now
Before time, this
Never not already here
Older than any fear

This is what we're dying to see
Its mystery holding all history

Feeling it now
We realize we've always felt it

Feeling is the first and last tongue
Revealing more than can be said or sung
Feeling is relational electricity
Rendering us capable of intimacy
The feeling of Being
Homing us
Whatever the scene
Whatever the dream
Wherever we may be
Our every emotion
Both sail and ocean

A Meditative Practice for Establishing Grounded Spaciousness

Find a comfortable place to sit on the floor or in a chair, making sure that you will not be interrupted within the next fifteen minutes or so. (Turn off your phone and electronic devices; close or lock your door.) Also be sure to wear clothing that's loose enough to allow easy, unrestricted breathing.

Once you've settled into sitting, close your eyes and bring your attention to your breathing. Don't try to change it in any way, but simply notice it, allowing your belly to soften. Remain comfortably upright.

At the *end* of your next exhalation, softly say the word "one." At the *end* of the following exhalation, softly say the word "two." Continue counting your breaths this way until you've reached five, then begin at one again. Do nothing to change your breathing as you do this.

When you reach the fifth breath a second time, begin counting at one again, but now do so silently. If at any point you forget what number you're on, simply begin at one again. It doesn't matter how often you forget.

Now, as you continue counting silently, notice how your belly rises or expands with your inhale, and falls back as you exhale. Be aware of the sensations of this movement for each breath. So as you inhale, observe the feeling of your belly rising; as you exhale, observe the feeling of your belly falling back, and count at the end of the exhalation.

So you are doing two things: silently counting at the end of each out-breath, and observing the sensations in your belly that are generated by each inhalation and exhalation. Remember to start at one again if you lose track of the counting. As you settle into this practice, allow your entire body to soften, letting your concentration be as easeful as it is focused. No matter what you're thinking or feeling, stay with the practice. Let your belly continue to relax—so too your shoulders, your jaw, your forehead, your back, your entire body.

Stay with this for ten minutes or so, then stop the counting and simply remain aware of the movement of your belly with each breath. After a few minutes of this, let go of any effort to be aware of your breathing. Make no effort to do anything in particular. Sit like this for another three or four minutes, simply resting, simply being.

And last, take a deep breath and let it go fully. Then slowly open your eyes. Take another, even deeper breath, and exhale it fully. Stay here as long as you like.

Acknowledgments

THE FIRST INCARNATION OF THIS book was a collection of my writings on emotions, assembled for the benefit of those doing work with my wife, Diane, and me. I mentioned this collection to Tami Simon of Sounds True in an email about an unrelated creative project. I was surprised when she said she'd be interested in taking a look at these writings, and a few months later I signed a contract with Sounds True to publish a full-length version of them. Over the next year the collection of writings metamorphosed into a book that incorporated and expanded upon what I'd learned over three decades of doing very deep emotional work with many people. So I send my heartfelt appreciation to Tami for offering me this unexpected opportunity and for believing in me.

Also, big thanks to my very skilled editor at Sounds True, Haven Iverson. Without her keen, detailed, and panoramic eye, I would have had much less of a book. And gratitude to my expert copyeditor, Laurel Kallenbach, for helping me make this a better book. Thanks also to Marj Hahne, Iyeshka Farmer, and Jessica Bahr for their insightful comments on my gender chapter.

It has been wonderful to channel my thirty-five years of investigating and working with emotions into this book; I am grateful to all of those who came to me for psychological and spiritual work, for each one contributed something to my understanding of emotion.

I am especially grateful to those currently training with Diane and me in order to learn how to teach/transmit our way of working—a far from easy task! Their dedication to this process and wonderful support of us coexists with their trusting us to do exceptionally deep work with them, work that has further instructed me in the ways of getting to the heart of emotion. So immeasurable thanks to Saleem Berryman, Brett Butler, Laura Calderon de la Barca, Iyeshka Farmer, Rochelle Jaffe, and Laura Loescher! Your coming into our lives has made, and is making, a huge difference to us.

And, of course, thanks beyond thanks to Diane. She was side by side with me through all my ups and downs in the writing and rewriting of *Emotional Intimacy,* and she also carefully read its various incarnations, providing me with directional clues and insights that deepened this book.

About the Author

ROBERT AUGUSTUS MASTERS, PHD, is a relationship expert, a spiritual teacher, and a psychospiritual guide with a doctorate in psychology. He is the cofounder, with his wife Diane, of the Masters Center for Transformation (MCT), a school featuring relationally rooted psychospiritual work devoted to deep healing and fully embodied awakening. A substantial portion of his work involves training MCT practitioners. He is also the author of thirteen books, including *Transformation through Intimacy* and *Spiritual Bypassing*.

His uniquely integral, intuitive work, which he developed over the past thirty-five years, dynamically blends the psychological and physical with the spiritual, emphasizing full-blooded embodiment, authenticity, emotional openness and literacy, deep shadow work, and the development of relational maturity.

At essence his writing and work are about becoming more intimate with all that we are—high and low, dark and light, dying and undying—in the service of the deepest possible healing, awakening, and integration. He works side by side and in very close conjunction with Diane. They live and work in Ashland, Oregon. His website is robertmasters.com.

About Sounds True

SOUNDS TRUE is a multimedia publisher whose mission is to inspire and support personal transformation and spiritual awakening. Founded in 1985 and located in Boulder, Colorado, we work with many of the leading spiritual teachers, thinkers, healers, and visionary artists of our time. We strive with every title to preserve the essential "living wisdom" of the author or artist. It is our goal to create products that not only provide information to a reader or listener, but that also embody the quality of a wisdom transmission.

For those seeking genuine transformation, Sounds True is your trusted partner. At SoundsTrue.com you will find a wealth of free resources to support your journey, including exclusive weekly audio interviews, free downloads, interactive learning tools, and other special savings on all our titles.

To learn more, please visit SoundsTrue.com/bonus/free_gifts or call us toll free at 800-333-9185.

SOUNDS TRUE
many voices, one journey